W. Jones

**Dissertations and Miscellaneous Pieces**

relating to the History and antiquities the Arts, Sciences and literature of Asia, Vol.2

W. Jones

**Dissertations and Miscellaneous Pieces**
*relating to the History and antiquities the Arts, Sciences and literature of Asia, Vol.2*

ISBN/EAN: 9783337385552

Printed in Europe, USA, Canada, Australia, Japan

Cover: Foto ©ninafisch / pixelio.de

More available books at **www.hansebooks.com**

# DISSERTATIONS
### AND
## MISCELLANEOUS PIECES
#### RELATING TO THE
## HISTORY AND ANTIQUITIES,
#### THE
## ARTS, SCIENCES, AND LITERATURE
#### OF
## *A S I A.*

---

### VOL. II.

# DISSERTATIONS
AND
## MISCELLANEOUS PIECES
RELATING TO THE
## HISTORY AND ANTIQUITIES,
THE
## ARTS, SCIENCES, AND LITERATURE,
OF
## *A S I A,*
BY

| | |
|---|---|
| SIR W. JONES, | J. RAWLINS, ESQ. |
| W. CHAMBERS, ESQ. | J. SHORE, ESQ. |
| W. HASTINGS, ESQ. | J. WILLIAMS, ESQ. |
| GEN. CARNAC, | ARCH. KEIR, ESQ. |
| M. VANSITTART, ESQ. | COL. PEARSE, |
| C. WILKINS, ESQ. | LIEUT. COL. POLIER; |

AND OTHERS.

## VOLUME THE SECOND,
CONTAINING THE
### MISCELLANEOUS PIECES,
BY

PRINTED FOR G. NICOL, BOOKSELLER TO HIS MAJESTY,
PALL-MALL; J. WALTER, CHARING-CROSS; AND
J. SEWELL, CORNHILL.
M DCC XCII.

# THE CONTENTS OF THE SECOND VOLUME.

|     |     | Page |
| --- | --- | --- |
| I. | On the Ruins at *Mavalipuram*, | 1 |
| II. | An Interview with the Young *Lama*, | 38 |
| III. | A Journey to *Tibet*, | 49 |
| IV. | On the *Sic'hs* and their College, | 68 |
| V. | On the *Indian* Trial by Ordeal, | 76 |
| VI. | On the Literature of the *Hindus*, | 98 |
| VII. | On the Descent of the *Afghans* from the *Jews*, | 119 |
| VIII. | On extracting the Essential Oil of Roses, | 130 |
| IX. | A Description of *Asam*, | 135 |
| X. | On the Mountaineers of *Tipra*, | 156 |

XI. On

## THE CONTENTS.

|  | Page |
|---|---|
| XI. On the *Indian* Grosbeak, | 166 |
| XII. An Account of *Nipál* | 169 |
| XIII. On two *Indian* Festivals, and the *Sphinx*, | 193 |
| XIV. On the Isle of *Carnicobar*, | 198 |
| XV. On the Cure of the *Elephantiasis*, | 210 |
| XVI. On the Cure of Persons bitten by Snakes, | 222 |
| ✓ XVII. On the City of *Tagara*, | 231 |
| ✓ XVIII. A Royal Grant found at *Thana*, | 241 |
| XIX. A Royal Grant found at *Mongueer*, | 255 |
| XX. On an Ancient Building in *Hájipur*, | 266 |
| XXI. On the Mode of Distilling at *Chitra*, | 271 |
| XXII. On the *Pangolin* of *Bahar*, | 288 |
| XXIII. On the *Lac* Insect, | 299 |
| XXIV. An Inscription at *Buddha Gayá*, | 304 |
| XXV. An Inscription on a Pillar near *Buddal*, | 309 |
| XXVI. On a Cave with an Inscription near *Gayá*, | 324 |
| XXVII. Translation of a *Sanscrit* Inscription, | 331 |
| XXVIII. An Inscription found near *Islamabad*, | 338 |

APPENDIX.

## THE CONTENTS.

Page.

## APPENDIX

I. Hymn to CAMDEO, by Sir WILLIAM JONES, 347

II. Hymn to NARAYENA, by the fame, 353

III. An Account of Embaſſies and Letters between the Emperor of *China* and Sultan SHAHROKH, tranſlated by W. CHAMBERS, Eſq. 357

IV. A ſhort Account of the *Marratta* State, tranſlated by W. CHAMBERS, Eſq. 380

# MISCELLANEOUS PIECES
RELATING TO THE
## HISTORY AND ANTIQUITIES,
THE
## ARTS, SCIENCES, AND LITERATURE,
OF
# ASIA.

AN ACCOUNT OF THE SCULPTURES AND RUINS
AT
## MAVALIPURAM[*].

BY WILLIAM CHAMBERS, ESQ.

AS amidst inquiries after the histories and antiquities of *Asia* at large, those of that division of it in which this Society resides may seem on many accounts to lay claim to a particular share of its attention, a few hints put down from recollection, concerning some monuments of *Hindoo* antiquity, which, though situated in the neighbourhood of *European* settlements on the *Choromandel* coast, have hitherto been little observed, may, it is conceived, be acceptable at least; as they may possibly give rise

[*] A place a few miles north of SADRAS, and known to Seamen by the name of THE SEVEN PAGODAS.

hereafter to more accurate observations, and more complete discoveries on the same subject. The writer of this account went first to view them in the year 1772, and curiosity led him thither again in 1776; but as he neither measured the distances nor size of the objects, nor committed to writing at the time the observations he made on them, he hopes to be excused if, after the lapse of so many years, his recollection should fail him in some respects, and his account fall far short of that precision and exactness which might have been expected had there then existed in *India* so powerful an incentive to diligent enquiry and accurate communication as the establishment of this Society must now prove.

The Monuments he means to describe appear to be the remains of some great city that has been ruined many centuries ago; they are situated close to the sea, between *Covelong* and *Sadras*, somewhat remote from the high road that leads to the different *European* settlements. And when he visited them in 1776, there was still a native village adjoining to them, which retained the antient name, and in which a number of *Bramins* resided that seemed perfectly well acquainted with the subjects of most of the sculptures to be seen there.

The rock, or rather hill of stone, on which great part of these works are executed, is one
of

of the principal marks for mariners as they approach the coast, and to them the place is known by the name of the *Seven Pagodas*, possibly because the summits of the rock have presented them with that idea as they passed: but it must be confessed, that no aspect which the hill assumes as viewed on the shore, seems at all to authorize this notion; and there are circumstances, which will be mentioned in the sequel, that would lead one to suspect that this name has arisen from some such number of Pagodas that formerly stood here, and in time have been buried in the waves. But, be that as it may, the appellation by which the natives distinguish it is of a quite different origin: in their language, which is the *Tamulic* (improperly termed *Malabar*), the place is called *Māvalipuram*, which in *Shanscrit*, and the languages of the more northern *Hindoos*, would be *Mahābalipūr*, or the *City of the great Bali*. For the *Tamulians* (or *Malabars*), having no *b* in their alphabet, are under a necessity of shortening the *Shanscrit* word Mahā, *great*, and write it *mā*[*]. They are obliged also for a similar reason to substitute a *v* for a *b*, in words of *Shanscrit*, or other foreign original, that be-

[*] They do indeed admit a substitute, but the abbreviation is most used.

gin with that letter, and the syllable *am* at the end is merely a termination, which, like *um* in *Latin*, is generally annexed to neuter substantives*. To this etymology of the name of this place it may be proper to add, that *Bali* is the name of an hero very famous in *Hindoo* romance, and that the river *Mávaliganga*, which waters the eastern side of *Ceylone*, where the *Tamulic* language also prevails, has probably taken its name from him, as, according to that orthography, it apparently signifies the *Ganges* of the great *Bali*.

The rock or hill of stone above mentioned is that which first engrosses the attention on approaching the place; for as it rises abruptly out of a level plain of great extent, consists chiefly of one single stone, and is situated very near to the sea-beach, it is such a kind of object as an inquisitive traveller would naturally turn aside to examine. Its shape is also singular and romantic, and, from a distant view, has an appearance like some antique and lofty edifice. On coming near to the foot of the rock from the north,

works

* This explains also, why the *Shanscrit* word Vèd, by which the *Hindoos* denominate the books of the law of their religion, is written by the *Tamulians* Védam, which is according to the true orthography of their language, and no mistake of *European* travellers, as some have supposed; while the same word is called Bèd by the *Bengalies*, who have in effect no v in their alphabet.—See Dow, Differt. vol. I.

works of imagery * and sculpture croud so thick upon the eye, as might seem to favour the idea of a petrified town, like those that have been fabled in different parts of the world by too credulous travellers †. Proceeding on by the foot of the hill on the side facing the sea, there is a pagoda rising out of the ground of one solid stone, about sixteen or eighteen feet high, which seems to have been cut upon the spot out of a detached rock that has been found of a proper size for that purpose. The top is arched, and the stile of architecture according to which it is formed different from any now used in those parts. A little further on there appears upon an huge surface of stone, that juts out a little from the side of the hill, a numerous group of human figures in bass relief, considerably larger than life, representing the most remarkable persons whose actions are celebrated in the *Mahábharit*, each of them in an attitude, or with weapons, or other insignia, expressive of his character, or of some one of his most famous exploits. All these figures are, doubtless, much less distinct than they were at first; for

---

* Among these, one object, though a mean one, attracts the attention on account of the grotesque and ridiculous nature of the design; it consists of two monkies cut out of one stone, one of them in a stooping posture, while the other is taking the insects out of his head.

† See SHAW's Travels, p. 155. et seq.

upon comparing these and the rest of the sculptures that are exposed to the sea air, with others at the same place, whose situation has afforded them protection from that element, the difference is striking, the former being everywhere much defaced, while the others are fresh as recently finished. This defacement is nowhere more observable, than in the piece of sculpture which occurs next in the order of description. This is an excavation in another part of the east side of the great rock, which appears to have been made on the same plan and for the same purpose that Chowltries are usually built in that country, that is to say, for the accommodation of travellers. The rock is hollowed out to the size of a spacious room, and two or three rows of pillars are left, as a seeming support to the mountainous mass of stone which forms the roof. Of what pattern these pillars have originally been, it is not easy now to conjecture, for the air of the sea has greatly corroded them, as well as all the other parts of the cave. And this circumstance renders it difficult to discover, at first sight, that there is a scene of sculpture on the side fronting the entrance. The natives, however, point it out, and the subject of it is manifestly that of *Krishen* attending the herds of *Nund Ghose*, the *Admetus* of the *Hindoos*, from which circumstance *Krishen* is also called *Gopaul*, or the Cowherd, as *Apollo* was entitled *Nomius*.

THE

THE objects that seem next to claim regard, are those upon the hill itself, the ascent of which, on the north, is, from its natural shape, gradual and easy at first, and is in other parts rendered more so, by very excellent steps cut out in several places, where the communication would be difficult or unpracticable without them. A winding stair of this sort leads to a kind of temple cut out of the solid rock, with some figures of idols in high relief upon its walls, very well finished and perfectly fresh, as it faces the west, and is therefore sheltered from the sea air. From this temple again there are flights of steps that seem to have led to some edifice, formerly standing upon the hill; nor does it seem absurd to suppose, that this may have been a palace, to which this temple, as a place of worship, may have appertained. For besides the small detached ranges of stairs that are here and there cut in the rock, and seem as if they had once led to different parts of one great building, there appear in many places, small water channels cut also in the rock, as if for drains to an house, and the whole top of the hill is strewed with small round pieces of brick, which may be supposed from their appearance to have been worn down to their present form during the lapse of many ages. On ascending the hill by its slope on the north, a very a very singular piece of sculpture presents itself to view. On a plain surface of the rock, which may once have served as the floor of some apartment, there is a platform of stone, about eight or nine feet long, by three or four wide, in a situation rather elevated, with two or three steps leading up to it, perfectly resembling a couch or bed, and a lion very well executed at the upper end of it by way of pillow, the whole of one piece, being part of the hill itself. This the *Bramins*, inhabitants of the place, call the *bed of Dbermarájah* or *Judishter*, the eldest of the five brothers whose fortunes and exploits are the leading subject in the *Mahabharit*. And at a considerable distance from this, at such a distance indeed as the apartment of the women might be supposed to be from that of the men, is a bath excavated also from the solid rock, with steps in the inside, which the *Bramins* call the bath of *Dropedy*, the wife of *Judishter* and his brothers. How much credit is due to this tradition, and whether this stone couch may not have been anciently used as a kind of throne rather than a bed, is matter for future inquiry. A circumstance, however, which may seem to favour this idea is, that a throne in the *Shanscrit* and other *Hindoo* languages is called *Singhásen*, which is composed of the words *Sing* a lion, and *ásen* a seat.

These

THESE are all that appear on that part of the upper surface of the hill, the ascent to which is on the north; but on descending from thence you are led round the hill to the opposite side, in which there are steps cut from the bottom to a place near the summit, where is an excavation that seems to have been intended for a place of worship, and contains various sculptures of *Hindoo* Deities. The most remarkable of these, is a gigantic figure of *Vishnoo*, asleep on a kind of bed, with a huge snake wound about in many coils by way of pillow for his head, and these figures, according to the manner of this place, are all of one piece hewn from the body of the rock.

BUT though these works may be deemed stupendous, they are surpassed by others that are to be seen at the distance of about a mile, or a mile and an half, to the southward of the hill. They consist of two Pagodas of about thirty feet long by twenty feet wide, and about as many in height, cut out of the solid rock, and each consisting originally of one single stone. Near these also stand an elephant full as big as life, and a lion much larger than the natural size, but very well executed, each hewn also out of one stone. None of the pieces that have fallen off in cutting these extraordinary sculptures, are now to be found near or any where

where in the neighbourhood of them, so that there is no means of ascertaining the degree of labour and time that has been spent upon them, nor the size of the rock or rocks from which they have been hewn, a circumstance which renders their appearance the more striking and singular. And though their situation is very near the sea-beach, they have not suffered at all by the corrosive air of that element, which has provided them with a defence against itself, by throwing up before them a high bank that completely shelters them. There is also great symmetry in their form, though that of the Pagodas is different from the style of architecture according to which idol temples are now built in that country. The latter resembles the *Egyptian*, for the towers are always pyramidical, and the gates and roofs flat and without arches; but these sculptures approach nearer to the *Gothic* taste, being surmounted by arched roofs or domes that are not semicircular, but composed of two segments of circles meeting in a point at top. It is also observable that the lion in this group of sculptures, as well as that upon the stone couch above mentioned, are perfectly just representations of the true lion, and the natives there give them the name which is always understood to mean a lion in the *Hindoo* language, to wit, *Sing*; but the
figure

figure which they have made to represent that animal in their idol temples for centuries past, though it bears the same appellation, is a distorted monster totally unlike the original; insomuch that it has from hence been supposed, that the lion was not anciently known in this country, and that *Sing* was a name given to a monster that existed only in *Hindoo* romance. But it is plain that that animal was well known to the authors of these works, who in manners as well as arts seem to have differed much from the modern *Hindoos*.

THERE are two circumstances attending these monuments, which cannot but excite great curiosity, and on which future inquiries may possibly throw some light. One is, that on one of the Pagodas last mentioned, there is an inscription of a single line, in a character at present unknown to the *Hindoos*. It resembles neither the *Deyvu-nágre*, nor any of the various characters connected with or derived from it, which have come to the writer's knowledge from any part of *Hindostan*. Nor did it, at the time he viewed it, appear to correspond with any character, *Asiatick* or *European*, that is commonly known. He had not then, however, seen the alphabet of the *Balie*, the learned language of the *Siamese*, a sight of which has since raised in his mind a suspicion, that there is a near affinity between them, if the character

be

be not identically the same. But as these conjectures, after such a lapse of time, are somewhat vague, and the subject of them is perhaps yet within the reach of our researches, it is to be hoped that some method may be fallen upon of procuring an exact copy of this inscription.

THE other circumstance is, that though the outward form of the Pagodas is complete, th ultimate design of them has manifestly not been accomplished, but seems to have been defeated by some extraordinary convulsion of nature. For the western side of the most northerly one is excavated to the depth of four or five feet, and a row of pillars left on the outside to support the roof; but here the work has been stopped, and an uniform rent of about four inches breadth has been made throughout the solid rock, and appears to extend to its foundations, which are probably at a prodigious depth below the surface of the ground. That this rent has happened since the work begun, or while it was carrying on, cannot be doubted, for the marks of the mason's tools are perfectly visible in the excavated part on both sides of the rent, in such a manner as to show plainly, that they have been divided by it. Nor is it reasonable to suppose, that such a work would ever have been designed or begun, upon a rock that had previously been rent in two.

NOTHING

NOTHING less than an earthquake, and that a violent one, could apparently have produced such a fissure in the solid rock; and that this has been the case in point of fact, may be gathered from other circumstances, which it is necessary to mention in an account of this curious place.

THE great rock above described is at some small distance from the sea, perhaps fifty or an hundred yards, and in that space the *Hindoo* village before mentioned stood in 1776. But close to the sea are the remains of a Pagoda built of brick, and dedicated to *Sib*, the greatest part of which has evidently been swallowed up by that element; for the door of the innermost apartment, in which the idol is placed, and before which there are always two or three spacious courts surrounded with walls, is now washed by the waves; and the pillar used to discover the meridian at the time of founding the Pagoda *, is seen standing at some distance in the sea. In the neighbourhood of this building, there are some detached rocks, washed also by the waves, on which there appear sculptures, though now much worn and defaced. And the natives of the place declared to the writer of this account, that the more aged people among them remembered to have seen the tops of several Pago-

* See Voyage du M. Gentil, Vol. I. page 158.

das far out in the sea, which being covered with copper (probably gilt) were particularly visible at sun-rise, as their shining surface used then to reflect the sun's rays, but that now that effect was no longer produced, as the copper had since become incrusted with mould and verdegrise.

These circumstances look much like the effects of a sudden inundation, and the rent in the rock above described makes it reasonable to conjecture, that an earthquake may have caused the sea to overflow its boundaries, and that these two formidable enemies may have joined to destroy this once magnificent city. The account which the *Bramins*, natives of the place, gave of its origin and downfal, partly it should seem on the authority of the *Mahabhirit*, and partly on that of later records, at the same time that it countenances this idea, contains some other curious particulars which may seem to render it worthy of attention. Nor ought it to be rejected on account of that fabulous garb in which all nations, but especially those of the East, have always clad the events of early ages.

"Hirinachkren, said they, was a gigan-
"tick prince that rolled up the earth into a
"shapeless mass, and carried it down to the
"abyss, whither *Vishnoo* followed him in the
"shape

"shape of an hog, killed him with his tusks,
"and replaced the earth in its original situa-
"tion. The younger brother of HIRINACHE-
"SEN was HIRINAKASSAP, who succeeded
"him in his kingdom, and refused to do ho-
"mage to VISHNOO. He had a son named
"PRALHAUD, who at an early age openly
"disapproved this part of his father's conduct,
"being under the tuition of SOKERACHARJ. His
"father persecuted him on this account, ba-
"nished him, and even sought to kill him, but
"was prevented by the interposition of heaven,
"which appeared on the side of PRALHAUD.
"At length HIRINAKASSAP was softened, and
"recalled his son to his court, where, as he
"sat in full assembly, he began again to argue
"with him against the supremacy of VISHNOO,
"boasted that he himself was lord of all the
"visible world, and asked what VISHNOO
"could pretend to more. PRALHAUD replied,
"that VISHNOO had no fixed abode, but was
"present everywhere. "Is he," said his father,
"in that pillar?" "Yes," returned PRALHAUD.
"Then let him come forth" said HIRINAKAS-
"SAP; and, rising from his seat, struck the pil-
"lar with his foot: upon which VISHNOO,
"in the *Narasinghah Avtár*, that is to say,
"with a body like a man, but an head like a
                                        "lion,

"lion, came out of the pillar and tore Hi-
"rinakassap in pieces. Vishnoo then
"fixed Pralhaud on his father's throne, and
"his reign was a mild and virtuous one, and
"as such was a contrast to that of his father.
"He left a son named Namachee, who
"inherited his power and his virtues, and
"was the father of Balee, the founder of the
"once magnificent city of Mahábalipoor, the
"situation of which is said to be described in
"a verse in the Mahabhárit, the sense of which
"is literally this:

"South of the Ganges two hundred Yojen
"Five Yojen * westward from the eastern sea."

Such is the Bramin account of the origin of this place. The sequel of its history, according to them, is as follows:

"The son of Balee was Banacheren, who
"is represented as a giant with a thousand hands.

* The *Yojen* is a measure often mentioned in the *Shanscrit* books, and according to some accounts is equal to nine, according to others twelve *English* miles. But at that rate the distance here mentioned, between this place and the *Ganges*, is prodigiously exaggerated, and will carry us far south of *Ceylon*; this, however, is not surprising in an *Hindoo* poem; but from the second line it seems pretty clear that this city at the time this verse was composed must have stood at a great distance from the sea.

"Anuredh,

"ANUREDH, the son of KRISHEN, came to his
"court in disguise and seduced his daughter,
"which produced a war, in the course of
"which ANUREDH was taken prisoner, and
"brought to *Mahabalipoor*, upon which KRI-
"SHEN came in person from his capital *Dwarri-
"kab*, and laid siege to the place. SIB guarded
"the gates and fought for BANACHEREN, who
"worshipped him with his thousand hands, but
"KRISHEN found means to overthrow SIB, and
"having taken the city cut off all BANACHE-
"REN's hands except two, with which he obliged
"him to do him homage. He continued in sub-
"jection to KRISHEN till his death, after which
"a long period ensued, in which no mention
"is any where made of this place, till a Prince
"arose whose name was MALECHEREN, who
"restored the kingdom to great splendour, and
"enlarged and beautified the capital. But in his
"time the calamity is said to have happened by
"which the city was entirely destroyed, and
"the cause and manner of it have been wrapt
"up by the *Bramins* in the following fabu-
"lous narration. MALECHEREN, say they, in
"an excursion which he made one day alone
"and in disguise, came to a garden in the en-
"virons of the city, where was a fountain so
"inviting, that two celestial nymphs had come
"down to bathe there. The *Rajah* became
"enamoured of one of them, who conde-

Vol. II.           C            " scended

"scended to allow of his attachment to her,
"and she and her sister nymph used thence-
"forward to have frequent interviews with
"him in that garden. On one of those occa-
"sions, they brought with them a male inha-
"bitant of the heavenly regions, to whom
"they introduced the *Rajah*; and between him
"and MALECHEREN a strict friendship ensued;
"in consequence of which he agreed, at the *Ra-
"jah*'s earnest request, to carry him in disguise
"to see the court of the divine INDER, a favour
"never before granted to any mortal. The
"*Rajah* returned from thence, with new ideas
"of splendour and magnificence, which he
"immediately adopted in regulating his court
"and his retinue, and in beautifying his seat
"of government. By this means *Mahâbali-
"poor* became soon celebrated beyond all the
"cities of the earth, and an account of its
"magnificence having been brought to the
"Gods assembled at the court of INDER, their
"jealousy was so much excited at it, that they
"sent orders to the God of the sea to let loose
"his billows, and overflow a place which im-
"piously pretended to vie in splendour with
"their celestial mansions. This command he
"obeyed, and the city was at once overflowed
"by that furious element, nor has it ever since
"been able to rear its head."

SUCH

Such is the mode in which the *Bramins* chuse to account for the signal overthrow of a place devoted to their wretched superstitions.

It is not, however, improbable, that the rest of this history may contain, like the mythology of *Greece* and *Rome*, a great deal of real matter of fact, though enveloped in dark and figurative representations. Through the disguise of these, we may discern some imperfect records of great events, and of revolutions that have happened in remote times, and they perhaps merit our attention the more, as it is not likely that any records of ancient *Hindoo* history exist, but in this obscure and fantastic dress. Their poets seem to have been their only historians, as well as divines, and whatever they relate, is wrapt up in this burlesque garb, set off, by way of ornament, with circumstances hugely incredible and absurd, and all this without any date, and in no other order or method than such as the poet's fancy suggested and found most convenient. Nevertheless, by comparing names and grand events recorded by them, with those interspersed in the histories of other nations, and by calling in the assistance of ancient monuments, coins, and inscriptions, as occasion shall offer, some probable conjectures at least, if not important discoveries, may, it is hoped, be made on these interesting

interesting subjects. It is much to be regretted, that a blind zeal, attended with a total want of curiosity, in the *Mohammedan* governors of this country, have been so hostile to the preservation of *Hindoo* monuments and coins. But a spirit of enquiry among *Europeans* may yet perhaps be successful, and an instance which relates to the place above described, though in itself a subject of regret, leaves room to hope, that futurity may yet have in store some useful discoveries. The *Kanzy* of *Madras*, who had often occasion to go to a place in the neighbourhood of *Mahabalipoor*, assured the writer of this account, that within his remembrance, a ryot of those parts had found, in plowing his ground, a pot of gold and silver coins, with characters on them which no one in those parts, *Hindoo* or *Mohammedan*, was able to decypher. He added, however, that all search for them would now be vain, for they had doubtless been long ago devoted to the crucible, as, in their original form, no one there thought them of any value.

THE inscription on the Pagoda mentioned above, is an object, which, in this point of view, appears to merit great attention. That the conjecture, however, which places it among the languages of *Siam*, may not seem in itself chimerical, the following passages from

from some authors of repute are here inserted to shew, that the idea of a communication having formerly subsisted between that country and the coast of *Choromandel*, is by no means without foundation, nay that there is some affinity, even at this day, between the *Balic* and some of the *Hindoo* languages, and that the same mode of worship seems formerly to have prevailed in the *Deckan*, which is now used by the *Siamese*.

MONSIEUR DE LA LOUBERE, in his excellent account of *Siam*, speaks thus of the origin of the *Balic* language:

" THE *Siamese*," says he, " do not mention
" any country where the *Balic* language, which
" is that of their laws and their religion, is at
" present in use. They suppose, indeed, on
" the report of some among them, who have
" been on the coast of *Choromandel*, that it
" bears some resemblance to some of the dia-
" lects of that country, but they at the same
" time allow, that the character in which it is
" written, is not known but among themselves.
" The secular Missionaries settled at *Siam* be-
" lieve that this language is not entirely a dead
" one; because they have seen in their hospital
" a man from the neighbourhood of *Cape Co-*
" *morin*, who mixed several *Balic* words in his
" discourse, declaring that they were in use in
" his country, and that he himself had never
" studied

"studied nor knew any other than his mother
"tongue. They at the same time mention, as
"matter of certainty, that the religion of the
"*Siamese* comes from those parts; as they have
"read in a *Balic* book that SOMMONACODOM,
"the idol of the *Siamese*, was the son of a
"King of *Ceylone* \*."

THE language of the man mentioned in this
passage, who came from the neighbourhood of
*Cape Comorin*, could be no other than the *Tamulic*, but the words here alluded to may very
possibly have been derivatives from the *Shanscrit*,
common to both that and the *Balic*.

IN another part of the same work, where
the author treats of the history of SOMMONACO-

\* " Les Siamois ne nomment aucun païs ou la langue
" Bali, qui est celle de leurs loix et de leur religion, soit
" aujourdhuy en usage. Ils soupçonnent à la verité, sur le
" rapport de quelques-uns d'entre eux, qui ont été à la
" côte de Coromandel, que la langue Balic a quelque resem-
" blance avec quelqu'un des dialects de ce païs là : mais ils
" conviennent en même temps que les lettres de la langue
" Balic ne sont connues que chez eux. Les Missionnaires
" seculiers à Siam croyent que cette langue n'est pas entiere-
" ment morte; parce qu'ils ont vu dans leur hopital un
" homme des environs du Cap de Comorin, qui mettoit plu-
" sieurs mots Balis dans son langage, assurant qu'ils etoient
" en usage en son païs, et que lui n'avoit jamais etudié, et
" ne savoit que sa langue maternelle. Ils donnent d'ailleurs
" pour certain que la religion des Siamois vient de ces quar-
" tiers là, parce quils ont lu dans un livre Balic que Som-
" monacodom que les Siamois adorent, etoit fils d' un Roy
" de l'isle de Ceylone."

DOM

dom at large, on the authority of the *Balic* books, he says:

"The father of Sommonacodom, according to the same *Balic* book, was a King of *Teve Lanca*, that is to say, of the famous *Ceylone* \*."

Here it is observable, that while the country of *Siam* seems to be utterly unknown, both to the natives of *Ceylone* and *Hindoſtan*, *Ceylone* should nevertheleſs be ſo well known to the *Siameſe*, and under the ſame appellation it bears in the *Shanſcrit*. An epithet is alſo here prefixed to it, which ſeems to be the ſame as that uſed by the *Hindoos* in ſpeaking of that iſland, for they alſo call it in *Shanſcrit Déve Lanca* or *the Sacred Lanca*. From ſeveral paſſages in the ſame work it alſo appears, that the *Shanſcrit* word *Mahá*, which ſignifies *great*, is conſtantly uſed in the *Balic* language in the ſame ſenſe. And the names of the days of the week are moſt of them the ſame in *Shanſcrit* and in *Balic*, as may be ſeen in the following compariſon of them.

| *Shanſcrit* | *Balic* | |
|---|---|---|
| Aditta-vâr, | Van Athit, | Sunday. |

\* "Le pere de Sommonacodom etoit, ſelon ce meſme
"livre Bali, un Roy de Teve Lanca, c'eſt à dire un Roy de
"la celebre Ceylan."

Soma-

| Shanscrit. | Balie. | |
|---|---|---|
| Soma-vâr, | Van *Tchân, | Monday, |
| Mungela-vâr, | Van Angkaan, | Tuesday. |
| Bouci-vâr, | Van Pout, | Wednesday, |
| Brahspati-vâr, | Van Prahou, | Thursday. |
| Soucra-vâr, | Van Souc, | Friday. |
| Sany-vâr, | Van Saon, | Saturday. |

The same author gives, in another place, an account of a pretended print of a foot on a rock, which is an object of worship to the *Siamese*, and is called *Prabát*, or the venerable foot. For *prá* in *Balie*, he says, signifies *venerable*, which agrees with *práper* and *pramesht* in *Shanscrit*, and *Bát* in the same tongue is a foot, as *Pád* in *Shanscrit*. After which he goes on to say:

" We know that in the island of Ceylone,
" there is a pretended print of a human foot,
" which has long been held in great veneration.
" It represents, doubtless, the left foot, for
" the *Siamese* say that Sommonacodom set his
" right foot on their *Prabat*, and his left foot
" at *Lanca* †."

From Knox's history of *Ceylone* it appears, that the impression here spoken of is upon the

* Here one *Hindoo* word is substituted for another, for *Tchin* in *Hindostany*, and *Tchander* in *Shanscrit*, signify the moon, as well as Soma.

† " On fait que dans l'isle de Ceylan, il y a un pretendu
" vestige de pié humain, que depuis long temps y est grande
" veneration. Il represente sans doute le pie gauche; car
" les Siamois disent que Sommonacodom posa le pie droit à
" leur *prabat*, et le pie gauche à Lanca."

hill

hill called by the *Chingelays Hamaleil*, by Europeans *Adam's Peak*, and that the natives believe it to be the foot-step of their great idol BUDDOU; between the worship of whom, as described by KNOX, and that of SOMMONACODOM, as related by M. DE LA LOUBERE, there is a striking resemblance in many particulars, which it may be proper here to enumerate.

1*st*. BESIDES the foot-steps above mentioned, there is a kind of tree (which from description appears to be the *Pipel* tree, so well known in *India*) which the *Chingelays* hold sacred to BUDDOU and the *Siamese* to SOMMONACODOM; insomuch that the latter deem it meritorious to hang themselves upon it. The *Chingelays* called it *Bogahah*; for *gahah*, in their language, signifies a tree, and *bo* seems to be an abbreviation of BOD or BUDDOU; and the *Siamese* call it in *Balic*, *Prass Mahà Pout*, which, according to DE LA LOUBERE'S interpretation, signifies the tree of the great *Pout* \*. This he supposes to mean MERCURY, for he observes that *Pout* or *Poot* is the name of that planet in the *Balic* term for *Wednesday*; and in another place, he says, POUT is one of the names of SOMMONACODOM. It is certain that *Wednesday* is called the day of BOD or BUDD in all the *Hindoo* languages, among which the *Tamulic*, having no *b*, begins the word

\* " In vulgar *Siamese* they call it *Ten-ps*.

with

with a *p*, which brings it very near the *Balic* mode of writing it. It is equally certain, that the days of the week in all thefe languages, are called after the planets in the fame order as with us, and that BOD, BUDD, or POOR, holds the place of MERCURY. From all which it fhould appear, that POUT, which among the *Siamefe* is another name for SOMMONACODOM, is itfelf a corruption of BUDDOU, who is the MERCURY of the *Greeks*. And it is fingular that, according to M. DE LA LOUBERE, the mother of SOMMONA-CODOM is called in *Balic* MAHA-MANIA, or THE GREAT MANIA, which refembles much the name of MAIA, the mother of MERCURY; at the fame time that the *Tamulic* termination *en*, which renders the word *Pooden*, creates a refemblance between this and the WODEN of the *Gothic* nations, from which the fame day of the week is denominated, and which, on that and other accounts, is allowed to be the MERCURY of the *Greeks*.

2*dly*. THE temples of SOMMONACODOM are called *Pihán*, and round them are habitations for the priefts refembling a college, fo thofe of BUDDOU are called *Vihár*, and the principal priefts live in them as in a college. The word *Vihár*, or as the natives of *Bengal* would write it *Bihár*, is *Shanfcrit*; and FERISHTAH, in his hiftory of *Bengal*, fays, that this name was

given

given by the *Hindoos* to the Province of *Behár*, because it was formerly so full of *Bramins* as to be, as it were, one great *seminary of Learning*, as the word imports.

*3dly.* The *Siamese* have two orders of priests, and so have the worshippers of Buddou. Both the one and the other are distinguished by a yellow habit, and by another circumstance which must be mentioned in the words of the respective authors. Knox says of the Buddou priests, "They have the honour of carrying "the *Tallipot* with the broad end over their "heads foremost, which none but the King "does." And M. DE LA LOUBERE says of the *Siamese* priests, "To defend themselves "from the sun they have the *Talapat*, which "is their little umbrella in the form of a "screen *."

The word here used is common to most of the *Hindoo* languages, and signifies *the leaf of the Palmyra tree*. M. DE LA LOUBERE mentions it as a *Siamese* word, without seeming to know its origin or primary signification.

*4thly.* The priests of Buddou, as well as those of Sommonacodom, are bound to celibacy, as long as they continue in the profession; but both the one and the other are allowed to lay it down and marry.

* " Pour se garentir du soleil ils ont le Talapat, qui est
" leur petit parasol en forme d'ecran."

*5thly.*

5*thly.* They both eat flesh, but will not kill the animal.

6*thly.* The priests of either nation are of no particular tribe, but are chosen out of the body of the people.

These circumstances plainly shew, that this is a system of religion different from that of the *Vèds*, and some of them are totally inconsistent with the principles and practice of the *Bramins*. And indeed it is manifest, from Knox's whole account, that the religion of the *Chingelays* is quite distinct from that which prevails at this day among the *Hindoos*, nor does it appear that there is such a race of men as that of the *Bramins* among them. The only part in which there seems to be any agreement is in the worship of the *Debtahs*, which has probably crept in among them from their *Tamulian* neighbours, but that is carried on in a manner very different from the *Braminical* system, and appears to be held by the nation at large in very great contempt, if not abhorrence. Knox's account of it is this: " Their temples (i. e. those of the " *Debtahs*) are, he says, called *Covels*," which is the *Tamulic* word for *Pagoda*. He then goes on to say, " A man piously disposed " builds a small house at his own charge, " which is the *temple*, and *himself becomes priest* " *thereof*. This house is seldom called *God's* " *House*,

"House, but most usually *Jacc's the Devil's.*" But of the prevailing religion he speaks in very different terms, and describes it as carried on with much parade and splendour, and attended with marks of great antiquity. "The Pagodas
" or temples of their Gods," says he, "are so
" many that I cannot number them. Many
" of them are of rare and exquisite work, built
" of hewn stone, engraven with images and
" figures, but by whom and when I could
" not attain to know, the inhabitants them-
" selves being ignorant therein. But sure I
" am they were built by far more ingenious
" artificers than the *Chingelays* that now are
" on the land. For the *Portugnese* in their in-
" vasions have defaced some of them, which
" there is none found that hath skill enough
" to repair to this day." In another place he says, " Here are some antient writings engraven
" upon rocks which puzzle all that see them.
" There are divers great rocks in divers parts
" in *Cande Uda*, and in the northern parts.
" These rocks are cut deep with great letters
" for the space of some yards, so deep that
" they may last to the world's end. Nobody
" can read them, or make any thing of them.
" I have asked *Malabars* and *Gentoos*, as well as
" *Chingelays* and *Moors*, but none of them un-
" derstood them. There is an antient temple,

"*Goddiladenni* in *Tattanour*, stands by a place where there are some of these letters." From all which the antiquity of the nation and their religion is sufficiently evident; and from other passages it is plain, that the worship of BUDDOU in particular, has been from remote times a very eminent part of that religion; for the same author, speaking of the tree at *Anurodgburro*, in the northern part of the island, which is sacred to BUDDOU, says, "The due performance of this worship they reckon not a little meritorious: insomuch that, as they report, ninety Kings have reigned there successively, where by the ruins that still remain, it appears they spared not for pains and labour to build temples and high monuments to the honour of this God, as if they had been born to hew rocks and great stones, and lay them up in heaps. These Kings are now happy spirits, having merited it by these labours." And again he says, "For this God above all other, they seem to have an high respect and devotion," &c.

AND from other authorities it will appear, that this worship has formerly been by no means confined to *Ceylone*, but has prevailed in several parts of *India* prior to that of the *Bramins*, nay that this has been the case even so late as the ninth and twelfth centuries of the *Christian Æra*.

IN

In the well-known *Anciennes Relations* *, translated from the *Arabic* by that eminent Orientalist Eusebius Renaudot, the *Arabian* traveller gives this account of the custom of dancing-women, which continues to this day in the *Decan*, but it is not known among the *Hindoos* of *Bengal* or *Hindostan* proper.

" There are in *India* public women, called
" *women of the idol*, and the origin of this
" custom is this: When a woman has made a
" vow for the purpose of having children, if
" she brings into the world a pretty daughter,
" she carries it to Bod so they call the idol
" which they adore, and leaves it with him †."

This is a pretty just account of this custom, as it prevails at this day in the *Decan*, for children are indeed devoted to this profession by their parents, and when they grow up in it, they are called in *Tamulic Devadasi*, or *female slaves of the idol*. But it is evident they have changed their master since this *Arabian* account

---

* Anciennes Relations des Indes et de la Chine, de deux Voyageurs Mohametans, qui y allerent dans le neuvieme Siecle. *Paris*, 1718, 8vo.

† " Il y a dans les Indes des femmes publiques, appellée
" femmes de l'idole; l' origine de cette coustume est telle:
" Lors qu'une femme a fait un voeu pour avoir des enfans,
" si elle met au monde une belle fille, elle l' apporte au Bod,
" c'est ainsi qu' ils appellent l' idole qu'ils adorent, auprès
" duquel elle la laisse, &c." Anc. Rel. p. 109.

was written, for there is no idol of the name of BOD now worshipped there. And the circumstance of this custom being unknown in other parts of *India* would lead one to suspect, that the *Bramins*, on introducing their system of religion into that country, had thought fit to retain this part of the former worship, as being equally agreeable to themselves and their new disciples.

THE same *Arabian* travellers give us an account of a very powerful race of *Hindoo* Kings, according to them indeed the most powerful in *India*, who then reigned on the *Malabar* Coast with the title of *Balhara*. Their dominion appears to have extended over *Guzerat*, and the greatest part, if not the whole, of the ancient kingdom of *Visiapoor*. For the *Arabian* geographer quoted by M. RENAUDOT, makes *Nahelwarah* the metropolis of these princes, which is doubtless *Nahercalah*, the ancient capital of *Guzerat*, though M. RENAUDOT seems not to have known that place; and the rest of the description sufficiently shews the great extent of their dominion southward. M. D'ANVILLE speaks of this race of Kings on the authority of the *Arabian* geographer EDRISI, who wrote in the twelfth century, according to whom it appears that their religion was, even so late as that period, not the *Braminical*, but that of which

we

we are now speaking. M. D'Anville's words are these: "Edrisi acquaints us with the reli-
"gion which this Prince professed in saying,
"that his worship was addressed to *Beddu*,
"who, according to St. Jerome and Clemens
"Alexandrinus, was the founder of the sect
"of the *Gymnosophists*, in like manner as the
"*Bramins* were used to attribute their insti-
"tution to *Brahma* *."

The authority of Clemens Alexandri-
nus is also cited on the same subject by Relan-
dus in his 11th Dissertation, where, treating of
the language of *Ceylone*, he explains the word
*Vebdr*, above spoken of, in these terms.

"*Vebdr* signifies a temple of their principal
"God Buddou, who, as Clemens Alexan-
"drinus has long ago observed, was worship-
"ped as a God by the *Hindoos* †."

After the above quotations, the following extract from the voyage of that inquisitive and ingenious traveller M. Gentil, published in

---

\* "L'Edrisi nous instruit sur la religion que professoit ce
" Prince, en disant que son culte s' addressoit a Bodda, que
" selon St. Jerome et St. Clement d' Alexandrie
" avoit ete l'instituteur des Gymnosophistes, comme les
" Brachmanes rapportoient à Brahma leur institut." Ant.
Geog. de L'Inde, p. 94.

† "*Vebdr*, templum dei primarii *Buddou* sacrum quem In-
" dos ut Deum venerari jam olim notavit Clemens Alex-
" andrinus." Strom. lib. 1. p. 273. Rel. Diss. pars
tertia, p. 85.

Vol. II.      D      1779,

1779, is given as a further and very remarkable illustration of this subject.

"This system is also that of the *Bramins* of our time; it forms the basis of that religion which they have brought with them into the southern parts of the Peninsula of *Hindostan*, into *Madura*, *Tanjore*, and *Maissore*.

"There was then in those parts of *India*, and principally on the Coast of *Choromandel* and *Ceylone*, a sort of worship, the precepts of which we are quite unacquainted with. The God Baouth, of whom at present they know no more in *India* than the name, was the object of this worship; but it is now totally abolished, except that there may possibly yet be found some families of *Indians*, who have remained faithful to Baouth, and do not acknowledge the religion of the *Bramins*, and who are on that account separated from and despised by the other Casts.

"I have not indeed heard that there are any such families in the neighbourhood of *Pondichery*, but there is a circumstance well worthy of remark, which none of the travellers that have treated of the Coast of *Choromandel* and *Pondichery* seem to have noticed. It is this: That at a short league's distance to the south of this town, in the plain
"of

" of *Virapatnam*, and pretty near the river, we
" had a statue of Granite very hard and beau-
" tiful. This statue, which is from three
" feet to three and a half in height, is sunk
" in the sand to the waist, and weighs, doubtless,
" many thousand weight; it is, as it were,
" abandoned in the midst of this extensive plain.
" I cannot give a better idea of it, than by
" saying, that it exactly agrees with and re-
" sembles the *Sommonocodom* of the *Siamese*;
" its head is of the same form, it has the same
" features, its arms are in the same attitude,
" and its ears are exactly similar. The form
" of this divinity, which has certainly been
" made in the country, and which in no respect
" resembles the present idols of the *Gentoos*,
" struck me as I passed this plain. I made va-
" rious inquiries concerning this singular
" figure; and the *Tamulians* one and all af-
" fured me that this was the God BAOUTH,
" who was now no longer regarded, for that
" his worship and his festivals had been abo-
" lished ever since the *Bramins* had made
" themselves masters of the people's faith *."

* " Ce système est aussi celui des Bramnes de nos jours;
" il fait la base de la religion qu' ils ont apportée dans le sud
" de la presqu' isle de l' Indostan, le Madure, le Tan-
" jaour, et le Maissour.
" Il y avoit alors dans ces parties de l' Inde, et princi-
" palement à la Côte de Coromandel et à Ceylan, un culte
" dont

D 2

M. GENTIL then goes on to say a good deal more upon this subject, in the course of which he supposes, that this Deity is the *Fo* of the *Chinese*, whose worship, by their own accounts, was brought from *India*. And indeed the abridgement of the name *Poet*, mentioned in a note of this paper, which the vulgar *Siamese* reduce to the single syllable *Po*, seems to countenance this opinion. But as this is foreign to our present purpose, and the above passages, it is hoped, are sufficient to establish what was

" dont on ignore absolument les dogmes : le Dieu Baouth,
" dont on ne connoit aujourd'hui dans l' Inde que le nom,
" etoit l'objet de ce culte ; mais il est tout-a-fait aboli, si ce
" n'est qu'il se trouve encore quelques familles d' Indiens sé-
" parées et méprisées des autres Castes, qui sont restées fideles
" a Baouth, et qui ne reconnoissent point la religion des
" Brames.

" Je n' ai pas entendu dire qu'il y ait de ces familles aux en-
" virons de Pondichery; cependant, une chose tres digne
" de remarque, & a laquelle aucun des Voyageurs qui
" parlent de la Côte de Coromandel & de Pondichery n'ont
" fait attention, est, que l' on trouve a une petite lieue au
" sud de cette ville, dans la plaine de Virapatnam, assez
" pres de la riviere, une statue de Granit tres dur & tres
" beau : cette statue, d' environ trois pieds a trois pieds &
" demi de hauteur, est enfoncée dans le sable jusqu' a la cein-
" ture, & pese sans doute plusieurs milliers ; elle est comme
" abandonnée au milieu de cette vaste plaine : je ne peux
" mieux en donner une idée, qu'en disant qu' elle est ex-
" actement conforme & ressemblante a *Sommonacadam* des
" Siamois ; c'est la même forme de tête, ce sont les
" mêmes traits dans le visage, c'est la même attitude dans les
" bras, and les oreilles sont absolument semblables. La
" forme

proposed, it seems high time to take leave of this subject, with an apology for that prolixity which is inseparable from this kind of discussion. *17th June 1784.*

" forme de cette divinité, qui certainement a été fait dans
" le pays, & qui ne ressemble en rien aux divinités actuelles
" des Gentils, m'avoit frappé lorsque je passai dans cette
" plaine. Je fis diverses informations sur cette figure singu-
" liere, les Tamoulas m'assurerent tous que c'etoit Baouth,
" qu' on ne regardoit plus ; que son culte & ses fêtes etoient
" cessées depuis que les Brames s' etoient rendus les maitres
" de la croyance du peuple."

[ 38 ]

# ACCOUNT
## OF AN
# INTERVIEW
### BETWEEN
TEESHOO LAMA and Lieut. SAMUEL TURNER

(WHO WAS APPOINTED ON AN EMBASSY TO TIBET),

AT THE MONASTERY OF TERPALING:

COMMUNICATED IN A LETTER FROM

*Lieutenant* SAMUEL TURNER

TO THE

Honourable JOHN MACPHERSON, Esq.

GOVERNOR-GENERAL OF BENGAL.

---

PATNA, *March* 2, 1784.

DURING my residence in *Tibet*, it was an object I had much at heart to obtain an interview of the infant TEESHOO LAMA, but the Emperor of *China*'s general orders, restricting his guardians to keep him in the strictest privacy, and prohibiting indiscriminately the admission of all persons to his presence, even his votaries, who should come from a distance, appeared to me an obstacle almost insurmountable:

able: yet, however, the Rajah, mindful of the amity subsisting between the Governor and him, and unwilling, I believe, by any act to hazard its interruption, at length consented to grant me that indulgence. As the meeting was attended with very singular and striking circumstances, I could not help noting them with most particular attention; and though the repetition of such facts, interwoven and blended as they are with superstition, may expose me to the imputation of extravagance and exaggeration, yet I should think myself reprehensible to suppress them; and while I divest myself of all prejudice and assume the part of a faithful narrator, I hope, however tedious the detail I propose to enter into may be found, it will be received with candour, and merit the attention of those for whose perusal and information it is intended, were it only to mark a strong feature in the national character, of implicit homage to the great religious sovereign, and to instance the very uncommon, I may say almost unheard-of, effects of early tuition.

I SHALL, perhaps, be still more justified in making this relation, by adverting to that very extraordinary assurance the Rajah of TEESHOO LOOMBOO made me but a few days before my departure from his court, which, without further introduction, I will beg leave literally to recite.

AT an interview he allowed me, after having given me my audience of leave, said he, "I had yesterday a vision of our tutelary deity, and to me it was a day replete with much interesting and important matter. This guardian power, who inspires us with his illuminations on every momentous and great occasion, indulged me with a divination, from which I have collected that every thing will be well: set your heart at rest, for tho' a separation is about to take place between us, yet our friendship will not cease to exist; but through the favour of interposing Providence you may rest assured it will increase, and terminate eventually in that which will be for the best."

I should have paid less regard to so strange an observation but for this reason, that however different from other doctrines their positions may be found, yet I judge they are the best foundation to build our reliances upon, and superstition combining with inclination to implant such friendly sentiments in their minds, will ever constitute, the opinion having once obtained, the strongest barrier to their preservation. Opposed to the prejudices of a people, no plan can reasonably be expected to take place: agreeing with them success must be the result.

ON the 3d of December 1783, I arrived at *Terpaling*, situated on the summit of a high hill, and it was about noon when I entered the gates of the Monastery, which was not long since erected for the reception and education of TEESHOO LAMA. He resides in a palace in the center of the Monastery, which occupies about a mile of ground in circumference, and the whole is encompassed by a wall. The several buildings serve for the accommodation of three hundred *Gylongs* appointed to perform religious service with TEESHOO LAMA, until he shall be removed to the Monastery and Musnud of *Teeshoo Loomboo*. It is unusual to make visits either here or in *Bootan* on the day of arrival: we therefore rested this day, only receiving and sending messages of compliment.

ON the 4th in the morning, I was allowed to visit TEESHOO LAMA, and found him placed in great form upon his Musnud; on the left side stood his father and mother, on the other the officer particularly appointed to wait upon his person. The Musnud is a fabrick of silk cushions piled one upon the other until the seat is elevated to the height of four feet from the floor; an embroidered silk covered the top, and the sides were decorated with pieces of silk of various colours suspended from the upper edge and hanging down. By the particular request

quest of TEESHOO LAMA's father, Mr. SAUN-
DERS and myself wore the *English* dress.

I ADVANCED, and, as is the custom, presented a white pelong handkerchief, and delivered also into the LAMA's hands the Governor's present of a string of pearls and coral,
while the other things were set down before
him. Having performed the ceremony of the
exchange of handkerchiefs with his father and
mother, we took our seats on the right of
TEESHOO LAMA.

A MULTITUDE of persons, all those ordered
to escort me, were admitted to his presence,
and allowed to make their prostrations. The
infant LAMA turned towards them, and received them all with a chearful and significant
look of complacency. His father then addressed me in the *Tibet* language, which was
explained to me by the interpreter, that
TEESHOO LAMA had been used to remain at
rest until this time of the day, but he had
awoke very early this morning, and could not
be prevailed on to remain longer in bed, for,
added he, " the *English* Gentlemen were ar-
" rived, and he could not sleep." During
the time we were in the room, I observed the
LAMA's eyes were scarce ever turned from us,
and when our cups were empty of tea, he appeared uneasy, and throwing back his head
and contracting the skin of his brow, he kept
making

making a noise, for he could not speak, until they were filled again. He took out of a golden cup, containing confects, some burnt sugar, and stretching out his arm made a motion to his attendants to give them to me. He then sent some in like manner to Mr. SAUNDERS, who was with me. I found myself, though visiting an infant, under the necessity of saying something, for it was hinted to me, that notwithstanding he is unable to reply, it is not to be inferred that he cannot understand. However, his incapacity of answering excused me many words, and I just briefly said, That the Governor-General on receiving the news of his decease in *China*, was overwhelmed with grief and sorrow, and continued to lament his absence from the world until the cloud that had overcast the happiness of this nation by his reappearance was dispelled and then, if possible, a greater degree of joy had taken place than he had experienced of grief on receiving the first mournful news. The Governor wished he might long continue to illumine the world with his presence, and was hopeful that the friendship which had formerly subsisted between them would not be diminished, but rather that it might become still greater than before, and that by his continuing to shew kindness to my countrymen, there might be an extensive communication between his votaries and the dependants

pendants of the *British* nation. The little creature turned, looking ftedfaftly towards me with the appearance of much attention while I fpoke, and nodded with repeated but flow movements of the head, as though he underftood and approved every word, but could not utter a reply. The parents, who ftood by all the time, eyed their fon with a look of affection, and a fmile expreffive of heartfelt joy at the propriety of the young LAMA's conduct. His whole regard was turned to us; he was filent and fedate, never once looking towards his parents, as if under their influence at the time; and with whatever pains his manners may have been formed fo correct, yet I muft own his behaviour on this occafion appeared perfectly natural and fpontaneous, and not directed by any action or fign of authority.

The fcene in which I was here brought to take a part was too new and extraordinary, however trivial, if not abfurd, as it may appear to fome, not to claim from me great attention and confequently minute remark.

TEESHOO LAMA is at this time about 18 months of age. He did not fpeak a word, but made moft expreffive figns, and conducted himfelf with aftonifhing dignity and decorum. His complexion is of that hue which in *England* we fhould term rather brown, but not
without

without colour. His features good—small black eyes—an animated expreſſion of countenance—and altogether I thought him one of the handſomeſt children I had ever ſeen. I had but little converſation with the father. He told me he had directions to entertain me three days on account of TESHOO LAMA, and entreated me with ſo much earneſtneſs to paſs another on his own account, that I could not refiſt complying with his requeſt. He then invited us for to-morrow to an entertainment he propoſed to make at a ſmall diſtance from the Monaſtery; which invitation having accepted, we took our leave and retired.

In the courſe of the afternoon I was viſited by two officers of the LAMA's houſhold, both of whom are immediately attendant on his perſon. They ſat and converſed with me ſome time; enquired after Mr. BOGLE, whom both of them had ſeen; and then remarking how extremely fortunate it was the young LAMA's having regarded us with very particular notice, obſerved on the very ſtrong partiality of the former TESHOO LAMA for the *Engliſh*, and that the preſent one often tried to utter the name of the *Engliſh*. I encouraged the thought, hopeful that they would teach the prejudice to ſtrengthen with his increaſing age; and they aſſured me that ſhould he, when he begins to
ſpeak,

speak, have forgot, they would early teach him to repeat the name of HASTINGS.

ON the morning of the 6:th, I again waited on TESHOO LAMA to present some curiosities I had brought for him from *Bengal*. He was very much struck with a small clock, and had it held to him, watching for a long time the revolutions of the moment-hand; he admired it, but with gravity and without any childish emotion. There was nothing in the ceremony different from the first day's visit. The father and mother were present. I staid about half an hour, and retired to return and take leave in the afternoon.

THE votaries of TESHOO LAMA already begin to flock in numbers to pay their adorations to him. Few are yet admitted to his presence. Those who come esteem it a happiness if he is but shown to them from the window, and they are able to make their prostrations before he is removed. There came to-day a party of *Kilmaaks (Calmuc Tartars)* for purposes of devotion and to make their offerings to the LAMA. When I returned from visiting him, I saw them standing at the entrance of the square in front of the palace, each with his cap off, his hands being placed together elevated, and held even with his face. They remained upwards of half an hour in this

this attitude, their eyes fixed upon the apartment of the LAMA, and anxiety very visibly depicted in their countenances. At length, I imagine, he appeared to them, for they began all together by lifting their hands, still closed, above their heads, then bringing them even with their faces, and after lowering them to their breasts, then separating them; to assist them in sinking and rising, they dropt upon their knees and struck their heads against the ground. This with the same motions was repeated nine times. They afterwards advanced to deliver their presents, consisting of talents of gold and silver, with the products of their country, to the proper officer, who having received them, they retired apparently with much satisfaction.

Upon enquiry I learnt that offerings made in this manner are by no means unfrequent, and in reality constitute one of the most copious sources from which the LAMAS of *Tibet* derive their wealth.

No one thinks himself degraded by performing these humiliations. The persons I allude to, who came for this devout purpose, were attendant on a man of superior rank, that seemed to be more engrossed than the rest in the performance of the ceremony. He wore a rich satin garment lined with fox skins, and a

cap

cap with a tassel of scarlet silk flowing from the center of the crown upon the sides all round, and edged with a broad band of *Siberian* fur.

ACCORDING to appointment, I went in the afternoon to make my last visit to TEESHOO LAMA. I received his dispatches for the Governor General, and from his parents two pieces of satin for the Governor, with many compliments.

THEY presented me with a vest lined with lambskins, making many assurances of a long remembrance, and observing, that att his time TEESHOO LAMA is an infant and incapable of conversing, but they hoped to see me again when he shall have become of age. I replied, that by favour of the LAMA I might again visit this country: I looked forward with anxiety to the time when he should mount the Musnud, and should then be extremely happy in the opportunity of paying my respects. After some expressions and protestations of mutual regard, my visit was concluded: I received the handkerchiefs and took my leave; and am to pursue my journey towards *Bengal* to-morrow at the dawn of day.

# AN ACCOUNT OF A JOURNEY TO TIBET,

MADE BY POORUNGEER, a GOSSEYN,

AND OF HIS RECEPTION BY TEESHOO LAMA:

COMMUNICATED IN A LETTER FROM Lieutenant SAMUEL TURNER

TO THE Honourable JOHN MACPHERSON, Esq.

GOVERNOR-GENERAL OF BENGAL.

---

HONOURABLE SIR,

HAVING, in obedience to the instructions with which you were pleased to honour me, examined POORUNGEER, the *Gosseyn*, who has at different times been employed in deputations to the late TEESHOO LAMA, formerly accompanied him to the court of *Pekin*, and who is lately again returned from *Tibet*, and having collected from him such an account of the journey he has just performed, and other information

tion as he could give me relative to the countries he has left; I beg leave to submit it to you in the following narrative.

In the beginning of last year POORUNGEER having received dispatches from Mr. HASTINGS, a short time previous to his departure from *Bengal*, for TESHOO LAMA and the Regent of TEESHO LOOMBOO, immediately set about preparing for the distant journey he had engaged to undertake, which employed him until the beginning of the following month of March, when I beg leave to recal to your remembrance I had the honour to present him to you for his dismission. He then commenced his journey from *Calcutta*, and early in the month of April had passed, as he relates, the limits of the Company's Provinces, and entered the mountains that constitute the kingdom of *Bootan*, where, in the prosecution of his journey, he received from the subjects of the DAIB RAJA the most ample and voluntary assistance to the frontier of his territory, nor met with any impediment to oppose his progress until he came upon the borders of *Tibet*. Here he was compelled to halt for near a fortnight by a heavy fall of snow, that commenced upon his arrival, and continued incessantly for the space of six days, covering the face of the country to so great a depth as totally to put a stop to all travelling,

and

and render it impracticable for him to proceed until a thaw succeeded to open the communication. During the time of his confinement at *Phari*, he says, such was the severity of the cold, and the injurious effect so rapid a transition from a temperate climate had on the health of himself and his companions, that it left him little room to doubt, if an early change had not fortunately taken place and permitted his advance, that they must all have fallen victims to the inclemency of the weather.

However, as early as it was possible for him to leave *Phari*, he proceeded by long stages on his journey, and without encountering any farther difficulty, on the 8th of May following, reached *Teshoo Loomboo*, the capital of *Tibet*. Immediately upon entering the Monastery, he went to the Durbar of the Regent Ponjur Intinnee Nemohein to announce his arrival and the purpose of his commission. Quarters were then allotted for his residence, and an hour fixed for him to wait upon Teeshoo Lama; who, he was informed, the following morning intended to leave the palace to occupy one of his gardens, situated on the plain within sight of the Monastery, where it was visible a considerable encampment had been formed. The Lama quitted his apartment at the first dawn of day, and was lodged in the

tent.

tents pitched for his accommodation before the sun had rifen.

In the courfe of the morning, at the hour appointed for his admiffion, POORUNGEER went down to the LAMA's tents. He heard, on entering the gates of the enclofure, that the young LAMA was taking his recreation in the garden, ranging about, which became with him a very favourite amufement. As it was at this time in *Tibet* the warmeft part of the year, that he might enjoy the benefit of the air, his attendants had chofen a fpot where the trees afforded a complete fhade to place an elevated feat of cufhions for the young LAMA, after his exercife, to reft upon. In this fituation POORUNGEER found him, when fummoned to his prefence, attended by the Regent, his parents, SOOPOON CHOOMBOO, the cup-bearer, and the principal officers of the court. After making three obeifances at as remote a diftance as it was poffible, POORUNGEER approached, and prefented to the LAMA, according to the cuftom of *Tibet*, a piece of white pelong, and then delivered the letters and prefents with which he had been charged. The packages were all immediately opened before the LAMA, who had every article brought near to him, and viewed them feparately one by one. The letter he took into his own hand, himfelf broke the

feal,

seal, and taking from under the cover a string of pearls, which it enclosed, run them over between his fingers, as they read their rosaries, and then with an arch air placed them by his side, nor would, while the narrator was in his presence, permit any one to take them up. Poorungeer says, the young LAMA regarded him with a very kind and significant look, spoke to him in the *Tibet* language, and asked him if he had had a fatiguing journey. The interview lasted more than an hour, during all which time the LAMA sat with the utmost composure, not once attempting to quit his seat, nor discovering the least froward uneasiness at his confinement. Tea was twice brought in, and the LAMA drank a cup each time. When ordered to accept his dismission, POORUNGEER approached the LAMA, and bowing before him, presented his head uncovered to receive his blessing, which the young LAMA gave by stretching out his hand and laying it upon his head. He then ordered him, for as long as he resided at *Teeshoo Loombo*, to come to him once every day.

THE following morning POORUNGEER waited upon the Regent at his apartments in the palace, to whom, after observing the customary forms of introduction, he delivered his dispatches. After this he visited SOOPOON CHOOMBOO,

Choomboo, the Lama's parents, and others to whom he was before known, and says, he experienced from all quarters the most cordial and kind reception; for they had been long used to consider him as an agent of the Government of *Bengal*. He found no change whatever to have ensued in the Administration since his attendance upon me in *Tibet*. The country enjoyed perfect tranquillity, and the only event that had taken place of importance in their annals was the inauguration of the infant Lama, which happened the preceding year; and as this constitutes a concern of the highest moment, whether considered in a political or religious point of view, being no less than the recognizance in an infant form of their re-generated immortal Sovereign and ecclesiastical Supreme, I was induced to bestow more than common pains to trace the ceremonies that attended the celebration of such a great event, conceiving that the novelty of the subject might render the account curious, if even it should be found to contain no information of real utility. I shall therefore, without further apology, subjoin the result of my enquiries, premising only that my authority for the description is derived principally from Poorungeer, and confirmed, with some additional particulars, by the concurring reports of of a *Goffyen*, who was at the time himself present on the spot.

The Emperor of *China* appears on this occasion to have assumed a very conspicuous part in giving testimony of his respect and zeal for the great religious Father of his faith. Early in the year 1784, he dismissed ambassadors from the court of *Pekin* to *Teeshoo Loomboo*, to represent their sovereign in supporting the dignity of the High Priest, and do honour to the occasion of the assumption of his office. Dalai Lama and the Viceroy of *Lassa*, accompanied by all the court, one of the *Chinese* Generals stationed at *Lassa*, with a part of the troops under his command, two of the four magistrates of the city, the heads of every Monastery throughout *Tibet*, and the Emperor's ambassadors, appeared at *Teeshoo Loomboo* to celebrate this epocha in their theological institutions. The 28th day of the seventh moon, corresponding nearly, as their year commences with the vernal equinox, to the middle of October 1784, was chosen as the most auspicious for the ceremony of inauguration; a few days previous to which the Lama was conducted from *Terpaling*, the Monastery in which he had passed his infancy, with every mark of pomp and homage that could be paid by an enthusiastick people. So great a concourse as assembled

sembled either from curiosity or devotion was never seen before, for not a person of any condition in *Tibet* was absent who could join the suite. The procession was hence necessarily constrained to move so slow, that though *Terpaling* is situated at the distance of twenty miles only from *Teeshoo Loomboo*, three days expired in the performance of this short march. The first halt was made at *Tsondue*; the second at *Summaar*, about six miles off, whence the most splendid parade was reserved for the Lama's entry on the third day; the account of which is given me by a person who was present in the procession. The road, he says, was previously prepared by being whitened with a wash, and having piles of stones heaped up, with small intervals between, on either side. The retinue passed between a double row of priests, who formed a street extending all the way from *Summaar* to the gates of the palace. Some of the priests held lighted rods of a perfumed composition, that burn like decayed wood, and emit an aromatick smoke; the rest were furnished with the different musical instruments they use at their devotions, such as the gong, the cymbal, hautboy, trumpets, drums, and sea-shells, which were all sounded in union with the hymn they chanted. The crowd of spectators were kept without the street, and
none

none admitted on the high road but such as properly belonged to or had a prescribed place in the procession, which was arranged in the following order.

THE van was led by three military commandants or governors of districts at the head of 6 or 7000 horsemen armed with quivers, bows, and matchlocks. In their rear followed the ambassador, with his suite, carrying his diploma, as is the custom of *China*, made up in the form of a large tube, and fastened on his back. Next the *Chinese* General advanced with the troops under his command, mounted and accoutred after their way with fire-arms and sabres; then came a very numerous group bearing the various standards and insignia of state; next to them moved a full band of wind and other sonorous instruments; after which were led two horses richly caparisoned, each carrying two large circular stoves disposed like panniers across the horse's back, and filled with burning aromatic woods. These were followed by a senior priest, called a LAMA, who bore a box containing books of their form of prayer and some favourite idols. Next nine sumptuary horses were led loaded with the LAMA's apparel; after which came the priests immediately attached to the LAMA's person for the performance of daily offices in the temple,
amounting

amounting to about 700: following them were two men, each carrying on his shoulder a large cylindrical gold infignium emboffed with emblematical figures (a gift from the Emperor of *China*). The *Dulmanniers* and *Soopeons*, who were employed in communicating addreffes and diftributing alms, immediately preceded the LAMA's bier, which was covered with a gaudy canopy, and borne by eight of the fixteen *Chinefe* appointed for this fervice. On one fide of the bier attended the Regent, on the other the LAMA's father. It was followed by the heads of the different Monafteries, and as the proceffion advanced, the priefts who formed the ftreet fell in the rear and brought up the fuite, which moved at an extremely flow pace, and about noon was received within the confines of the Monaftery amidft an amazing difplay of colours, the acclamations of the croud, folemn mufick, and the chanting of their priefts.

The LAMA being fafely lodged in the palace, the Regent and SOOPOON CHOOMBOP went out, as is a cuftomary compliment paid to vifitors of high rank on their near approach, to meet and conduct DALAI LAMA and the Viceroy of *Laffa*, who were on the way to *Teefhoo Loomboo*. Their retinues encountered the following morning at the foot of *Painom* caftle, and the next day together entered the Monaftery

Monastery of *Teeshoo Loomboo*, in which both DALAI LAMA and the Viceroy were accommodated during their stay.

THE following morning, which was the third after TESHOO LAMA's arrival, he was carried to the great temple, and about noon seated upon the throne of his progenitors; at which time the Emperor's ambassador delivered his diploma, and placed the presents with which he had been charged at the LAMA's feet.

THE three next ensuing days, DALAI LAMA met TESHOO LAMA in the temple, where they were assisted by all the priests in the invocation and public worship of their Gods. The rites then performed completed, as I understand, the business of inauguration. During this interval all who were at the capital were entertained at the public expence, and alms were distributed without reserve. In conformity likewise to previous notice circulated every where for the same space of time, universal rejoicings prevailed throughout *Tibet*. Banners were unfurled on all their fortresses, the peasantry filled up the day with music and festivity, and the night was celebrated by general illuminations. A long period was afterwards employed in making presents and publick entertainments to the newly-inducted LAMA.

Lama, who at the time of his accession to the Musnud, or, if I may use the term, pontificate, of *Teeshoo Loomboo*, was not three years of age. The ceremony was begun by Dalai Lama, whose offerings are said to have amounted to a greater value, and his publick entertainments to have been more splendid, than the rest. The second day was dedicated to the Viceroy of *Lassa*; the third to the *Chinese* General. Then followed the Culloong or Magistrates of *Lassa*, and the rest of the principal persons who had accompanied Dalai Lama. After which the Regent of *Teeshoo Loomboo*, and all that were dependent on that government, were severally admitted, according to pre-eminence of rank, to pay their tributes of obeisance and respect. As soon as the acknowledgements of all those were received who were admissible to the privilege, Teeshoo Lama made, in the same order, suitable returns to each, and the consummation lasted forty days.

Many importunities were used with Dalai Lama to prolong his stay at *Teeshoo Loomboo*, but he excused himself from encumbering the capital any longer with so numerous a concourse of people as attended on his movements; and deeming it expedient to make his absence as short as possible from the seat of his authority, at the expiration of forty days he withdrew with all his suite to *Lassa*, and the Emperor's ambassador

ambassador received his dismission to return to *China*; and thus terminated this famous festival.

With respect to the lately-established commercial intercourse, POORUNGEER informs me, that though so early, he found himself not the first person who had arrived at *Teeshoo Loomboo* from *Bengal*. Many merchants had already brought their commodities to market, and others followed before he left it. He heard from no quarter any complaint of impediment or loss; and concludes, therefore, that all adventurers met the same easy access and ready aid as he himself had every where experienced. The markets were well stocked with *English* and *Indian* articles, yet not in so great a degree as to lower the value of commodities below the prices of the two or three last preceding years. Bullion was somewhat reduced in worth in comparison with the year 1783. A Pootree, or bulse, of gold dust, the same quantity that then sold for twenty-one Indermillees, was procurable of a purer quality for nineteen and twenty Indermillees. A talent of silver, which was then 500, was 450 Indermillees; so that the exchange was much in favour of the trader.

POORUNGEER, during his residence at *Teeshoo Loomboo*, had very frequent interviews with the Regent and the ministers, and assures me he found the heartiest dispositions in them to encourage

courage the commercial intercourse established under the auspices of the late Governor General, whose departure, however, the Regent regretted, as the loss of the first friend and ally he became connected with of, I believe it may be said, any foreign nation; in whom was acknowledged also the original means of opening the communication and of commencing a correspondence between the Governments of *Bengal* and *Tibet*; and although it may be observed that, in consequence of his having from the beginning been used exclusively to address himself to, and acknowledge alone the agents of, Mr. HASTINGS, his attachments to the *English* nation had grown not without a great degree of personality; yet, free from an unworthy capriciousness of temper, he descended not to take advantage of the opening offered by his friend's departure to close the new connection. For such was the respect he had learnt to entertain for our national integrity of character, that, under the apparent conviction our views tended to no scheme of ambition, but were confined merely to objects of utility and curiosity, POONUNGEER assures me he expressed an anxious desire for continuing with the succeeding Governor General the exercise of those offices of friendship so long supported by his predecessor; and in the hope that his would be met with equal wishes, determined to invite you to join him in preserving the same intercourse of commerce and correspondence so essentially calculated for the benefit of both countries. In consequence of which the LAMA and the Regent addressed the letters POORUNGEER had the honor to deliver to you, translations of which having, in obedience to your directions, been applied for to your *Persian* translator, I now subjoin them.

*Copy of a Letter from* TEESHOO LAMA.

" GOD be praised, that the situation of these
" countries is in peace and happiness, and I am
" always praying at the altar of the Almighty
" for your health and preservation. This is
" not unknown: you are certainly employed
" in protecting and assisting the whole world,
" and you promote the good and happiness of
" mankind. We have made no deviation from
" the union and unanimity which existed
" during the time of the first of nobles Mr.
" HASTINGS and the deceased LAMA, and
" may you also grant friendship to these
" countries, and always make me happy with
" the news of your health, which will be the
" cause of ease to my heart and confirmation
" to my soul. At this time, as friendly offer-
" ings of union and unanimity, I send one
" handkerchief, one ketoo of silver, and one
" piece of cochin. Let them be accepted."

*From*

*From the* Rajah *of* Teeshoo Loomboo.

"God be praised, that the situation of these countries is in peace and happiness, and I am always praying at the altar of the Almighty for your health and preservation. This is not unknown: I am constantly employed in promoting the advantage of the subjects and the service of the newly-seated Lama, because the newly-seated Lama is not distinct from the deceased Lama, and the light of his countenance is exalted. Grant your friendship to Poorungeer *Gosseyn.*

"Maintain union and unanimity and affection, like the first of nobles, and every day make me happy with the news of your health and prosperity, and bestow favours like the first of nobles, and make me happy with letters, which are causes of consolation. At this time, as friendly offerings of union and affection and unanimity, I send one handkerchief, three tolah of gold, and one piece of cochin. Let them be accepted."

Poorungeer, having received these dispatches in the beginning of October, after a residence of five months at *Teeshoo Loomboo,* took leave of the Lama and the Regent, and set out on his return, by the same route he came to *Bengal.* The weather at this season of the year being most extremely favourable for travelling,

ling, he experienced no delay or interruption in the course of his journey through *Tibet* and *Bootan*, but arrived at *Rungpore* early in December, whence he proceeded as expeditiously as possible to the Presidency; where, to his great mortification and concern, he finds upon his arrival his affairs involved in great distress; the little territory his adopted Chela was left in charge of, having during his absence been violently invaded by RAJA CHUND, a neighbouring *Zemeendar*, and to the amount of fifty begas forcibly taken out of his hands. Prevailed on by his earnest repeated solicitations, I am induced to say for him, that in your justice and favour are his only hopes of relief from his embarrassments, and he humbly supplicates your protection in restoring and securing him in the possession of his invaded right. The liberty of this intercession I am confident to think would be forgiven, were it not in favour of one who has rendered to this Government various useful services; but as, though of trivial importance, it affords an authentic instance of the encroaching disposition of inferior *Zemeendars*, yet another circumstance it may not be improper to point out. The ground alluded to is a part of the land situated upon the western bank of the river opposite *Calcutta*, that was formerly granted under a Sunnud of this Government to

TEESHOO LAMA, for the foundation of a temple of worship, and as a resort for such pilgrims of their nation as might occasionally make visits to the consecrated *Ganges*.

HAVING, in conformity to your desires, done my best endeavours literally to translate all the information POORUNGEER could give me, I have now only to apologize for the prolixity of the account, which I have been induced to be particularly minute in, as I conceived every circumstance, however trivial, might be in some degree interesting, that tends to illustrate any trait in the national character of a people we are but recently become acquainted with, and with whom in its extended views it has been an object of this Government to obtain a closer alliance.

I WILL not now presume to intrude longer on your time by adding any observations or conjectures deducible from the elevated importance your young ally seems rising to, in consequence of the signal respect paid him by the most exalted political characters known to his nation; but beg leave to repeat, that it is with infinite satisfaction I learn from the reports of POORUNGEER the flourishing state of the lately projected scheme of trade; to promote which, he assures me, not any thing had been wanting in facility of intercourse: that the adventurers who had invested their property had experienced

rienced perfect security in conducting their commerce, carried their articles to an exceeding good market, and found the rate of exchange materially in their favour.

Those advantages authorize the inference, that it will no doubt encourage more extensive enterprize; and permit me to add, I derive a confidence from the success of this infant essay, that inspires me with the strongest hopes, that the commission which your Honourable Board was pleased to commit to my charge, will eventually be productive of essential benefits to the political and commercial interests of the Company.

I have the honour to be, &c. &c.

SAMUEL TURNER.

Calcutta, Feb. 8, 1786.

## OBSERVATIONS AND INQUIRIES

CONCERNING THE

## SEEKS* and their COLLEGE,

AT PATNA, IN THE EAST-INDIES,

## By CHARLES WILKINS, Esq.

WRITTEN MARCH 1781.

---

I FOUND the College of the *Seeks* situated in one of the narrow streets of *Patna*, at no very considerable distance from the Custom-house. I was permitted to enter the outward gate, but, as soon as I came to the steps which led up into the Chapel, or public hall, I was civilly accosted by two of the Society. I asked them if I might ascend into the hall: they said it was a place of worship open to me and to all men; but at the same time intimated that I must take off my shoes. As I consider this ceremony in the same light as uncovering my head upon entering any of our temples dedicated to the Deity, I did not hesitate to comply, and I was then politely conducted into the hall, and seated upon a carpet, in the midst

---

\* A sect of people distinguished by that appellation from the Worshippers of BRAHMA and the followers of MAHOMMED.

of the assembly, which was so numerous as almost to fill the room. The whole building forms a square of about forty feet, raised from the ground about six or eight steps. The hall is in the center, divided from four other apartments by wooden arches, upon pillars of the same materials, all neatly carved. This room is rather longer than it is broad. The floor was covered with a neat carpet, and furnished with six or seven low desks, on which stood as many of the books of their law; and the walls, above the arches, were hung with *Europe* looking-glasses in gold frames, and pictures of *Muſſulman* Princes and *Hindoo* Deities. A little room, which, as you enter, is situated at the left-hand end of the hall, is the chancel, and is furnished with an altar covered with a cloth of gold, upon which was laid a round black shield over a long broad sword, and, on either side, a *chowry* of peacock's feathers, mounted in a silver handle. The altar was raised a little above the ground, in a declining position. Before it stood a low kind of throne plated with silver; but rather too small to be useful; about it were several silver flower-pots and rose-water bottles, and on the left hand stood three small *Urns* which appeared to be copper, furnished with notches to receive the donations of the charitable. There stood also

near

near the altar, on a low defk, a great book of a folio fize, from which fome portions are daily read in their divine fervice. It was covered over with a blue mantle, on which were printed, in filver letters, fome felect paffages of their law.

After I had had a long converfation with two of the congregation, who had politely feated themfelves, on each fide of me, on the carpet, and whom I found very intelligent, notice was given, that it was noon, and the hour of divine fervice. The congregation arranged themfelves upon the carpet, on each fide of the hall, fo as to leave a fpace before the altar from end to end. The great book, defk, and all, was brought with fome little ceremony from the altar, and placed at the oppofite extremity of the hall. An old man, with a reverend filver beard, kneeled down before the defk with his face towards the altar ; and on one fide of him fat a man with a fmall drum, and two or three with cymbals. The book was now opened, and the old man began to chant to the time of the drum and the cymbals; and, at the conclufion of every verfe, moft of the congregation joined chorus in a refponfe, with countenances exhibiting great marks of joy. Their tones were by no means har ; the time was quick ; and I learnt that

the

the subject was a Hymn in praise of the Unity, the Omnipresence, and the Omnipotence, of the Deity. I was singularly delighted with the gestures of the old man: I never saw a countenance so expressive of inselt joy, whilst he turned about from one to another, as it were bespeaking their assents to those truths which his very soul seemed to be engaged in chanting forth. The Hymn being concluded, which consisted of about twenty verses, the whole congregation got up and presented their faces with joined hands towards the altar, in the attitude of prayer. A young man now stood forth; and, with a loud voice and distinct accent, solemnly pronounced a long prayer or kind of liturgy, at certain periods of which all the people joined in a general response, saying, *Wà Gooroo!* They prayed against temptation; for grace to do good; for the general good of mankind; and a particular blessing to the *Seeks*; and for the safety of those who at that time were on their travels. This prayer was followed by a short blessing from the old man, and an invitation to the assembly to partake of a friendly feast. The book was then closed and restored to its place at the altar, and, the people being seated as before, two men entered bearing a large iron caldron, called a *Carray*, just taken from the fire, and placed it in the center of the hall upon a low stool. These were followed by others with five or six dishes, some of which were of silver, and a large pile of leaves sewed together with fibres in the form of plates. One of these plates was given to each of the company without distinction, and the dishes being filled from the caldron, their contents were served out till every one had got his share: myself was not forgotten; and, as I was resolved not to give them the smallest occasion for offence, I ate up my portion. It was a kind of sweetmeat, of the consistence of soft brown sugar, composed of flour and sugar mixed up with clarified butter, which is called *Ghee*. Had not the *Ghee* been rancid, I should have relished it better. We were next served with a few sugar-plums; and here ended the feast and the ceremonies of the day. They told me the religious part of the ceremony was daily repeated five times. I now took my leave, inviting some of the principal men amongst them, who were about to return to their own country through *Banares*, to pay me a visit.

In the course of the conversation I was engaged in with the two *Seeks* before the service, I was able to gather the following circumstances. That the founder of their faith was called *Náneek Sah*, who flourished about four hundred

hundred years ago at *Punjab*, and who, before his apostacy, was a *Hindoo* of the *Kshetry*, or military tribe; and that his body disappeared as the *Hindoos* and the *Muffulmans* were disputing for it; for upon their removing the cloth which covered it, it was gone. That he left behind him a book, composed by himself, in verse and the language of *Punjab*, but a character partly of his own invention; which teaches the doctrines of the faith he had established. That they call this character, in honour of their founder, *Gooroo-Mookhee: from the mouth of the preceptor*. That this book, of which that standing near the altar, and several others in the hall, were copies, teaches that there is but one God, omnipotent and omnipresent, filling all space, and pervading all matter, and that he is to be worshipped and invoked; that there will be a day of retribution, when virtue will be rewarded and vice punished (I forgot to ask in what manner); that it not only commands universal toleration, but forbids disputes with those of another persuasion; that it forbids murder, theft, and such other deeds as are, by the majority of mankind, esteemed crimes against society; and inculcates the practice of all the virtues, but particularly an universal philanthropy, and a general hospitality to strangers and travellers. This is all my short
visit

visit would permit me to learn of this book. It is a folio volume, containing about four or five hundred pages.

They told me further, that some years after this book of *Náneek Sab* had been promulgated, another made its appearance, now held in almost as much esteem as the former. The name of the author has escaped my memory; but they favoured me with an extract from the book itself in praise of the Deity. The passage had struck my ear on my first entering the hall, when the students were all engaged in reading. From the similarity of the language to the *Hindoovee*, and many *Shanscrit* words, I was able to understand a good deal of it, and I hope, at some future period, to have the honour of laying a translation of it before the Society. They told me I might have copies of both their books if I would be at the expence of transcribing them.

I next enquired why they were called *Seeks*, and they told me it was a word borrowed from one of the commandments of their founder which signifies " *Learn thou* ;" and that it was adopted to distinguish the sect soon after he disappeared. The word, as is well known, has the same import in the *Hindoovee*.

I asked them what were the ceremonies used in admitting a proselyte. A person having
shewn

shewn a sincere inclination to renounce his former opinions, to any five or more *Seeks* assembled together, in any place, as well on the highway as in a house of worship, they send to the first shop where sweetmeats are sold, and procure a small quantity of a particular sort, which is very common, and as I recollect they call *Batafa*, and having diluted it in pure water, they sprinkle some of it on the body, and into the eyes of the convert, whilst one of the best instructed repeats to him, in any language with which he is conversant, the chief canons of their faith, exacting from him a solemn promise to abide by them the rest of his life. This is the whole of the ceremony. The new convert may then choose a *Gooroo*, or preceptor, to teach him the language of their scriptures, who first gives him the alphabet to learn, and so leads him on, by slow degrees, until he wants no further instruction. They offered to admit me into their Society; but I declined the honour; contenting myself with the alphabet, which they told me to guard as the apple of my eye, as it was a sacred character. I find it differs but little from the *Dewnager*: the number, order, and powers of the letters are exactly the same. The language itself is a mixture of *Persian*, *Arabic*, and some *Shanscrit*, grafted upon the provincial dialect of *Punjab*, which is a kind of *Hindovee*, or, as it is vulgarly called by us, *Moors*.

ON

## ON THE
## TRIAL BY ORDEAL
### AMONG THE
## HINDUS.

BY ALI' IBRA'HI'M KHA'N, CHIEF MAGISTRATE
AT BANARES.

COMMUNICATED BY WARREN HASTINGS, ESQ.

---

THE modes of trying offenders by an appeal to the Deity, which are described at large in the *Mitácsherá*, or comment on the *Dherma Sástra*, in the *Chapter of Oaths*, and other ancient books of *Hindu* law, are here sufficiently explained, according to the interpretation of learned *Pandits*, by the well-wisher to mankind, ALI' IBRA'HI'M KHA'N.

THE word *Divya* in *Sanscrit* signifies the same with *parikshá* or *parikhyá* in *Bháshá*, *kasam* in *Arabick*, and *saucand* in *Persian*; that is, an *oath*, or the form of invoking the Supreme Being to attest the truth of an allegation; but it is generally understood to mean the trial by *Ordeal*,

*Ordeal*, or the form of appealing to the *immediate* interpofition of the Divine Power.

Now this trial may be conducted in *nine* ways: firſt, by the *balance*; ſecondly, by *fire*; thirdly, by *water*; fourthly, by *poiſon*; fifthly, by the *Cóſha*, or water in which an idol has been waſhed; ſixthly, by *rice*; ſeventhly, by *boiling* oil; eighthly, by *red-hot iron*; ninthly, by *images*.

I. Ordeal by the balance is thus performed. The beam having been previouſly adjuſted, the cord fixed, and both ſcales made perfectly even, the perſon accuſed and a *Pandit* faſt a whole day; then, after the accuſed has been bathed in ſacred water, the *hóma*, or *oblation*, preſented to *Fire*, and the deities worſhipped, he is carefully weighed; and, when he is taken out of the ſcale, the *Pandits* proſtrate themſelves before it, pronounce a certain *mentra* or *incantation*, agreeably to the *Sáſtras*, and, having written the ſubſtance of the accuſation on a piece of paper, bind it on his head. Six minutes after, they place him again in the ſcale; and, if he weigh more than before, he is held guilty; if leſs, innocent; if exactly the ſame, he muſt be weighed a third time; when, as it is written in the *Mitácſherá*, there will certainly be a difference in his weight. Should the balance, though well fixed, break down, this would be conſidered as a proof of his guilt.

II. Fox

II. For the *fire-ordeal* an excavation, nine hands long, two spans broad, and one span deep, is made in the ground, and filled with a fire of *pippal* wood: into this the person accused must walk bare-footed; and, if his foot be unhurt, they hold him blameless; if burned, guilty.

III. Water-ordeal is performed by causing the person accused to stand in a sufficient depth of water, either flowing or stagnant, to reach his navel; but care should be taken that no ravenous animal be in it, and that it be not moved by much air: a *Bráhman* is then directed to go into the water, holding a staff in his hand; and a soldier shoots three arrows on dry ground from a bow of cane: a man is next dispatched to bring the arrow which has been shot farthest: and after he has taken it up, another is ordered to run from the edge of the water; at which instant the person accused is told to grasp the foot or the staff of the *Bráhman*, who stands near him in the water, and immediately to dive into it. He must remain under water till the two men who went to fetch the arrows are returned; for, if he raise his head or body above the surface before the arrows are brought back, his guilt is considered as fully proved. In the villages near *Banáres*, it is the practice for the person who is to be tried by this kind of *Ordeal* to stand in water up to his navel, and then, holding the foot of a *Bráhman*, to dive under it as long as a man can walk fifty paces very gently: if, before the man has walked thus far, the accused rise above the water, he is condemned; if not, acquitted.

IV. THERE are two sorts of trial by *poison*. First, the *Pandits* having performed their *hóma*, and the person accused his ablution, two *retti's* and a half, or seven barley-corns, of *vishanagá*, a poisonous root, or of *sunc'hyá*, that is, white arsenick, are mixed in eight *máshas*, or sixty-four *retti's*, of clarified *butter*, which the accused must eat from the hand of a *Bráhman*: if the poison produce no visible effect, he is absolved; otherwise, condemned. Secondly, the hooded snake, called *nága*, is thrown into a deep earthen pot, into which is dropped a ring, a seal, or a coin: this the person accused is ordered to take out with his hand; and, if the serpent bite him, he is pronounced guilty; if not, innocent.

V. TRIAL by the *Císha* is as follows: the accused is made to drink three draughts of the water, in which the images of the *Sun*, of *Déví*, and other deities, have been washed for that purpose; and if, within fourteen days, he has any sickness or indisposition, his crime is considered as proved.

VI. WHEN

VI. WHEN several persons are suspected of theft, some dry rice is weighed with the sacred stone called *salgràm*; or certain *slócas* are read over it; after which the suspected persons are severally ordered to chew a quantity of it: as soon as they have chewed it, they are to throw it on some leaves of *pippal*, or, if none be at hand, on some *b'hùrja patra*, or bark of a tree from *Nepàl* or *Cashmìr*. The man from whose mouth the rice comes dry or stained with blood, is holden guilty; the rest are acquitted.

VII. THE ordeal by *hot oil* is very simple: when it is heated sufficiently, the accused thrusts his hand into it; and if he be not burned, is held innocent.

VIII. IN the same manner they make an *iron ball*, or the *head of a lance*, red-hot, and place it in the hands of the person accused; who, if it burn him not, is judged guiltless.

IX. To perform the ordeal by *dharmárch*, which is the name of the *slóca* appropriated to this mode of trial, either an image named *Dharma*, or the Genius of Justice, is made of silver, and another, called *Adharma*, of clay or iron, both of which are thrown into a large earthen jar, and the accused, having thrust his hand into it, is acquitted if he bring out the silver image, but condemned if he draw forth the iron: or, the figure of a deity is painted on
white

white cloth, and another on black; the first of which they name *sharma*, and the second, *adharma*. These are severally rolled up in cow-dung, and thrown into a large jar without having ever been shewn to the accused; who must put his hand into the jar, and is acquitted or convicted, as he draws out the figure on white, or on black, cloth.

It is written in the Comment on the *Dherma Sástra*, that each of the four principal Casts has a sort of ordeal appropriated to it; that a *Brahman* must be tried by the *balance*, a *Chatriya* by *fire*, a *Vaifya* by *water*, and a *Súdra* by *poison*; but some have decided, that any ordeal, except that by *poison*, may be performed by a *Bráhman*, and that a man of any Cast may be tried by the *balance*; it has been determined, that a woman may have any trial except those by poison and by water.

CERTAIN months and days also are limited in the *Mitácsherá* for the different species of ordeal; as *Agrahan*, *Pauſh*, *Mágh*, *P'hálgun*, *Sriáwan*, and *B'hádr* for that by *fire*; *A'ſwin*, *Cártic*, *Jaiſht*, and *A'ſhádh*, for that by *water*; *Pauſh*, *Mágh*, and *P'hálgun*, for that by *poiſon*; and regularly there should be no *water ordeal* on the *Aſhtemí*, or *eighth*, the *Cheturdaſh*, or *fourteenth* day of the new or full moon, in the intercalary month, in the month of

VOL. II. G *B'hádr*,

*B'hadr*, on *Sanaifcher*, or *Saturday*, and on *Mangal*, or *Tuefday:* but whenever the Magiftrate decides that there fhall be an *Ordeal*, the regular appointment of months and days needs not be regarded.

The *Mitácfherá* contains alfo the following diftinctions: in cafes of theft or fraud to the amount of a hundred gold mohrs, the trial by *poifon* is proper; if eighty mohrs be ftolen, the fufpected perfon may be tried by *fire*; if forty, by the *balance*; if from thirty to ten, by the *image-water*; if two only, by *rice*.

An infpired Legiflator, named CA'TYA'YANA, was of opinion, that though a theft or fraud could be proved by witneffes, the party accufed might be tried by *Ordeal*: he fays too, that, where a thoufand *puna*'s are ftolen, or fraudulently withheld, the proper trial is by *poifon*; where feven hundred and fifty, by *fire*; where fix hundred and fixty-fix, and a fraction, by *water*; where five hundred, by the *balance*, where four hundred, by *hot oil*; where three hundred, by *rice*; where an hundred and fifty, by the *Cofha*; and where one hundred, by the *dharmarch*, or images of filver and iron.

The mode of conducting the *Ordeal* by redhot balls, or *heads of fpears*, is thus particularly defcribed in the Commentary on YA'GYA-WELCYA.

AT

AT day-break the place where the ceremony is to be performed, is cleared and washed in the customary form; and at sun-rise, the *Pandits*, having paid their adoration to GANĔSA, the God of Wisdom, draw nine circles on the ground with cow-dung, at intervals of sixteen fingers; each circle containing sixteen fingers of earth, but the ninth either smaller or larger than the rest: then they worship the Deities in the mode prescribed by the *Sáſtra*, present oblations to the *fire*, and having a second time worshipped the Gods, read the appointed *Mentra's*. The person to be tried then performs an ablution, puts on moist clothes, and, turning his face to the East, stands in the first ring, with both his hands fixed in his girdle: after this the presiding Magistrate and *Pandits* order him to rub some rice in the husk between his hands, which they carefully inspect; and if the scar of a former wound, a mole, or other mark appear on either of them, they stain it with a dye, that, after the trial, it may be distinguished from any new mark. They next order him to hold both his hands open and close together; and, having put into them seven leaves of the *trembling tree*, or *pippal*, seven of the *sami* or *jend*, seven blades of *darbha* grass, a little barley moistened with curds, and a few flowers, they fasten the leaves on his hand with

seven threads of raw cotton. The *Pandits* then read the *slocas* which are appointed for the occasion; and, having written a state of the case and the point in issue on a *Palmyra-leaf*, together with the *Mentra* prescribed in the *Vida*, they tie the leaf on the head of the accused. All being prepared, they heat an iron-ball, or the head of a lance, weighing two *ser* and a half, or five pounds, and throw it into water; they heat it again, and again cool it in the same manner: the third time they keep it in the fire till it is red-hot; then they make the person accused stand in the first circle; and, having taken the iron from the fire and read the usual incantation over it, the *Pandits* place it with tongs in his hands. He must step gradually from circle to circle, his feet being constantly within one of them, and, when he has reached the eighth, he must throw the iron into the ninth, so as to burn some grass, which must be left in it for that purpose. This being performed, the Magistrate and *Pandits* again command him to rub some rice in the husk between both his hands, which they afterwards examine; and, if any mark of burning appear on either of them, he is convicted; if not, his innocence is considered as proved. If his hand shake through fear, and by his trembling any other part of his body is burned, his veracity

city remains unimpeached; but if he let the iron drop before he reach the eighth circle, and doubt arise in the minds of the spectators, whether it had burned him, he must repeat the whole ceremony from the beginning.

In the year of the MESSIAH 1783, a man was tried by the hot ball at *Benáres* in the presence of me ALI IBRA'HIM KHA'N, on the following occasion: A man had appealed one SANCAR of larceny, who pleaded that he was not guilty; and as the theft could not be proved by legal evidence, the trial by *Fire-ordeal* was tendered to the appellee, and accepted by him. This well-wisher to mankind advised the learned Magistrates and *Pandits* to prevent the decision of the question by a mode not conformable to the practice of the Company's Government, and recommended an oath by the water of the *Ganges* and the leaves of *tulasí* in a little vessel of brass, or by the book *Herivansa*, or the stone *Sálgrám*, or by the hallowed ponds or basons; all which oaths are used at *Benáres*. When the parties obstinately refused to try the issue by any one of the modes recommended, and insisted on a trial by the *hot ball*, the Magistrates and *Pandits* of the Court were ordered to gratify their wishes, and, setting aside those forms of trial in which there could be only a distant fear of death, or loss of property, as the just punishment of perjury by

the sure yet slow judgment of *Heaven*, to perform the ceremony of *Ordeal* agreeably to the *Dherma Sástra:* but it was not till after mature deliberation for four months, that a regular mandate issued for a trial by the *red-hot ball*; and this was at length granted for four reasons: first, because there was no other way of condemning or absolving the person accused: secondly, because both parties were *Hindus*, and this mode of trial was specially appointed in the *Dherma Sástra* by the ancient law-givers: thirdly, because this *Ordeal* is practised in the dominions of the *Hindu* RA'JA's: and fourthly, because it might be useful to enquire how it was possible for the heat of fire to be resisted, and for the hand that held it to avoid being burned. An order was accordingly sent to the *Pandits* of the Court and of *Benares* to this effect: " Since the parties
" accusing and accused are both *Hindus*, and
" will not consent to any trial but that by the
" *hot ball*, let the *Ordeal* desired be duly per-
" formed in the manner prescribed by the *Mi-*
" *táchsrá*, or Commentary on *Yágyawalcya*."

WHEN preparations were made for the trial, this well-wisher to mankind, attended by all the learned Professors, by the Officers of the Court, the *Sipáhis* of CAPTAIN HOGAN's battalion, and many inhabitants of *Benares*, went to the place prepared, and endeavoured to dissuade the appellor from requiring the accused to be tried by fire, adding, "if his hand be not burned, you shall certainly be imprisoned." The accuser, not deterred by this menace, persisted in demanding the trial: the ceremony, therefore, was thus conducted in the presence of me ALI IBRAHI'M KHA'N.

THE *Pandits* of the Court and the City having worshipped the God of Knowledge, and presented their oblation of clarified butter to the fire, formed nine circles of cow-dung on the ground; and, having bathed the appellee in the *Ganges*, brought him with his clothes wet; when, to remove all suspicion of deceit, they washed his hands with pure water; then, having written a state of the case and the words of the *Mentra* on a *Palmyra-leaf*, they tied it on his head; and put into his hands, which they opened and joined together, seven leaves of *pippal*, seven of *jend*, seven blades of *darbha* grass, a few flowers, and some barley moistened with curds, which they fastened with seven threads of raw white cotton. After this they made the iron-ball red-hot, and taking it up with tongs, placed it in his hands: he walked with it step by step, the space of three gaz and a half, through each of the seven intermediate rings, and threw the ball into the ninth, where it

it burnt the grafs that had been left in it. He
next, to prove his veracity, rubbed some rice
in the hufk between his hands; which were
afterwards examined, and were so far from
being burned, that not even a blifter was raifed
on either of them. Since it is the nature of
fire to burn, the Officers of the Court, and
people of *Benares*, near five hundred of whom
attended the ceremony, were aftonifhed at the
event; and this well-wifher to mankind was
perfectly amazed. It occurred to his weak ap-
prehenfion, that probably the frefh leaves and
other things which, as it has been mentioned,
were placed on the hands of the accufed, had
prevented their being burned; befides that, the
time was but fhort between his taking the ball
and throwing it down: yet it is pofitively declared in the *Dherma Saftra*, and in the written
opinions of the moft refpectable *Pandits*, that
the hand of a man who fpeaks truth cannot be
burned; and ALI IBRA'HIM KHA'N certainly
faw with his own eyes, as many others alfo
faw with theirs, that the hands of the appellee
in this caufe were unhurt by the fire: he was
confequently difcharged; but, that men might
in future be deterred from demanding the trial
by *Ordeal*, the appellor was committed for a
week. After all, if fuch a trial could be feen
once or twice by feveral intelligent men, acquainted

quainted with natural philosophy, they might be able to assign the true reason why a man's hand may be burned in some cases and not in others.

ORDEAL by the vessel of *hot oil*, according to the Comment on the *Dherma Sástra*, is thus performed: The ground appointed for the trial is cleared and rubbed with cow-dung, and the next day, at sun-rise, the *Pandit* worships GANE'SA, presents his oblations, and pays adoration to other Deities, conformably to the *Sástra*: then, having read the incantation prescribed, he places a round pan of gold, silver, copper, iron, or clay, with a diameter of sixteen fingers, and four fingers deep; and throws into it one *ser*, or eighty *sicca* weight, of clarified butter or oil of *sesamum*. After this, a ring of gold, or silver, or iron, is cleaned and washed with water, and cast into the oil; which they proceed to heat, and when it is very hot put into it a fresh leaf of *pippula*, or of *bilwa*: when the leaf is burned, the oil is known to be sufficiently hot. Then, having pronounced a *mentra* over the oil, they order the party accused to take the ring out of the pan; and, if he take it out without being burned, or without a blister on his hand, his innocence is considered as proved; if not, his guilt.

A *Bráh-*

A *Bráhman* named RISHI'SWARA BHATTA accused one RA'MDAYA'L, a linen-painter, of having stolen his goods: RA'MDAYA'L pleaded not guilty; and, after much altercation, consented to be tried, as it had been proposed, by the *vessel of oil*. This well-wisher to mankind advised the *Pandits* of the Court to prevent, if possible, that mode of trial; but, since the parties insisted on it, an *Ordeal* by *hot oil*, according to the *Sástra*, was awarded for the same reasons which prevailed in regard to the trial by the *ball*. The *Pandits* who assisted at the ceremony were, BHISH'MA BHATTA, NA'NA'PA'T'HAC, MANIRA'MA', *Páthaca*, MENIRA'MA BHATTA, SIVA, ANANTARA'MA BHATTA, CRIPA'RA'MA, VISHNUHERI, CHRISHNACHANDRA, RA'MENDRA, GO'VINDARA'MA, HERICRISHNA BHATTA, CA'LIDA'SA: the three last were *Pandits* of the Court. When GANE'SA had been worshipped, and the *hóma* presented, according to the *Sástra*, they sent for this well-wisher to mankind; who, attended by the two *Dároghas* of the *Díváni* and *Faujdári* Courts, the *Cotwál* of the town, the other Officers of the Court, and most of the inhabitants of *Benáres*, went to the place of trial; where he laboured to dissuade RA'MDAYA'L and his father from submitting to the *Ordeal*; and apprized them, that if the hand

of

of the accused should be burned, he would be compelled to pay the value of the goods stolen, and his character would be disgraced in every company. RA'MDAYAL would not desist: he thrust his hand into the vessel, and was burned. The opinion of the *Pandits* was then taken; and they were unanimous, that, by the burning of his hand, his guilt was established, and he bound to pay RISHI'SWARA BHATTA the price of what he had stolen; but if the sum exceeded five hundred *ashrafi's*, his hand must be cut off, by an express law in the *Sástra*; and a mulct also must be imposed on him according to his circumstances.

THE chief Magistrate therefore caused RA'MDAYA'L to pay RISHI'SWARA seven hundred rupees in return for the goods which had been stolen; but as amercements in such cases are not usual in the Courts of Judicature at *Benáres*, the mulct was remitted and the prisoner discharged.

THE record of this conviction was transmitted to *Calcutta* in the year of the MESSIAH 1783; and in the month of *April* 1784, the Governor General IMA'DU'DDAU'LAH JELA'DET JANG BEHA'DER, having seen the preceding account of trials by *Ordeal*, put many questions concerning the meaning of *Sanscrit* words, and the cases here reported; to which he he received respectful answers. He first desired to know the precise meaning of *hóma*, and was informed, that it meant the oblations made to please the Deities, and comprised a variety of things: thus in the *agni hóma*, they throw into the fire several sorts of wood and grass, as *palás wood, c'hadira wood, racta chandan*, or red *sandal, pippal-wood sami*, and *cusha grass, dubha*, together with some sorts of grain, fruit, and other ingredients; as black *sesamum*, barley, rice, sugar-cane, clarified butter, almonds, dates, and gugal or bdellium.

To his next question, "how many species of *hóma* there were," it was answered, that different species were adapted to different occasions; but that, in the *Ordeals* by hot iron, and hot oil, the same sort of oblation was used. When he desired to know the meaning of the word *mantra*, he was respectfully told, that in the language of the *Pandits*, there were three such words, *mantra, yantra*, and *tantra*: that the first meant a passage from one of the *Védas*, in which the names of certain Deities occurred; the second, a scheme of figures, which they write with a belief that their wishes will be accomplished by it; and the third, a medical preparation, by the use of which all injuries may be avoided; for they are said to rub it on their hands, and afterwards to touch red-hot iron

iron without being burned. He then asked, how much barley moistened with curds was put into the hands of the accused person; and the answer was, nine grains.

His other questions were thus answered: "that the leaves of *pippala* were spread about in the hands of the accused, not heaped one above another: that the man who performed the *Fire-ordeal* was not much agitated, but seemed in full possession of his faculties: that the person tried by hot oil was at first afraid, but persisted, after he was burned, in denying the theft; nevertheless, as he previously had entered into a written agreement, that if his hand should be hurt, he would pay the value of the goods, the Magistrate for that reason thought himself justified in compelling payment: that when the before-mentioned ingredients of the *homa* were thrown into the fire, the *Pandits* sitting round the hearth sung the *sléens* prescribed in the *Sastra*: that the form of the hearth is established in the *Véda* and in the *Dherma Sástra*; and this fire-place is also called *Védi*: that for the smaller oblations they raise a little ground for the hearth, and kindle fire on it; for the higher oblations, they sink the ground to receive the fire, where they perform the *homa*; and this sacred hearth they call *cunda*." The Governor then asked, why

the

the trials by fire, by the hot ball, and the vessel of oil, if there be no essential difference between them, are not all called *Fire-ordeals*; and it was humbly answered, that, according to some *Pandits*, they were all three different; whilst others insisted, that the trial by fire was distinct from that by the vessel, though the trial by the hot ball and the head of a lance were the same; but that, in the apprehension of his respectful servant, they were all ordeals by fire.

---

## *The* INDIAN LAW *of* ORDEAL, *verbally translated from* YA'GYAWALCYA.

1. THE balance, fire, water, poison, the idol — these are the ordeals used here below for the proof of innocence, when the accusations are heavy, and when the accuser offers to hazard a mulct (if he should fail):

2. ONE party may be tried, if he please, by ordeal, and the other must then risque an amercement; but the trial may take place even without any wager, if the crime committed be injurious to the prince.

3. THE sovereign, having summoned the accused, while his clothes are yet moist from bathing,

bathing, at sunrise, before he has broken his aft, shall cause all trials by ordeal to be conducted in the presence of *Bráhmens*.

4. The balance is for women, children, old men, the blind, the lame, *Bráhmens*, and the sick: for the *Súdra*, fire or water, or seven barley-corns of poison.

5. Unless the loss of the accuser amount to a thousand pieces of silver, the accused must not be tried by the red-hot ball, nor by poison, nor by the scales; but if the offence be against the king, or if the crime be heinous, he must acquit himself by one of those trials in all cases.

6. He who has recourse to the balance, must be attended by persons experienced in weighing, and go down into one scale, with an equal weight placed in the other, and a groove (with water in it) marked on the beam.

7. " Thou, O balance, art the mansion of
" truth; thou wast anciently contrived by
" Deities; declare the truth, therefore, O giver
" of success, and clear me from all suspicion.

8. " If I am guilty, O venerable as my own
" mother, then sink me down; but if inno-
" cent, raise me aloft." Thus shall he address the balance.

9. If he sink, he is convicted, or if the scales be broken; but if the string be not broken, and he rise aloft, he must be acquitted.

10. On

10. On the trial by fire, let both hands of the accused be rubbed with rice in the husk, and well examined: then let seven leaves of the *Afwatt'ha* (the religious fig-tree) be placed on them, and bound with seven threads.

11. "Thou, O fire, pervadest all beings! "O cause of purity, who givest evidence of "virtue and of sin, declare the truth in this "my hand."

12. When he has pronounced this, the priest shall place in both his hands an iron-ball, red-hot, and weighing fifty \* *pala's*.

13. Having taken it, he shall step gradually into seven circles, each with a diameter of sixteen fingers, and separated from the next by the same space.

14. If, having cast away the hot ball, he shall again have his hands rubbed with rice in the husk, and shall show them unburned, he will prove his innocence. Should the iron fall during the trial, or should a doubt arise (on the regularity of the proceedings), he must be tried again.

15. "Preserve me, O Varuna, by de- "claring the truth." Thus having invoked the God of waters, the accused shall plunge

---

\* A *pala* is four *carsha's*, and b. *carsha*, eighty *racticá'l*, or seeds of the *Gunja* creeper, each weighing above a grain and a quarter, or, correctly, 1 7/16 gr.

his

his head into the river or pool, and hold both thighs of a man, who shall stand in it up to his navel.

16. A swift runner shall then hasten to fetch an arrow shot at the moment of his plunging; and if, while the runner is gone, the priest shall see the head of the accused under water, he must be discharged as innocent.

17. "THOU, O poison, art the child of "BRAHMA', stedfast in justice and in truth: "clear me then from this heavy charge, and, "if I have spoken truly, become nectar to "me."

18. SAYING this, he shall swallow the poison *Sárrnga*, from the tree which grows on the mountain *Himálaya*; and, if he digest it without any inflammation, the prince shall pronounce him guiltless.

19. OR the priest shall perform rites to the image of some tremendous deity, and, having bathed the idol, shall make the accused to drink three handfuls of the water that has dropped from it:

20. IF, in fourteen days after, he suffer no dreadful calamity from the act of the deity or of the king, he must indubitably be acquitted.

# ON THE
# LITERATURE
# OF THE
# HINDUS,
### FROM THE SANSCRIT,
COMMUNICATED BY GOVERDHAN CAUL:
WITH A SHORT COMMENTARY.

---

## THE TEXT.

THERE are eighteen *Vidyá's*, or parts of *true Knowledge*, and some branches of Knowledge *falsely so called*; of both which a short account shall here be exhibited.

The first *four* are the immortal *Véda's* evidently revealed by GOD; which are entitled, in one compound word, *Rigyajuhsámát'harva*, or, in separate words, *Rich*, *Yajush*, *Sáman*, and *At'harvan*: the *Rigvéda* consists of *five* sections; the *Yajurvéda*, of *eighty-six*; the *Sámavéda*, of a *thousand*; and the *At'harvavéda*, of *nine*; with eleven hundred *sác'ha's*, or branches, in various divisions and subdivisions. The *Véda's* in truth are infinite; but were

were reduced by VYA'SA to this number and order: the principal part of them is that which explains the Duties of Man in a methodical arrangement; and in the *fourth* is a fystem of divine ordinances.

FROM thefe are deduced the four *Upavédas*, namely, *Ayufh, Gándharva, Dhanufh*, and *St'hápatya*: the firft of which, or *Ayurvéda*, was delivered to mankind by BRAHMA', INDRA, DHANWANTARI, and *five* other Deities; and comprizes the theory of Diforders and Medicines, with the practical methods of curing Difeafes. The fecond, or Mufick, was invented and explained by BHARATA: it is chiefly ufeful in raifing the mind by devotion to the felicity of the Divine nature. The third *Upavéda* was compofed by VISWAMITRA on the fabrication and ufe of arms and implements handled in war by the tribe of *Cfhatriya's*. VISWACARMAN revealed the *fourth* in various treatifes on *fixty-four* Mechanical Arts, for the improvement of fuch as exercife them.

SIX *Anga's*, or *Bodies* of Learning, are alfo derived from the fame fource: their names are, *Sicfhà, Calpa, Vyácarana, Ch'handas, Jyótifh*, and *Niructi*. The *firft* was written by PA'NINI, an infpired Saint, on the *pronunciation* of vocal founds; the *fecond* contains a detail of religious acts and ceremonies from the firft to the laft; and

and from the branches of these works a variety of rules have been framed by A'SWALA'YANA, and others: the *third*, or the Grammar, entitled *Pániníya*, consisting of *eight* lectures or chapters (*Vriddhirádaij*, and so forth), was the production of three *Rishi's*, or holy men, and teaches the proper determinations of words in construction; but other less abstruse Grammars, compiled merely for popular use, are not considered as *Anga's*: the *fourth*, or *Prosody*, was taught by a *Muni*, named PINGALA, and treats of charms and incantations in verses aptly framed and variously measured, such as the *Gáyatri*, and a thousand others. *Astronomy* is the *fifth* of the *Védánga's*, as it was delivered by SU'RYA, and other divine persons: it is necessary in calculations of time. The *sixth*, or *Nirutti*, was composed by YA'SCA (so is the manuscript; but, perhaps, it should be VYA'SA) on the signification of difficult words and phrases in the *Véda's*.

LASTLY, there are four *Upánga's*, called *Purána*, *Nyáya*, *Mimánsá*, and *Dherma Sástra*. Eighteen *Purána's*, that of *Brahma*, and the rest, were composed by VYA'SA for the instruction and entertainment of mankind in general. *Nyáya* is derived from the root *ní*, to *acquire* or *apprehend*; and, in this sense, the books on *apprehension*, *reasoning*, and *judgement*,

*ment*, are called *Nyáya*: the principal of these are the work of GAUTAMA in *five* chapters, and that of CANA'DA in *ten*: both teaching the meaning of sacred texts, the difference between just and unjust, right and wrong, and the principles of knowledge, all arranged under *twenty-three* heads. *Mimansa* is also *two-fold*; both shewing what acts are pure or impure, what objects are to be desired or avoided, and by what means the soul may ascend to the First Principle: the *former*, or *Carma Mimánsá*, comprized in *twelve* chapters, was written by JAIMINI, and discusses questions of Moral Duties and Law; next follows the *Upásaná Cánda* in four lectures (*Sancarshana* and the rest), containing a survey of Religious Duties; to which part belong the rules of SA'NDILYA, and others, on devotion and duty to GOD. Such are the contents of the *Púrva*, or *former Mimánsá*. The *Uttara*, or *latter*, abounding in questions on the Divine Nature and other sublime speculations, was composed by VYA'SA, in *four* chapters and *sixteen* sections; it may be considered as the brain and spring of all the *Anga's*; it exposes the heretical opinions of RA'MA'NUJA, MA'DHWA, VALLABHA, and other Sophists; and, in a manner suited to the comprehension of adepts, it treats on the true nature of GANE'SA, BHA'SCARA, or the Sun,

H 3      NI'LA-

Ni'LACANTA, LACSHMI', and other *forms* of One Divine Being. A similar work was written by SRI' SANCARA, demonstrating the Supreme Power, Goodness, and Eternity of GOD.

THE Body of *Law*, called *Smriti*, consists of *eighteen* books, each divided under three general heads, the duties of *religion*, the administration of *justice*, and the punishment or *expiation* of crimes: they were delivered, for the instruction of the human species, by MENU, and other sacred personages.

As to *Ethicks*, the *Véda's* contain all that relates to the duties of Kings; the *Purána's*, what belongs to the relation of husband and wife; and the duties of friendship and society (which complete the triple division) are taught succinctly in both: this double division of *Anga's* and *Upánga's* may be considered as denoting the double benefit arising from them in *theory* and *practice*.

THE *Bhárata* and *Rámáyana*, which are both *Epick Poems*, comprize the most valuable part of ancient History.

FOR the information of the lower classes in religious knowledge, the *Pásupata*, the *Pancharátra*, and other works, fit for nightly meditation, were composed by SIVA, and others,

in

in an hundred and ninety-two parts on different subjects.

WHAT follow are not really divine, but contain infinite contradictions. *Sánc'hya* is two-fold, that with IS'WARA and that without IS'WARA: the *former* is entitled *Pátanjala* in one chapter of four sections, and is useful in removing doubts by pious contemplation; the *second*, or *Cápila*, is in six chapters on the production of all things by the union of PRACRITI, or *Nature*, and PURUSHA, or the *First Male*: it comprizes also, in eight parts, rules for devotion, thoughts on the invisible power, and other topicks. Both these works contain a studied and accurate *enumeration* of natural bodies and their principles; whence this philosophy is named *Sánc'hya*. Others hold, that it was so called from its *reckoning three sorts of pain*.

THE *Mimánsá*, therefore, is in *two* parts; the *Nyáya*, in *two*; and the *Sánc'hya*, in *two*; and these *six* Schools comprehend all the doctrine of the Theists.

LAST of all appears a work written by BUDDHA; and there are also *six* Atheistical Systems of Philosophy, entitled *Yógáchára, Saudhánta, Vaibháshica, Mádhyamica, Digambara*, and *Chárvác*; all full of indeterminate phrases, errors in sense, confusion between distinct qualities, incomprehensible notions, opinions not duly weighed,

weighed, tenets destructive of natural equality; containing a jumble of Atheism and Ethicks; distributed, like our Orthodox books, into a number of sections, which omit what ought to be expressed, and express what ought to be omitted; abounding in false propositions, idle propositions, impertinent propositions; some assert, that the heterodox Schools have no *Upánga's*; others, that they have six *Anga's*, and as many *Sánga's*, or *Bodies*, and other *Appendices*.

Such is the analysis of universal knowledge, *Practical* and *Speculative*.

## THE COMMENTARY.

This first Chapter of a rare *Sanscrit* Book, entitled *Vidyádersa*, or a *View of Learning*, is written in so close and concise a style, that some parts of it are very obscure, and the whole requires an explanation. From the beginning of it we learn, that the *Véda's* are considered by the *Hindus* as the fountain of all knowledge human and divine; whence the verses of them are said in the *Gítá* to be the leaves of that holy tree, to which the Almighty Himself is compared.

"*Ûrdhva múlam adhah sác'ham aswattham práhuravyayám*
*chhandánsi yasya pernáni yastam véda sa védavit.*

"The

"The wise have called the Incorruptible One an *Aswatt'ha* with its roots above and its branches below; the leaves of which are the sacred measures; he who knows this tree, knows the *Véda's*."

All the *Pandits* insist, that *Aswatt'ha* means the *Pippala* or *Religious Fig-tree* with heart-shaped pointed and tremulous leaves; but the comparison of heavenly knowledge, descending and taking root on earth, to the *Vat'a*, or great *Indian* Fig-tree, which has most conspicuously its roots on high, or at least has radicating branches, would have been far more exact and striking.

The *Véda's* consist of three *Cānd'a's* or General Heads; namely, *Carma*, *Jnyána*, *Upásaná*, or *Works*, *Faith*, and *Worship*; to the first of which the Author of the *Vidyáderſa* wisely gives the preference, as Menu himself prefers universal benevolence to the ceremonies of religion:

*Japyénaiva tu sansidhyédbráhmanó nátra sansayah: Curyádanyatrava curyánmaitrö bráhmana uchyaté:*

that is: "By silent adoration undoubtedly a *Bráhman* attains holiness; but every benevolent man, whether he performs or omits that ceremony, is justly styled a *Bráhman*." This triple division of the *Véda's* may seem at first to throw light on a very obscure line in the *Gítá*.

Traig-

*Traigunyavishayáh védá nistraigunya bhavárjuna:*

or, "The *Véda's* are attended with *three* qualities: be not thou a man of *three* qualities, O Arjuna."

But several *Pandits* are of opinion, that the phrase must relate to the three *guna's*, or *qualities* of the mind, that of *excellence*, that of *passion*, and that of *darkness*; from the last of which a Hero should be wholly exempt, though examples of it occur in the *Véda's*, where animals are ordered to be *sacrificed*, and where horrid incantations are inserted for the *destruction* of enemies.

It is extremely singular, as Mr. WILKINS has already observed, that, notwithstanding the fable of BRAHMA's *four* mouths, each of which uttered a *Véda*, yet most ancient writers mention only *three Véda's*, in order as they occur in the compound word *Rigyajuhsáma*; whence it is inferred, that the *At'harvan* was written or collected after the three first; and the two following arguments, which are entirely new, will strongly confirm this inference. In the eleventh book of MENU, a work ascribed to the *first* age of mankind, and certainly of high antiquity, the *At'harvan* is mentioned by name, and styled the *Véda of Véda's*; a phrase which countenances the notion of DA'RA' SHECU'H, who asserts in the preface to his *Upanishat*, that "the *three* first *Védas* are named separately,
"because

"because the *At'harvan* is a corollary from them all, and contains the quintessence of them." But this verse of MENU, which occurs in a modern copy of the work brought from *Banáras*, and which would support the antiquity and excellence of the *fourth Véda*, is entirely omitted in the best copies, and particularly in a very fine one written at *Gayá*, where it was accurately collated by a learned *Bráhman*; so that, as MENU himself in other places names only three *Véda's*, we must believe this line to be an interpolation by some admirer of the *At'harvan*; and such an artifice overthrows the very doctrine which it was intended to sustain.

THE next argument is yet stronger, since it arises from *internal* evidence; and of this we are now enabled to judge by the noble zeal of Colonel POLIER in collecting *Indian* curiosities; which has been so judiciously applied and so happily exerted, that he now possesses a complete copy of the *four Véda's* in eleven large volumes.

ON a cursory inspection of those books it appears, that even a learner of *Sanscrit* may read a considerable part of the *At'harvavéda* without a dictionary; but that the style of the other *three* is so obsolete, as to seem almost a different dialect: when we are informed, therefore,

fore, that few *Brahmans* at *Banáras* can understand any part of the *Véda's*, we must presume, that none are meant, but the *Rich*, *Yajush*, and *Sáman*, with an exception of the *At'harvan*, the language of which is comparatively modern; as the learned will, perceive from the following specimen:

*Yatra brahmavidŏ yánti déshayá tapasá saha ag- nirmántatra nayatwagnirmédhátumé, ag- nayé swáhá. váyurmán tatra nayatu váyuh pránán dedhátu mé, váyuvai swáhá. súryó mán tatra nayatu chacshuh súryó dedhátu mé, súryáya swáhá; chandró mán tatra nayatu manaschandró dedhátu mé, chandráya swáhá. sómŏ mán tatra nayatu payah sómŏ dedhátu mé, sómáya swáhá. Indrŏ mán tatra nayatu balamindrŏ dedhátu mé, indráya swáhá. ápó mán tatra nayatvamritam- máposhishtatu, adbhyah swáhá. yatra brahmavidŏ yánti déshayá tapasá saha, brahmá mán tatra nayatu brahma brahmá dedhátu mé, brahmané swáhá;*

that is, "Where they, who know the Great
"One, go, through holy rites and through
"piety, thither may *fire* raise me! May fire
"receive my sacrifices! Mysterious praise to
"fire! May *air* waft me thither! May air
"increase my spirits! Mysterious praise to
"air! May the *Sun* draw me thither! May
"the

ON THE LITERATURE OF THE HINDUS. 165

"the sun enlighten my eye! Mysterious
"praise to the sun! May the Moon bear me
"thither! May the moon receive my mind!
"Mysterious praise to the moon! May the
"plant *Sóma* lead me thither! May *Sóma* be-
"stow on me its hallowed milk! Mysterious
"praise to *Sóma*! May INDRA, or the *firma-
"ment*, carry me thither! May INDRA give
"me strength! Mysterious praise to INDRA!
"May water bear me thither! May water
"bring me the stream of immortality! Mys-
"terious praise to the waters! Where they,
"who know the Great One, go, through
"holy rites and through piety, thither may
"BRAHMA' conduct me! May BRAHMA'
"lead me to the Great One! Mysterious
"praise to BRAHMA'."

SEVERAL other passages might have been cited from the first book of the *At'harvan*, particularly a tremendous *incantation* with consecrated *grass*, called *Darbha*, and a sublime Hymn to *Cála*, or Time; but a single passage will suffice to show the style and language of this extraordinary work. It would not be so easy to produce a genuine extract from the other *Véda's*: indeed, in a book, entitled *Srócot'hinta*, written in *Sanscrit*, but in *Cáshmirian* letters, a stanza from the *Yajurvéda* is introduced, which deserves for its sublimity to be quoted
here;

here; though the regular cadence of the verses, and the polished elegance of the language, cannot but induce a suspicion, that it is a more modern paraphrase of some text in the ancient Scripture:

*natatra sūryŏ bháti nacha chandra tárocáu, nimá vidyutŏ bhánti
cuta ivo
vanaih: tamíva bhántam anubháti sarvam, tasya bháṣā sarva-
midam vibháti:*

that is, " There the sun shines not, nor the
" moon and stars: these lightnings flash not
" *in that place*; how should even fire blaze
" *there?* God irradiates all this bright sub-
" stance; and by its effulgence the universe is
" enlightened."

AFTER all, the books on divine *Knowledge*, called *Véda*, or what is *known*, and *Sruti*, or what has been *heard*, from revelation, are still supposed to be very numerous; and the *four* here mentioned are thought to have been selected, as containing all the information necessary for man. MOHSANI FA'NI', the very candid and ingenious author of the *Dabistán*, describes in his first chapter a race of old *Persian* Sages, who appear from the whole of his account to have been *Hindus*; and we cannot doubt, that the book of MAHA'BA'D, or MENU, which was written, he says, *in a celestial dialect*, means the *Véda*: so that, as ZERA'TUSHT was
only

only a reformer, we find in *India* the true source of the ancient *Persian* religion. To this head belong the numerous *Tantra, Mantra, Agama,* and *Nigama, Sástra's,* which consist of *incantations* and other texts of the *Véda's,* with remarks on the occasions on which they may be successfully applied. It must not be omitted, that the *Commentaries* on the *Hindu* Scriptures, among which that of VASISHTHA seems to be reputed the most excellent, are innumerable; but, while we have access to the fountains, we need not waste our time in tracing the rivulets.

FROM the *Véda's* are immediately deduced the practical arts of *Chirurgery* and *Medicine, Musick* and *Dancing, Archery,* which comprizes the whole art of war, and *Architecture,* under which the system of *Mechanical* arts is included. According to the *Pandits,* who instructed ABU'LFAZL, each of the *four* Scriptures gave rise to one of the *Upavéda's,* or *Sub-scriptures,* in the order in which they have been mentioned; but this exactness of analogy seems to favour of refinement.

INFINITE advantage may be derived by *Europeans* from the various *Medical* books in *Sanscrit,* which contain the names and descriptions of *Indian* plants and minerals, with their uses, discovered by experience, in curing disorders:

orders: there is a vast collection of them, from the *Cáchnca*, which is considered as a work of SIVA, to the *Reganirúpana* and the *Nádína*, which are comparatively modern. A number of books, in prose and verse, have been written on *Musick*, with specimens of Indian airs in a very elegant notation; but the *Silpa Sástra*, or Body of Treatises on *Mechanical Arts*, is believed to be lost.

Next in order to these are the six *Vedánga*'s, three of which belong to Grammar; one relates to religious ceremonies; a fifth to the whole compass of Mathematicks, in which the author of *Lílávatí* was esteemed the most skilful man of his time; and the *sixth*, to the explanation of obscure words or phrases in the *Vída*'s. The grammatical work of PA'NINI, a writer supposed to have been inspired, is entitled *Siddhánta Caumudí*, and is so abstruse, as to require the lucubrations of many years, before it can be perfectly understood. When *Cásinát'ha Serman*, who attended Mr. WILKINS, was asked what he thought of the *Pániniya*, he answered very expressively, that " it " was a forest;" but, since Grammar is only an instrument, not the end, of true knowledge, there can be little occasion to travel over so rough and gloomy a path; which contains, however, probably some acute speculations in

Meta-

*Metaphysicks.* The *Sanscrit* Prosody is easy and beautiful; the learned will find in it almost all the measures of the *Greeks*; and it is remarkable, that the language of the *Bráhmans* runs very naturally into *Sapphicks, Alcaicks* and *Iambicks*. Astronomical works in this language are exceedingly numerous: seventy-nine of them are specified in one list; and, if they contain the names of the principal stars visible in *India*, with observations on their positions in different ages, what discoveries may be made in Science, and what certainty attained in antient Chronology?

SUBORDINATE to these *Angàs* (though the reason of the arrangement is not obvious) are the series of *Sacred Poems*, the body of *Law*, and the *six* philosophical *Sastràs*; which the author of our text reduces to *two*, each consisting of *two* parts, and rejects a *third*, in *two* parts also, as not perfectly *orthodox*, that is, not strictly conformable to his own principles.

THE first *Indian* Poet was VA'LMI'CI, author of the *Rámáyana*, a complete Epick Poem on one continued, interesting, and heroick action; and the next in celebrity, if it be not superior in reputation for holiness, was the *Mahábhárata* of VYA'SA: to him are ascribed the sacred *Puráńa's*, which are called, for their excellence, *the Eighteen*, and which have the following titles:

titles: BRAHME, or the *Great One*, PEDMA, or the *Lotos*, BRA'HMA'ND'A, or the *Mundane Egg*, and AGNI, or *Fire* (these *four* relate to the *Creation*), VISHNU, or the *Pervader*, GARUD'A, or his *Eagle*, the Transformations of BRAHMA, SIVA, LINGA, NA'REDA son of BRAHMA', SCANDA son of SIVA, MARCANDEY'A, or the Immortal Man, and BHAWISHYA, or the *Prediction of Futurity* (these *nine* belong to the *attributes* and *powers* of the Deity), and *four* others, MATSYA, VARA'HA, CU'RMA, VA'MENA, or as many incarnations of the Great One in his character of *Preserver*; all containing antient traditions embellished by poetry or disguised by fable: the *eighteenth* is the BHA'GAWATA, or Life of CRISHNA, with which the same Poet is by some imagined to have crowned the whole series; though others, with more reason, assign them different composers.

THE system of *Hindu* Law, besides the fine work called MENUSMRITI, or "what is *remembered* from MENU," that of YA'JNYAWALCYA, and those of *sixteen* other *Muni's*, with Commentaries on them all, consists of many tracts in high estimation, among which those current in *Bengal* are an excellent treatise on *Inheritances* by JI'MU'TA VA'HANA, and a complete *Digest*, in *twenty-seven* volumes, compiled a few centuries ago by RAGHUNANDAN the TRI-
BONIAN

IONIAN of *India*, whofe work is the grand repofitory of all that can be known on a fubject fo curious in itfelf, and fo interefting to the *Britifh* government.

Of the Philofophical Schools it will be fufficient here to remark, that the firft *Nyáyá* feems analogous to the *Peripatetick*, the fecond fometimes called *Vaiséfhica* to the *Ionick*, the two *Mimánfa's*, of which the *fecond*, is often diftinguifhed by the name of *Védánta*, to the *Platonick*, the firft *Sánc'hya* to the *Italick*, and the fecond, or *Pátanjala*, to the *Stoick*, Philofophy; fo that GAUTAMA correfponds with ARISTOTLE; CANA'DA, with THALES; JAIMINI with SOCRATES; VYA'SA with PLATO; CAPILA with PYTHAGORAS; and PATANJALI with ZENO: but an accurate comparifon between the *Grecian* and *Indian* Schools would require a confiderable volume. The original works of thofe Philofophers are very fuccinct; but, like all the other *Súftras*, they are explained, or obfcured by the *Upadérfana* or *Commentaries* without end: one of the fineft compofitions on the Philofophy of the *Vedanta* is entitled *Yóga Vásifht'ha*, and contains the inftructions of the great VASISHTHA to his pupil, RA'MA, king of *Ayódhyá*.

It refults from this analyfis of *Hindu* Liteterature, that the *Véda*, *Upavéda*, *Védánga*, *Purána*, *rana*, *Dherma*, and *Derfana*, are the *six* great *Sáſtra's*, in which all knowledge, divine and human, is supposed to be comprehended. And here we must not forget, that the word *Sáſtra*, derived from a root signifying *to ordain*, means generally an *Ordinance*, and particularly a *Sacred Ordinance* delivered by inspiration: properly, therefore, this word is applied only to *sacred literature*, of which the text exhibits an accurate sketch.

The *Súdra's*, or *fourth* class of *Hindus*, are not permitted to study the *six* proper *Sáſtra's* before enumerated; but an ample field remains for them in the study of *profane literature*, comprized in a multitude of *popular* books, which correspond with the several *Sáſtra's*, and abound with beauties of every kind. All the tracts on *Medicine* must indeed be studied by the *Vaidya's*, or those who are born Physicians; and they have often more learning, with far less pride, than any of the *Bráhmans*: they are usually Poets, Grammarians, Rhetoricians, Moralists; and may be esteemed in general the most virtuous and amiable of the *Hindus*. Instead of the *Véda's* they study the *Rájaníti*, or *Instruction of Princes*, and instead of *law*, the *Nitiſáſtra*, or general system of *Ethicks*: their *Síbitia*, or *Cávya Sáſtra*, consists of innumerable poems, written chiefly by the *Medical* tribe, and supplying

plying the place of the *Purána's*, since they contain all the stories of the *Ramayana*, *Bhárata*, and *Bhágawata*; they have access to many treatises of *Alancars*, or Rhetorick, with a variety of works in modulated prose; to *Upác'hyana*, or Civil History, called also *Rájataranginí*; to the *Nátaca*, which answers to the *Gándharvavéda*, consisting of regular *Dramatick* pieces in *Sanscrit* and *Prácrit*: besides which they commonly get by heart some entire Dictionary and Grammar. The best Lexicon or Vocabulary was composed in verse, for the assistance of the memory, by the illustrious AMARASINHA; but there are *seventeen* others in great repute: the best Grammar is the *Mugdhabódha*, or the *Beauty of Knowledge*, written by a *Góswami*, named VO'PADE'VA, and comprehending in two hundred short pages, all that a learner of the language can have occasion to know. To the *Cósha's*, or dictionaries, are usually annexed very ample *Tícá's*, or *Etymological* Commentaries.

WE need say no more of the heterodox writings, than that those on the religion and philosophy of BUDDHA seem to be connected with some of the most curious parts of *Asiatick* History, and contain, perhaps, all that could be found in the *Páli*, or *sacred language* of the Eastern *Indian* peninsula. It is asserted in *Bengal*, that AMARASINHA himself was a Bauddha;

*Bauddha*; but he seems to have been a theist of tolerant principles, and, like ABU'LFAZL, desirous of reconciling the different religions of *India*.

WHEREVER we direct our attention to *Hindu* Literature, the notion of *infinity* presents itself; and the longest life would not be sufficient for the perusal of near five hundred thousand stanzas in the *Purana's*, with a million more perhaps in the other works before mentioned; we may, however, select the best from each *Sástra*, and gather the fruits of science, without loading ourselves with the leaves and branches; while we have the pleasure to find, that the learned *Hindus*, encouraged by the mildness of our government and manners, are at least as eager to communicate their knowledge of all kinds, as we can be to receive it. Since *Europeans* are indebted to the *Dutch* for almost all they know of *Arabick*, and to the *French* for all they know of *Chinese*, let them now receive from our nation the first accurate knowledge of *Sanscrit*, and of the valuable works composed in it; but, if they wish to form a correct idea of *Indian* religion and literature, let them begin with forgetting all that has been written on the subject, by ancients or moderns, before the publication of the *Gítà*.

ON

# ON THE DESCENT OF THE AFGHANS FROM THE JEWS.*

THE *Afghāns*, according to their own traditions, are the posterity of MELIC TA'LU'T (king SAUL), who, in the opinion of some, was a descendant of JUDAH the son of JACOB, and according to others, of BENJAMIN the brother of JOSEPH.

In

---

* This Article was communicated to Sir W*. JONES by HENRY VANSITTART, Esq. with the following introductory Letter, dated CALCUTTA, *March* 3, 1784.

"SIR,

"HAVING some time ago met with a *Persian* abridgement, composed by *Maulavi* KHAIRU'DDIN, of the *ásráru'l afghinah*, or the secrets of the *Afghāns*, a book written in the *Pushto* language by HUSAIN, the son of SA'BIR, the son of KHIZR, the disciple of *Hazret* SHA'H KA'SIM *Sulaimāni*, whose tomb is in *Chunārgar*, I was induced to translate it. Although it opens with a very wild description of the origin of that tribe, and contains a narrative, which can by no means be offered upon the whole as a serious and probable history, yet I conceive, that the knowledge of what a nation suppose themselves to be, may be interesting to a Society like ours, as well as of what
"they

In a war which raged between the Children of *Israel* and the *Amalekites*, the latter, being

"they really are: indeed the commencement of almost
"every history is fabulous; and the most enlightened na-
"tions, after they have arrived at that degree of civilization
"and importance, which has enabled and induced them to
"commemorate their actions, have always found a vacancy
"at their outset, which invention, or at best presumption,
"must supply. Such fictions appear at first in the form
"of traditions; and, having in this shape amused successive
"generations by a gratification of their national vanity, they
"are committed to writing, and acquire the authority of
"history.

"As a kingdom is an assemblage of component parts
"condensed by degrees, from smaller associations of indivi-
"duals, to their general union, so history is a combination
"of the transactions not only of the different tribes, but
"even of the individuals of the nation of which it treats:
"each particular narrative in such a general collection must
"be summary and incomplete. Biography therefore, as well
"as descriptions of the manners, actions, and even opinions
"of such tribes, as are connected with a great kingdom,
"are not only entertaining in themselves, but useful, as
"they explain and throw a light upon the history of the
"nation.

"Under these impressions, I venture to lay before the
"Society the translation of an abridged history of the
"*Afghans*, a tribe at different times subject to, and always
"connected with, the kingdoms of *Persia* and *Hindostan*.
"Their language is called by them *Pushto*; but this word
"is softened in *Persian* into *Pushtu*.

"I am, Sir,
"With the greatest respect,
"Your most obedient humble servant,
"Henry Vansittart."

victorious

victorious, plundered the *Jews*, and obtained
possession of the Ark of the Covenant. Considering this the God of the Jews, they threw
it into fire, which did not affect it. They
afterwards attempted to cleave it with axes,
but without success: every individual who
treated it with indignity, was punished for his
temerity. They then placed it in their temple,
but all their idols bowed to it. At length they
fastened it upon a cow, which they turned loose
in the wilderness.

WHEN the Prophet SAMUEL arose, the Children of *Israel* said to him: " We have been
" totally subdued by the *Amalekites*, and have
" no King. Raise to us a King, that we may
" be enabled to contend for the glory of God."
SAMUEL said: " In case you are led out to
" battle, are you determined to fight?" They
answered: " What has befallen us, that we
" should not fight against infidels? That
" nation has banished us from our country and
" children." At this time the Angel GABRIEL
descended, and delivering a wand, said: " It is
" the command of GOD, that the person whose
" stature shall correspond with this wand, shall
" be King of *Israel*."

MELIC TA'LU'T was at that time a man of
inferiour condition, and performed the humble
employ-

employment of feeding the goats and cows of others. One day a cow under his charge was accidentally loft. Being difappointed in his fearches, he was greatly diftreffed, and applied to SAMUEL, faying, "I have loft a cow, and do not poffefs the means of fatisfying the owner. Pray for me, that I may be extricated from this difficulty." SAMUEL perceiving that he was a man of lofty ftature, afked his name. He anfwered TA'LU'T, SAMUEL then faid: "Meafure TA'LU'T with the wand which the Angel GABRIEL brought." His ftature was equal to it. SAMUEL then faid: "GOD has raifed TA'LU'T to be your King." The Children of *Ifrael* anfwered: "We are greater than our King. We are men of dignity, and He is of inferior condition. How fhall He be our King?" SAMUEL informed them, they fhould know that GOD had conftituted TA'LU'T their King, by his reftoring the Ark of the Covenant. He accordingly reftored it, and they acknowledged him their fovereign.

AFTER TA'LU'T obtained the kingdom, he feized part of the territories of JALU'T, or GOLIAH, who affembled a large army, but was killed by DAVID. TA'LU'T afterwards died a martyr in a war againft the Infidels; and GOD conftituted DAVID King of the *Jews*.

MELIC

MELIC TA'LU'T had two sons, one called BERKIA, and the other IRMIA, who served DAVID, and were beloved by him. He sent them to fight against the Infidels; and, by GOD's assistance, they were victorious.

THE son of BERKIA was called AFGHA'N, and the son of IRMIA was named USBEC. Those youths distinguished themselves in the reign of DAVID, and were employed by SOLOMON. AFGHA'N was distinguished by his corporal strength, which struck terror into Demons and Genii. USBEC was eminent for his learning.

AFGHA'N used frequently to make excursions to the mountains; where his progeny, after his death, established themselves, lived in a state of independence, built forts, and exterminated the Infidels.

WHEN the select of creatures, MUHAMMED, appeared upon earth, his fame reached the AFGHA'NS, who sought him in multitudes under their leaders KHA'LID and ABDUL RASHI'D, sons of WALI'D. The Prophet honoured them with the most gracious reception, saying: " Come, O *Mulúc*, or Kings;" whence they assumed the title of *Melic*, which they enjoy to this day. The Prophet gave them his ensign, and said, that the faith would be strengthened by them.

MANY

MANY sons were born of KHA'LID, the son of WALI'D, who signalized themselves in the presence of the Prophet, by fighting against the Infidels. MUHAMMED honoured and prayed for them.

IN the reign of Sultan MAHMU'D of *Ghaznah*, eight men arrived, of the posterity of KHA'LID the son of WALI'D, whose names were KÁLUN, ALUN, DAUD, YALUA, AHMED, AWIN, and GUA'ZI'. The Sultan was much pleased with them, and appointed each a commander in his army. He also conferred on them the offices of *Vazir*, and *Vakili Mutlak*, or Regent of the Empire.

WHEREVER they were stationed, they obtained possession of the country, built Mosques, and overthrew the Temples of Idols. They encreased so much, that the army of MAHMU'D was chiefly composed of *Afghâns*. When HEBHIND, a powerful prince of *Hindustân*, meditated an invasion of *Ghaznah*, Sultan MAHMU'D dispatched against him the descendants of KHA'LID with twenty thousand horse: a battle ensued; the *Afghâns* made the attack; and, after a severe engagement, which lasted from day-break till noon, defeated HEBHIND, killed many of the Infidels, and converted some to the *Muhammedan* faith.

THE *Afghâns* now began to establish themselves in the mountains; and some settled in cities

cities with the permission of Sultan MAHMU'D. They framed regulations, dividing themselves into four classes, agreeably to the following description. The first is the *pure* class, consisting of those, whose fathers and mothers were *Afghans*. The second class consists of those, whose fathers were *Afghans*, and mothers of another nation. The third class contains those, whose mothers were *Afghans*, and fathers of another nation. The fourth class is composed of the children of women, whose mothers were *Afghans*, and fathers and husbands of a different nation. Persons, who do not belong to one of the classes, are not called *Afghans*.

AFTER the death of Sultan MAHMU'D they made another settlement in the mountains. SHIHA'BUDDI'N *Gauri*, a subsequent Sultan of *Ghaznah*, was twice repulsed from *Hindustan*. His *Vazir* assembled the people, and asked, if any of the posterity of KHA'LID were living. They answered: "Many now live in a state of "independence in the mountains, where they "have a considerable army." The *Vazir* requested them to go to the mountains, and by entreaties prevail on the *Afghans* to come; for they were the descendants of companions of the Prophet.

THE inhabitants of *Ghaznah* undertook this embassy, and, by entreaties and presents, conciliated

ciliated the minds of the *Afgháns*, who promised to engage in the service of the Sultan, provided he would himself come, and enter into an agreement with them. The Sultan visited them in their mountains; honoured them; and gave them dresses and other presents. They supplied him with twelve thousand horse, and a confiderable army of infantry. Being dispatched by the Sultan before his own army, they took *Dehli*, killed Roy Pahtoura the King, his Ministers and Nobles, laid waste the city, and made the infidels prisoners. They afterwards exhibited nearly the same scene in *Canauj*.

The Sultan, pleased by the reduction of those cities, conferred honours upon the *Afgháns*. It is said, that he then gave them the titles of *Patán* and *Khán*: the word *Patán* is derived from the *Hindi* verb *Paitna*, to rush, in allusion to their alacrity in attacking the enemy. The *Patáns* have greatly distinguished themselves in the History of *Hindustán*, and are divided into a variety of sects.

The race of *Afgháns* possessed themselves of the mountain of Solomon, which is near *Kandahár*, and the circumjacent country, where they have built forts: this tribe has furnished many Kings. The following monarchs of this race have sat upon the throne of *Dehli*:

Sultan

Sultan *Behlole*, *Afghán* LODI, Sultan SECANDER, Sultan IBRA'HI'M, SHI'R SHA'H, ISLA'M SHA'H, ADIL SH'AH SUR. They also number the following Kings of *Gaur*: SOLAIMA'N *Sháh Qarání*, BAYAZI'D *Sháh*, and KUTB *Sháh*, besides whom their nation has produced many conquerors of Provinces. The *Afghans* are called *Solaimáni*, either because they were formerly the subjects of SOLOMON, King of the Jews, or because they inhabit the mountain of SOLOMON.

THE translation being finished, I shall only add, that the country of the *Afghans*, which is a province of *Cábul*, was originally called *Roh*, and from hence is derived the name of the *Rohillahs*. The city, which was established in it by the *Afghans* was called by them *Paishwer*, or *Paishór*, and is now the name of the whole district. The sects of the *Afghans*, or *Patáns*, are very numerous. The principal are these: *Lodi*, *Lohauni*, *Súr*, *Serwáni*, *Yúsufzihi*, *Bangish*, *Dilazad*, *Khatti*, *Yasin*, *Khail*, and *Baloje*. The meaning of *Zihi* is offspring, and of *Khail*, sect. A very particular account of the *Afghans* has been written by the late HA'FIZ RAHMAT *Khán*, a Chief of the *Rohillahs*, from which the curious reader may derive much information. They are *Muselmans*, partly of the *Sunni*, and partly of the *Shiah*

per-

persuasion. They are great boasters of the antiquity of their origin, and reputation of their tribe; but other *Musulmans* entirely reject their claim, and consider them of modern, and even base extraction. However, their character may be collected from history. They have distinguished themselves by their courage, both singly and unitedly, as principals and auxiliaries. They have conquered for their own princes and for foreigners, and have always been considered the main strength of the army in which they have served. As they have been applauded for virtues, they have also been reproached for vices, having sometimes been guilty of treachery, and even acted the base part of assassins.

---

NOTE by SIR WILLIAM JONES.

THIS account of the *Afghans* may lead to a very interesting discovery. We learn from ESDRAS, that the Ten Tribes, after a wandering journey, came to a country called *Arsareth*; where, we may suppose, they settled: now the *Afghans* are said by the best *Persian* historians to be descended from the *Jews*; they have traditions among themselves of such a descent; and it is even asserted, that their families
milies

milies are distinguished by the names of *Jewish* tribes, although, since their conversion to the *Islām*, they studiously conceal their origin. The *Pushto* language, of which I have seen a dictionary, has a manifest resemblance to the *Chaldaick*; and a considerable district under their dominion is called *Hazáreh*, or *Hazáret*, which might easily have been changed into the word used by ESDRAS. I strongly recommend an inquiry into the literature and history of the *Afghāns*.

# PROCESS

### OF MAKING

# ATTAR,

### OR

## ESSENTIAL OIL OF ROSES.

#### BY LIEUT. COL. POLIER.

---

THE *Attar* is obtained from the roses by simple distillation, and the following is the mode in which I have made it.

A QUANTITY of fresh roses, for example forty pounds, are put in a still with sixty pounds of water, the roses being left as they are with their calyxes, but with the stems cut close. The mass is then well mixed together with the hands, and a gentle fire is made under the still: when the water begins to grow hot, and fumes to rise, the cap of the still is put on, and the pipe fixed; the chinks are then well luted with paste, and cold water put on the refrigeratory at top: the receiver is also adapted at the end of the pipe; and the fire is continued under the still, neither too violent nor too weak.

weak. When the impregnated water begins to come over, and the still is very hot, the fire is lessened by gentle degrees, and the distillation continued, till thirty pounds of water are come over, which is generally done in about four or five hours; this rose-water is to be poured again on a fresh quantity (forty pounds) of roses, and from fifteen to twenty pounds of water are to be drawn by distillation, following the same process as before: the rose-water thus made and cohobated, will be found, if the roses were good and fresh, and the distillation carefully performed, highly scented with the roses. It is then poured into pans either of earthen ware or tinned metal, and left exposed to the fresh air for the night. The *attar*, or *essence*, will be found in the morning congealed, and swimming on the top of the water; this is to be carefully separated and collected, either with a thin shell or a skimmer, and poured into a phial. When a certain quantity has thus been obtained, the water and fæces must be separated from the clear essence, which, with respect to the first, will not be difficult to do, as the essence congeals with a slight cold, and the water may then be made to run off. If, after that, the essence is kept fluid by heat, the fæces will subside, and may be separated; but if the operation has been neatly performed, these will be little or none. The fœces are as highly perfumed as the essence, and must be kept. After as much of the essence has been skimmed from the rose-water as could be, the remaining water should be used for fresh distillations, instead of common water, at least as far as it will go.

The above is the whole process of making genuine *attar* of roses. But as the roses of this country give but a very small quantity of essence, and it is in high esteem, various ways have been thought of to augment the quantity, though at the expence of the quality. In this country, it is usual to add to the roses, when put in the still, a quantity of sandal-wood raspings, some more, some less (from one to five *tolabs*, or half ounces). The sandal contains a deal of essential oil, which comes over freely in the common distillation; and, mixing with the rose-water and essence, becomes strongly impregnated with their perfume: the imposition however cannot be concealed; the essential oil of sandal will not congeal in common cold, and its smell cannot be kept under, but will be apparent and predominate, spite of every art. In *Cashemire* they seldom use sandal to adulterate the *attar*; but I have been informed, to encrease the quantity, they distill with the roses a sweet-scented grass, which does

not

not communicate any unpleasant scent, and gives the *attar* a clear high green colour: this essence also does not congeal in a slight cold, as that of roses. Many other ways of adulteration have been practised, but all so gross and palpable, that I shall say nothing of them.

The quantity of essential oil to be obtained from the roses, is very precarious and uncertain, as it depends not only on the skill of the distiller, but also on the quality of the roses, and the favourableness of the season: even in *Europe*, where the chemists are so perfect in their business, some, as TACHENIUS, obtained only half an ounce of oil from one hundred pounds of roses.—HAMBERG obtained one ounce from the same quantity; and HOFFMAN above two ounces.

(*N. B.* The roses in those instances were stripped of their calyxes, and only the leaves used).

In this country nothing like either can be had, and to obtain four *majhas* (about one drachm and half) from eighty pounds, which, deducting the calyxes, comes to something less than three drachms per hundred pounds of rose-leaves, the season must be very favourable, and the operation carefully performed.

In the present year 1787, I had only sixteen *tolabs*, or about eight ounces, of *attar* from fifty-

fifty-four maunds, twenty-three feers (4366lb.) of roses produced from a field of thirty-three biggahs, or eleven *English* acres, which comes to about two drachms per one hundred pounds.

The colour of the *attar of roses* is no criterion of its goodness, quality, or country. I have had this year, *attar* of a fine emerald green, of a bright yellow, and of a reddish hue, from the same ground, and obtained by the same process, only of roses collected at different days.

The calyxes do not in any shape diminish the quality of the *attar*; nor impart any green colour to it; though perhaps they may augment the quantity: but the trouble necessary to strip them must, and ought to, prevent its being ever put in practice.

A

DESCRIPTION of ASAM

BY MOHAMMED CAZIM,

TRANSLATED FROM THE PERSIAN

BY HENRY VANSITTART, ESQ.*

---

ASAM, which lies to the north-east of *Bengal*, is divided into two parts by the river *Brahmaputra*, that flows from *Khata*. The northern portion is called *Uttarcul*, and the southern *Dacshincul*. *Uttarcul* begins at *Gowabutty*, which is the boundary of his Majesty's territorial possessions, and terminates in mountains inhabited by a tribe called *Meeri Mechmi*. *Dacshincul* extends from the village *Sidea* to the hills of *Srinagar*. The most famous mountains to the northward of *Uttarcul*, are those of

* This account of *Asam* was translated for the Society, but afterwards printed by the learned translator as an appendix to his *Aálamgirnámah*. It is reprinted here, because our government has an interest in being as well acquainted as possible with all the nations bordering on the British territories.

*Duleh*

*Duleh* and *Landah*; and to the southward of *Dacshincul* are those of *Namrup* (*Câmrúp*), situated four days journey above *Ghergong*, to which the *Rájá* retreated. There is another chain of hills, which is inhabited by a tribe called *Nanac*, who pay no revenue to the *Rájá*, but profess allegiance to him, and obey a few of his orders. But the *Zemleh* * tribe are entirely independent of him, and, whenever they find an opportunity, plunder the country contiguous to their mountains. *Asâm* is of an oblong figure: its length is about two hundred standard cofs, and its breadth, from the northern to the southern mountains, about eight days journey. From *Gowahutty* to *Ghergong* are seventy-five standard cofs; and from thence it is fifteen days journey to *Khoten*, which was the residence of *Peeran Wifeh* †, but is now called *Ava* ‡, and is the capital of the *Rájá* of *Pegu*, who considers himself of the posterity of that famous General. The first five days journey from the

---

* In another copy this tribe are called *Duſleh*.

† According to *Khandamir*, *Peeran Wifeh* was one of the nobles of *Afrasiab*, King of *Turàn*, contemporary with *Kaicaus*, second Prince of the *Kianian* Dynasty. In the *Ferhung Jehangeery* and *Berhaun Kateâ* (two Persian Dictionaries), *Peeran* is described as one of the *Pehlavan* or heroes of *Turán*, and General under *Afrasiab*, the name of whose father was *Wifeh*.

‡ This is a palpable mistake. *Khoten* lies to the north of *Himálaya*; and *Pirán Vyfeh* could never have been *Ava*.

moun-

mountains of *Camrûp*, is performed through forests, and over hills, which are arduous and difficult to pass. You then travel eastward to *Ava* thro' a level and smooth country. To the northward is the plain of *Khatâ*, that has been before mentioned as the place from whence the *Brahmaputra* issues, which is afterwards fed by several rivers that flow from the southern mountains of *Asam*. The principal of these is the *Dhonee*, which has before occurred in this history. It joins that broad river at the village *Luckeigereh*.

BETWEEN these rivers is an island well inhabited, and in an excellent state of tillage. It contains a spacious, clear and pleasant country, extending to the distance of about fifty coss. The cultivated tract is bounded by a thick forest, which harbours elephants, and where those animals may be caught, as well as in four or five other forests of *Asam*. If there be occasion for them, five or six hundred elephants may be procured in a year. Across the *Dhonee*, which is the side of *Ghergong*, is a wide, agreeable, and level country, which delights the heart of the beholder. The whole face of it is marked with population and tillage; and it presents on every side charming prospects of ploughed fields, harvests, gardens, and groves. All the island before described lies in *Dacshineul*.

From

From the village of *Salagereh* to the city of *Ghergong* is a space of about fifty cofs, filled with such an uninterrupted range of gardens, plentifully stocked with fruit-trees, that it appears as one garden. Within them are the houses of the peasants, and a beautiful assemblage of coloured and fragrant herbs, and of garden and wild flowers blowing together. As the country is overflowed in the rainy season, a high and broad causeway has been raised for the convenience of travellers from *Salagereh* to *Ghergong*, which is the only uncultivated ground that is to be seen. Each side of this road is planted with shady bamboos, the tops of which meet, and are intertwined. Amongst the fruits which this country produces, are mangoes, plantains, jacks, oranges, citrons, limes, pine-apples, and *punialeh*, a species of *amlib*, which has such an excellent flavour, that every person who tastes it prefers it to the plum. There are also cocoa-nut trees, pepper vines, *Areca* trees, and the *Sádij* *, in great plenty. The sugar-cane excels in softness and sweetness, and is of three colours, red, black, and white. There is ginger free from fibres,

---

* The *Sádij* is a long aromatick leaf, which has a pungent taste, and is called in *Sanſcrit Tijupatra*. In our botanical books it bears the name of *Malabothrum*, or the *Indian* leaf.

and betel vines. The strength of vegetation and fertility of the soil are such, that whatever seed is sown, or slips planted, they always thrive. The environs of *Ghergong* furnish small apricots, yams and pomegranates; but as these articles are wild, and not assisted by cultivation and engraftment, they are very indifferent. The principal crop of this country consists in rice and * *mash*. *Ades* is very scarce, and wheat and barley are never sown. The silks are excellent, and resemble those of *China*; but they manufacture very few more than are required for use. They are successful in embroidering with flowers, and in weaving velvet and *taushund*, which is a species of silk of which they make tents and † *kenauts*. Salt is a very precious and scarce commodity. It is found at the bottom of some of the hills, but of a bitter and pungent quality. A better sort is in common use, which is extracted from the plantain tree. The mountains inhabited by the tribe called *Nanac* produce plenty of excellent *Lignum Aloes*, which a society of the natives imports every year into *Asâm*, and barters for salt and grain. This evil-disposed race of mountaineers are many degrees removed from the line of humanity, and are destitute of the characteristical

---

* *Mash* is a species of grain, and *Ades* a kind of pea.
† *Kenauts* are walls made to surround tents.

properties of a man. They go naked from head to foot, and eat dogs, cats, snakes, mice, rats, ants, locusts, and every thing of this sort which they can find. The hills of *Cámrúp*, *Sídea*, and *Luckeigereh*, supply a fine species of *Lignum Aloes*, which sinks in water. Several of the mountains contain musk-deer.

The country of *Uttarcul*, which is on the northern side of the *Brahmaputra*, is in the highest state of cultivation, and produces plenty of pepper and *Areca*-nuts. It even surpasses *Dacfhincul* in population and tillage; but, as the latter contains a greater tract of wild forests, and places difficult of access, the rulers of *Afam* have chosen to reside in it for the convenience of control, and have erected in it the capital of the kingdom. The breadth of *Uttarcul* from the bank of the river to the foot of the mountains, which is a cold climate, and contains snow, is various, but is nowhere less than fifteen cofs, nor more than forty-five cofs. The inhabitants of those mountains are strong, have a robust and respectable appearance, and are of a middling size. Their complexions, like those of the natives of all cold climates, are red and white; and they have also trees and fruits peculiar to frigid regions. Near the fort of *Jum Dereh*, which is on the side of *Gowabutty*, is a chain of mountains, called the country of
*Dereng*,

*Dereng*, all the inhabitants of which resemble each other in appearance, manners, and speech, but are distinguished by the names of their tribes, and places of residence. Several of these hills produce musk, *kataus* \*, *bhoat* †, *peres*, and two species of horses, called *goont* and *tanyans*. Gold and silver are procured here, as in the whole country of *Asám*, by washing the sand of the rivers. This, indeed, is one of the sources of revenue. It is supposed, that twelve thousand inhabitants, and some say, twenty thousand, are employed in this occupation; and it is a regulation, that each of these persons shall pay a fixed revenue of a *tóla* of gold to the *Rájá*. The people of *Asám* are a base and unprincipled nation, and have no fixed religion. They follow no rule but that of their own inclinations, and make the approbation of their own vicious minds the test of the propriety of their actions. They do not adopt any mode of worship practised either by *Heathens* or *Mohamme-*

---

\* Kataus is thus described in the *Berhaun Katea*: "This word, in the language of *Rúm*, is a sea-cow; the tail of which is hung upon the necks of horses, and on the summit of standards. Some say, that it is a cow which lives in the mountains of *Khotá*." It here means the mountain-cow, which supplies the tail that is made into *chowries*, and in *Sanscrit* is called *chámara*.

† *Bhoat* and *perse* are two kinds of blanket.

*dans;*

*dans*; nor do they concur with any of the known sects which prevail amongst mankind. Unlike the Pagans of *Hindostan*, they do not reject victuals which have been dressed by *Mufelmans*; and they abstain from no flesh except human. They even eat animals that have died a natural death; but, in consequence of not being used to the taste of ghee, they have such an antipathy to this article, that if they discover the least smell of it in their victuals, they have no relish for them. It is not their custom to veil their women; for even the wives of the *Rájá* do not conceal their faces from any person. The females perform work in the open air, with their countenances exposed and heads uncovered. The men have often four or five wives each, and publickly buy, sell, and change them. They shave their heads, beards, and whiskers, and reproach and admonish every person who neglects this ceremony. Their language has not the least affinity with that of *Bengal* *. Their strength and courage are apparent in their looks; but their ferocious manners and brutal tempers are also betrayed by their physiognomy. They are superior to most nations in corporal force and hardy exertions. They are enterprizing,

---

* This is an error: young *Brahmens* often come from *Ajam* to *Nadiyá* for instruction, and their vulgar dialect is understood by the *Bengal* teachers.

savage,

savage, fond of war, vindictive, treacherous, and deceitful. The virtues of compassion, kindness, friendship, sincerity, truth, honour, good faith, shame, and purity of morals, have been left out of their composition. The seeds of tenderness and humanity have not been sown in the field of their frames. As they are destitute of the mental garb of manly qualities, they are also deficient in the dress of their bodies. They tie a cloth round their heads and another round their loins, and throw a sheet upon their shoulder; but it is not customary in that country to wear turbans, robes, drawers, or shoes. There are no buildings of brick or stone, or with walls of earth, except the gates of the city of *Ghergong*, and some of their idolatrous temples. The rich and poor construct their habitations of wood, bamboos, and straw. The *Rájá* and his courtiers travel in stately litters; but the opulent and respectable persons amongst his subjects are carried in lower vehicles, called doolies. *Asâm* produces neither horses [*], camels, nor asses; but those cattle are sometimes brought thither from other countries. The brutal inhabitants, from a congenial impulse, are fond of seeing and keeping asses, and buy and

---

[*] As the Author has asserted that two species of horses, called *goont* and *tunyoni*, are produced in *Dereng*, we must suppose that this is a different country from *Asâm*.

sell

sell them at a high price; but they discover the greatest surprize at seeing a camel; and are so afraid of a horse, that if one trooper should attack a hundred armed *Asamians*, they would all throw down their arms and flee; or should they not be able to escape, they would surrender themselves prisoners. Yet should one of that detestable race encounter two men of another nation on foot, he would defeat them.

The antient inhabitants of this country are divided into two tribes, the *Asamians* and the *Cultanians*. The latter excel the former in all occupations except war, and the conduct of hardy enterprises, in which the former are superior. A body-guard of six or seven thousand *Asamians*, fierce as demons, of unshaken courage, and well provided with warlike arms and accoutrements, always keep watch near the *Rájá*'s sitting and sleeping apartments; these are his loyal and confidential troops and patrol. The martial weapons of this country are the musquet, sword, spear, and arrow and bow of bamboo. In their forts and boats they have also plenty of cannon, *zerbzen* *, and *ramchanger*, in the management of which they are very expert.

Whenever any of the *Rájás*, magistrates, or principal men, die, they dig a large cave for

* Swivels.

the

the deceased, in which they inter his women, attendants, and servants, and some of the magnificent equipage and useful furniture which he possessed in his lifetime, such as elephants, gold and silver, *badcash* (large fans), carpets, clothes, victuals, lamps, with a great deal of oil, and a torch-bearer; for they consider those articles as stores for a future state. They afterwards construct a strong roof over the cave upon thick timbers. The people of the army entered some of the old caves, and took out of them the value of ninety thousand rupees, in gold and silver. But an extraordinary circumstance is said to have happened, to which the mind of man can scarcely give credit, and the probability of which is contradicted by daily experience. It is this: All the Nobles came to the Imperial General, and declared, with universal agreement, that a golden betel-stand was found in one of the caves, that was dug eighty years before, which contained betel-leaf quite green and fresh; but the authenticity of this story rests upon report.

GHERGONG has four gates, constructed of stone and earth; from each of which the *Rájá's* palace is distant three cos. The city is encompassed with a fence of bamboos, and within it high and broad causeways have been raised for the convenience of passengers during the rainy season.

season. In the front of every man's house is a garden, or some cultivated ground. This is a fortified city, which incloses villages and tilled fields. The *Rája*'s palace stands upon the bank of the *Degoo*, which flows through the city. This river is lined on each side with houses, and there is a small market, which contains no shopkeepers except sellers of botel. The reason is, that it is not customary for the inhabitants to buy provisions for daily use, because they lay up a stock for themselves, which lasts them a year. The *Rájá*'s palace is surrounded by a causeway, planted on each side with a close hedge of bamboos, which serves instead of a wall. On the outside there is a ditch, which is always full of water. The circumference of the inclosure is one cofs and fourteen jereebs. Within it have been built lofty halls, and spacious apartments for the *Rájá*, most of them of wood, and a few of straw, which are called *chuppers*. Amongst these is a *dewán khánah*, or public saloon, one hundred and fifty cubits long, and forty broad, which is supported by sixty-six wooden pillars, placed at an interval of about four cubits from each other. The *Rájá*'s seat is adorned with lattice-work and carving. Within and without have been placed plates of brass, so well polished, that when the rays of the sun strike upon them, they

they shine like mirrors. It is an ascertained fact, that three thousand carpenters and twelve thousand labourers were constantly employed in this work, during two years before it was finished. When the *Rájá* sits in this chamber, or travels, instead of drums and trumpets they beat the \* *dhól* and *dand*. The latter is a round and thick instrument made of copper, and is certainly the same as the drum †, which it was customary, in the time of the antient kings, to beat in battles and marches.

The *Rájá's* of this country have always raised the crest of pride and vain-glory, and displayed an ostentatious appearance of grandeur, and a numerous train of attendants and servants. They have not bowed the head of submission and obedience, nor have they paid tribute or revenue to the most powerful monarch; but they have curbed the ambition, and checked the conquests of the most victorious Princes of *Hindustàn*. The solution of the difficulties attending a war against them, has baffled the penetration of heroes who have been stiled Conquerors of the World. Whenever an invading army has entered their territories, the *Asamians* have

\* The *dhól* is a kind of drum, which is beaten at each end.

† This is a kind of kettle-drum, and is made of a composition of several metals.

covered

covered themselves in strong posts, and have distressed the enemy by stratagems, surprises, and alarms, and by cutting off their provisions. If these means have failed, they have declined a battle in the field, but have carried the peasants into the mountains, burnt the grain, and left the country empty. But when the rainy season has set in upon the advancing enemy, they have watched their opportunity to make excursions, and vent their rage; the famished invaders have either become their prisoners, or been put to death. In this manner powerful and numerous armies have been sunk in that whirlpool of destruction, and not a soul has escaped.

FORMERLY HUSAIN SHAH, a King of *Bengal*, undertook an expedition against *Asam*, and carried with him a formidable force in cavalry, infantry and boats. The beginning of this invasion was crowned with victory. He entered the country, and erected the standard of superiority and conquest. The *Rájá* being unable to encounter him in the field, evacuated the plains, and retreated to the mountains. HUSAIN left his son, with a large army, to keep possession of the country, and returned to *Bengal*. The rainy season commenced, and the roads were shut up by the inundation. The *Rájá* descended from the mountains, surrounded the

*Bengal*

*Bengal* army, skirmished with them, and cut off their provisions, till they were reduced to such straits, that they were all, in a short time, either killed or made prisoners.

In the same manner Mohammed *Shâh*, the son of Togluc *Shâh*, who was king of several of the provinces of *Hindustân*, sent a well-appointed army of a hundred thousand cavalry to conquer *Asâm*; but they were all devoted to oblivion in that country of enchantment; and no intelligence or vestige of them remained. Another army was dispatched to revenge this disaster; but when they arrived in *Bengal*, they were panick-struck, and shrunk from the enterprize; because if any person passes the frontier into that district, he has not leave to return. In the same manner, none of the inhabitants of that country are able to come out of it, which is the reason that no accurate information has hitherto been obtained relative to that nation. The natives of *Hindustân* consider them as wizards and magicians, and pronounce the name of that country in all their incantations and counter-charms. They say, that every person who sets his foot there, is under the influence of witchcraft, and cannot find the road to return.

JOIDEJ SING *, the *Rája* of *Asam*, bears the title of *Swergi*, or *Celestial*. *Swerg*, in the *Hindustani* language, means Heaven. That frantick and vain-glorious prince is so excessively foolish and mistaken, as to believe that his vicious ancestors were sovereigns of the heavenly host; and that one of them, being inclined to visit the earth, descended by a golden ladder. After he had been employed some time in regulating and governing his new kingdom, he became so attached to it, that he fixed his abode in it, and never returned.

IN short, when we consider the peculiar circumstances of *Asam*: that the country is spacious, populous, and hard to be penetrated; that it abounds in perils and dangers; that the paths and roads are beset with difficulties; that the obstacles to the conquest of it are more than can be described; that the inhabitants are a savage race, ferocious in their manners, and brutal in their behaviour; that they are of a gigantic appearance, enterprizing, intrepid, treacherous, well armed, and more numerous than can be conceived; that they resist and attack the enemy from secure posts, and are always prepared for battle; that they possess forts as

* Properly *Jayadhwaja Sinha*, or the *Lion with Banners of Conquest*.

high

high as heaven, garrisoned by brave soldiers, and plentifully supplied with warlike stores, the reduction of each of which would require a long space of time; that the way was obstructed by thick and dangerous bushes, and broad and boisterous rivers: when we consider these circumstances, we shall wonder that this country, by the aid of God, and the auspices of his Majesty, was conquered by the imperial army, and became a place for erecting the standard of the faith. The haughty and insolent heads of several of the detestable *Asamians*, who stretch the neck of pride, and who are devoid of religion, and remote from God, were bruised by the hoofs of the horses of the victorious warriors. The *Muselman* heroes experienced the comfort of fighting for their religion; and the blessings of it reverted to the sovereignty of his just and pious Majesty.

The *Rájá*, whose soul had been enslaved by pride, and who had been bred up in the habit of presuming on the stability of his own government, never dreamt of this reverse of fortune; but being now overtaken by the punishment due to his crimes, fled, as has been before mentioned, with some of his nobles, attendants, and family, and a few of his effects, to the mountains of *Cámrúp*. That spot, by its bad air and water, and confined space, is rendered the worst place in the world, or rather it is one of the pits of hell. The *Rája's* officers and soldiers, by his orders, crossed the *Dhonec*, and settled in the spacious island between that and the *Brahmapútra*, which contains numerous forests and thickets. A few took refuge in other mountains, and watched an opportunity of committing hostilities.

Ca'mru'p is a country on the side of *Dacshincul*, situated between three high mountains, at the distance of four days journey from *Ghergong*. It is remarkable for bad water, noxious air, and confined prospects. Whenever the *Rájá* used to be angry with any of his subjects, he sent them thither. The roads are difficult to pass, insomuch that a foot-traveller proceeds with the greatest inconvenience. There is one road wide enough for a horse; but the beginning of it contains thick forests for about half a cofs. Afterwards there is a defile, which is stony and full of water. On each side is a mountain towering to the sky.

The Imperial General remained some days in *Ghergong*, where he was employed in regulating the affairs of the country, encouraging the peasants, and collecting the effects of the *Rájá*. He repeatedly read the *Khotbeh*, or prayer, containing the name and titles of the Prince of the Age, King of Kings, Alemguir, Conqueror

Conqueror of the World, and adorned the faces of the coins with the Imperial impreffion. At this time there were heavy fhowers, accompanied with violent wind, for two or three days; and all the figns appeared of the rainy feafon, which in that country fets in before it does in *Hinduftán*. The General exerted himfelf in eftablifhing pofts, and fixing guards, for keeping open the roads and fupplying the army with provifions. He thought now of fecuring himfelf during the rains, and determined, after the fky fhould be cleared from the clouds, the lightning ceafe to illuminate the air, and the fwelling of the water fhould fubfide, that the army fhould again be fet in motion againft the *Rájá* and his attendants, and be employed in delivering the country from the evils of their exiftence.

THE Author then mentions feveral fkirmifhes which happened between the *Rájá*'s forces and the Imperial troops, in which the latter were always victorious. He concludes thus:

AT length all the villages of *Dacflincul* fell into the poffeffion of the Imperial army. Several of the inhabitants and peafants, from the diffufion of the fame of his Majefty's kindnefs, tendernefs, and juftice, fubmitted to his government, and were protected in their
habitations

habitations and property. The inhabitants of *Uttarcul* also became obedient to his commands. His Majesty rejoiced, when he heard the news of this conquest, and rewarded the General with a costly dress, and other distinguishing marks of his favour.

The Narrative, to which this is a Supplement, gives a concise history of the military expedition into *Asam*. In this description the Author has stopt at a period, when the Imperial troops had possessed themselves of the Capital, and were masters of any part of the plain country which they chose to occupy or over-run. The sequel diminishes the credit of the conquest, by showing that it was temporary, and that the *Rájà* did not forget his usual policy of harrassing the invading army during the rainy season: but this conduct produced only the effect of distressing and disgusting it with the service, instead of absolutely destroying it, as his predecessors had destroyed former adventurers. Yet the conclusion of this war is far from weakening the panegyrick which the Author has passed upon the Imperial General, to whom a difference of situation afforded an opportunity of displaying additional virtues, and of closing that life with heroick fortitude, which he had always hazarded in the field with martial spirit. His name and titles were, *Mir Jumleh,*

Jumleh, Moazzim *Khán*, *Khání Khánán*, *Sipáhí* Sa'la'r.

## R E M A R K.

The preceding account of the *Aſamians*, who are probably ſuperior in all reſpects to the *Moguls*, exhibits a ſpecimen of the black malignity and frantick intolerance with which it was uſual, in the reign of Aurangzi'b, to treat all thoſe whom the crafty, cruel, and avaricious Emperor was pleaſed to condemn as infidels and barbarians.

## ON THE
## MANNERS, RELIGION, AND LAWS
## OF THE
## CUCIS,
## OR
## MOUNTAINEERS OF TIPRA,

COMMUNICATED IN PERSIAN,

BY JOHN RAWLINS, ESQ.

---

THE inhabitants of the mountainous districts to the east of *Bengal* give the name of PA'TIYA'N to the Being who created the Universe; but they believe, that a Deity exists in every Tree, that the Sun and Moon are Gods, and that, whenever they worship those subordinate divinities, PA'TIYA'N is pleased.

If any one among them put another to death the Chief of the Tribe, or other persons, who bear no relation to the deceased, have no concern in punishing the murderer; but if the murdered person have a brother, or other heir, he may take blood for blood; nor has any man whatever a right to prevent or oppose such retaliation.

WHEN

When a man is detected in the commission of theft or other atrocious offence, the Chieftain causes a recompence to be given to the complainant, and reconciles both parties; but the Chief himself receives a customary fine; and each party gives a feast of pork, or other meat, to the people of his respective tribe.

In ancient times it was not a custom among them to cut off the heads of the women whom they found in the habitations of their enemies; but it happened once, that a woman asked another, why she came so late to her business of sowing grain: she answered, that her husband was gone to battle, and that the necessity of preparing food and other things for him had occasioned her delay. This answer was overheard by a man at enmity with her husband; and he was filled with resentment against her, considering, that as she had prepared food for her husband for the purpose of sending him to battle against his tribe, so in general, if women were not to remain at home, their husbands could not be supplied with provision, and consequently could not make war with advantage. From that time it became a constant practice, to cut off the heads of the enemy's women; especially if they happen to be pregnant, and therefore confined to their houses; and this barbarity is carried so far,

that

that if a *Cúci* assail the house of an enemy, and kill a woman with child, so that he may bring two heads, he acquires honour and celebrity in his tribe, as the destroyer of two foes at once.

As to the marriages of this wild nation; when a rich man has made a contract of marriage, he gives four or five head of *gayáls* (the cattle of the mountains) to the father and mother of the bride, whom he carries to his own house: her parents then kill the *gayáls*, and, having prepared fermented liquors and boiled rice with other eatables, invite the father, mother, brethren, and kindred of the bridegroom to a nuptial entertainment. When a man of small property is inclined to marry, and a mutual agreement is made, a similar method is followed in a lower degree; and a man may marry any woman, except his own mother. If a married couple live cordially together, and have a son, the wife is fixed and irremoveable; but if they have no son, and especially if they live together on bad terms, the husband may divorce his wife, and marry another woman.

They have no idea of heaven or hell, the reward of good, or the punishment of bad, actions; but they profess a belief, that when a person dies, a certain spirit comes and seizes his soul, which he carries away; and that, whatever

whatever the spirit promises to give at the instant when the body dies, will be found and enjoyed by the dead; but that, if any one should take up the corpse and carry it off, he would not find the treasure.

The food of this people consists of elephants, hogs, deer, and other animals; of which if they find the carcasses or limbs in the forests, they dry them and eat them occasionally.

When they have resolved on war, they send spies, before hostilities are begun, to learn the stations and strength of the enemy, and the condition of the roads: after which they march in the night; and two or three hours before day-light, make a sudden assault with swords, lances, and arrows: if their enemies are compelled to abandon their station, the assailants instantly put to death all the males and females, who are left behind, and strip the houses of all their furniture; but, should their adversaries, having gained intelligence of the intended assault, be resolute enough to meet them in battle, and should they find themselves over-matched, they speedily retreat and quietly return to their own habitations. If at any time they see a star very near the moon, they say, "To-night "we shall undoubtedly be attacked by some "enemy;" and they pass that night under arms with extreme vigilance. They often lie in ambush in a forest near the path where their foes are used to pass and repass, waiting for the enemy with different sorts of weapons, and killing every man or woman who happens to pass by: in this situation, if a leech, or a worm, or a snake should bite one of them, he bears the pain in perfect silence; and whoever can bring home the head of an enemy, which he has cut off, is sure to be distinguished and exalted in his nation. When two hostile tribes appear to have equal force in battle, and neither has hopes of putting the other to flight, they make a signal of pacifick intentions, and sending agents reciprocally, soon conclude a treaty; after which they kill several head of *gayals*, and feast on their flesh, calling on the Sun and Moon to bear witness of the pacification: but if one side, unable to resist the enemy, be thrown into disorder, the vanquished tribe is considered as tributary to the victors; who every year receive from them a certain number of *gayals*, wooden dishes, weapons, and other acknowledgements of vassalage. Before they go to battle they put a quantity of roasted *élu's* (esculent roots like *potatoes*) and paste of rice-flour into the hollow of bambu's, and add to them a provision of dry rice with some leathern bags full of liquor: then they assemble, and march with such celerity, that in one day they

they perform a journey ordinarily made by letter-carriers in three or four days, since they have not the trouble and delay of dressing victuals. When they reach the place to be attacked, they surround it in the night, and at early dawn enter it, putting to death both young and old, women and children; except such as they chuse to bring away captive: they put the heads, which they cut off, into leathern bags; and, if the blood of their enemies be on their hands, they take care not to wash it off. When, after this slaughter, they take their own food, they thrust a part of what they eat into the mouths of the heads, which they have brought away, saying to each of them: " Eat; quench thy thirst; and satisfy " thy appetite: as thou hast been slain by my " hand, so may thy kinsmen be slain by my " kinsmen!" During their journey, they have usually two such meals; and every watch, or two watches, they send intelligence of their proceedings to their families: when any one of them sends word, that he has cut off the head of an enemy, the people of his family, whatever be their age or sex, express great delight, making caps and ornaments of red and black ropes; then filling some large vessels with fermented liquors, and decking themselves with all the trinkets they possess, they go forth to meet the conqueror, blowing large shells, and striking plates of metal, with other rude instruments of musick. When both parties are met, they show extravagant joy, men and women dancing and singing together; and, if a married man has brought an enemy's head, his wife wears a head-dress with gay ornaments, the husband and wife alternately pour fermented liquor into each other's mouths, and she washes his bloody hands with the same liquor which they are drinking: thus they go revelling, with excessive merriment, to their place of abode; and, having piled up the heads of their enemies in the court-yard of their chieftain's house, they sing and dance round the pile; after which they kill some *gayáls* and hogs with their spears, and, having boiled the flesh, make a feast on it, and drink the fermented liquor. The richer men of this race fasten the heads of their foes on a bambu, and fix it on the graves of their parents; by which act they acquire great reputation. He, who brings back the head of a slaughtered enemy, receives presents from the wealthy of cattle and spirituous liquor; and, if any captives are brought alive, it is the prerogative of those chieftains, who were not in the campaign, to strike off the heads of the captives. Their weapons are made by particular tribes; for some

some of them are unable to fabricate instruments of war.

In regard to their civil institutions; the whole management of their houshold affairs belongs to the women; while the men are employed in clearing forests, building huts, cultivating land, making war, or hunting game and wild beasts. Five days (they never reckon by months or years) after the birth of a male child, and three days after that of a female, they entertain their family and kinsmen with boiled rice and fermented liquor; and the parents of the child partake of the feast; they begin the ceremony with fixing a pole in the court-yard; and then, killing a *gayál* or a hog with a lance, they confecrate it to their deity; after which all the party eat the flesh and drink liquor, closing the day with a dance and with songs. If any one among them be so deformed, by nature, or by accident, as to be unfit for the propagation of his species, he gives up all thought of keeping house, and begs for his subsistence, like a religious mendicant, from door to door, continually dancing and singing. When such a person goes to the house of a rich and liberal man, the owner of the house usually strings together a number of red and white stones, and fixes one end of the string on a long cane, so that the other end may hang down to the ground; then, paying a kind of superstitious homage to the pebbles, he gives alms to the beggar; after which he kills a *gayál* and a hog, and some other quadrupeds, and invites his tribe to a feast: the giver of such an entertainment acquires extraordinary fame in the nation; and all unite in applauding him with every token of honour and reverence.

When a *Cúcí* dies, all his kinsmen join in killing a hog and a *gayál*; and, having boiled the meat, pour some liquor into the mouth of the deceased, round whose body they twist a piece of cloth by way of shroud: all of them taste the same liquor as an offering to his soul; and this ceremony they repeat at intervals for several days. Then they lay the body on a stage, and kindling a fire under it, pierce it with a spit and dry it; when it is perfectly dried, they cover it with two or three folds of cloth; and, enclosing it in a little case within a chest, bury it under ground. All the fruits and flowers, that they gather within a year after the burial, they scatter on the grave of the deceased; but some bury their dead in a different manner; covering them first with a shroud, then with a mat of woven reeds, and, hanging them on a high tree. Some, when the flesh is decayed, wash the bones, and keep

them

them dry in a bowl, which they open on every sudden emergence; and, fancying themselves at a consultation with the bones, pursue whatever measures they think proper; alledging, that they act by the command of their departed parents and kinsmen. A widow is obliged to remain a whole year near the grave of her husband, where her family bring her food; if she die within the year, they mourn for her; if she live, they carry her back to her house, where all her relations are entertained with the usual feast of the *Cúcí's*.

If the deceased leave three sons, the eldest and the youngest share all his property; but the middle son takes nothing: if he have no sons, his estate goes to his brothers, and, if he have no brothers, it escheats to the Chief of the tribe.

## NOTE.

A PARTY of *Cúcí's* visited the late CHARLES CROFTES, Esq. at *Jáfarabád* in the spring of 1776, and entertained him with a dance: they promised to return after their harvest, and seemed much pleased with their reception.

# ON THE
# BAYA,
## OR
# INDIAN GROSS-BEAK,
### BY ATHAR ALI KHAN, OF DEHLI.

THE little bird called *Bayā* in *Hindì*, *Barbera* in *Sanscrit*, *Babūī* in the dialect of *Bengal*, *Cibù* in *Persian*, and *Tenewwit* in *Arabick*, from his remarkably pendent nest, is rather larger than a sparrow, with yellow-brown plumage, a yellowish head and feet, a light-coloured breast, and a conick beak, very thick in proportion to his body. This bird is exceedingly common in *Hindustan*: he is astonishingly sensible, faithful, and docile, never voluntarily deserting the place where his young were hatched, but not averse, like most other birds, to the society of mankind, and easily taught to perch on the hand of his master. In a state of nature he generally builds his nest on the highest tree that he can find, especially on the palmyra,

palmyra, or on the *Indian* fig-tree, and he prefers that which happens to overhang a well or a rivulet: he makes it of grass, which he weaves like cloth, and shapes like a large bottle, suspending it firmly on the branches, but so as to rock with the wind, and placing it with its entrance downwards to secure it from birds of prey. His nest usually consists of two or three chambers; and it is the popular belief, that he lights them with fire-flies, which he catches alive at night, and confines with moist clay, or with cow-dung; that such flies are often found in his nest, where pieces of cow-dung are also stuck, is indubitable; but as their light could be of little use to him, it seems probable that he only feeds on them. He may be taught with ease to fetch a piece of paper, or any small thing that his master points out to him; it is an attested fact, that if a ring be dropped into a deep well, and a signal given to him, he will fly down with amazing celerity, catch the ring before it touches the water, and bring it up to his master with apparent exultation; and it is confidently asserted, that if a house or any other place be shown to him once or twice, he will carry a note thither immediately, on a proper signal being made. One instance of his docility I can myself mention with confidence, having often been an eye-witness of it. The young

young *Hindu* women at *Banáres*, and in other places, wear very thin plates of gold, called *tica's*, slightly fixed by way of ornament between their eye-brows, and when they pass through the streets, it is not uncommon for the youthful libertines, who amuse themselves with training *Bayás*, to give them a signal, which they understand, and send them to pluck the pieces of gold from the foreheads of their mistresses, which they bring in triumph to the lovers. The *Bayá* feeds naturally on grass-hoppers and other insects, but will subsist, when tame, on pulse macerated in water: his flesh is warm and drying, of easy digestion, and recommended in medical books, as a solvent of stone in the bladder or kidneys; but of that virtue there is no sufficient proof. The female lays many beautiful eggs resembling large pearls; the white of them, when they are boiled, is transparent, and the flavour of them is exquisitely delicate. When many *Bayá's* are assembled on a high tree, they make a lively din, but it is rather chirping than singing: their want of musical talents is, however, amply supplied by their wonderful sagacity, in which they are not excelled by any feathered inhabitants of the forest.

AN

# AN ACCOUNT

## OF THE

# KINGDOM OF NE'PA'L,

BY

FATHER GIUSEPPE, PREFECT OF THE
ROMAN MISSION.

COMMUNICATED BY JOHN SHORE, ESQ.

---

THE kingdom of *Népúl* is situated to the north east of *Patna* at the distance of ten or eleven days' journey from that city. The common road to it lies through the kingdom of *Macwanpur*; but the Missionaries and many other persons enter it on the *Bettia* quarter. Within the distance of four days' journey from *Népúl* the road is good in the plains of *Hindustân*, but in the mountains it is bad, narrow, and dangerous. At the foot of the hills the country is called *Teriáni*; and there the air is very unwholesome from the middle of *March* to the middle of *November*; and people in their passage catch a disorder called in the language of that country *Aul*, which is a putrid fever, and of which the generality of people who are attacked with it die in a few days; but on the plains there is no apprehension of it. Although the road be very narrow and inconvenient for three or four days at the passes of the hills, where it is necessary to cross and recross the river more than fifty times, yet, on reaching the interior mountain before you descend, you have an agreeable prospect of the extensive plain of *Népâl*, resembling an amphitheatre covered with populous towns and villages: the circumference of the plain is about two hundred miles, a little irregular and surrounded by hills on all sides, so that no person can enter or come out of it without passing the mountains.

There are three principal cities in the plain, each of which was the capital of an independent kingdom; the principal city of the three is situated to the northward of the plain, and is called *Cat'hmándú*: it contains about eighteen thousand houses; and this kingdom from south to north extends to the distance of twelve or thirteen days' journey as far as the borders of *Tibet*, and is almost as extensive from east to west. The king of *Cat'hmándú* has always about fifty thousand soldiers in his service. The second

second city to the southwest of *Cat'hmándù* is called *Lelit Pattan*, where I resided about four years; it contains near twenty-four thousand houses; the southern boundary of this kingdom is at the distance of four days' journey, bordering on the kingdom of *Macwanpur*. The third principal city to the east of *Lelit Pattan* is called *B'hátgán*; it contains about twelve thousand families, extends towards the east to the distance of five or six days' journey, and borders upon another nation, also independent, called *Ciratas*, who profess no religion. Besides these three principal cities, there are many other large and less considerable towns or fortresses, one of which is *Timi* and another *Cipoli*, each of which contains about eight thousand houses, and is very populous: all those towns both great and small are well built; the houses are constructed of brick, and are three or four stories high; their apartments are not lofty; they have doors and windows of wood well worked and arranged with great regularity. The streets of all their towns are paved with brick or stone, with a regular declivity to carry off the water. In almost every street of the capital towns there are also good wells made of stone, from which the water passes through several stone canals for the public benefit. In every town there are large square varandas well built, for the accommodation

modation of travellers and the public: these varandas are called *Pati*, and there are also many of them as well as wells in different parts of the country for public use. There are also, on the outside of the great towns, small square reservoirs of water faced with brick, with a good road to walk upon, and a large flight of steps for the convenience of those who choose to bathe. A piece of water of this kind on the outside of the city of *Cat'hmandu* was at least two hundred feet long on each side of the square, and every part of its workmanship had a good appearance.

The religion of *Népál* is of two kinds: the more antient is professed by many people who call themselves *Baryesu*; they pluck out all the hair from their heads; their dress is of coarse red woollen cloth, and they wear a cap of the same: they are considered as people of the religious order, and their religion prohibits them from marrying, as it is with the *Lamas* of *Tibet*, from which country their religion was originally brought; but in *Népál* they do not observe this rule, except at their discretion; they have large monasteries, in which every one has a separate apartment or place of abode; they observe also particular festivals, the principal of which is called *Yatrá* in their language, and continues a month or longer according to the pleasure

pleasure of the king. The ceremony consists in drawing an idol, which at *Lelit Pattan* is called BAGHERO [*], in a large and richly ornamented car, covered with gilt copper: round about the idol stand the king and the principal *Baryesus*; and in this manner the vehicle is almost every day drawn through some one of the streets of the city by the inhabitants, who run about beating and playing upon every kind of instrument their country affords, which make an inconceivable noise.

THE other religion, the more common of the two, is that of the *Bráhmens*, and is the same as is followed in *Hindustán*, with the difference, that in the latter country the *Hindus* being mixed with the *Mohammedans*, their religion also abounds with many prejudices, and is not strictly observed; whereas in *Népál*, where there are no *Muselmans* (except one *Cashmirian* merchant), the *Hindu* religion is practised in its greatest purity: every day of the month they class under its proper name, when certain sacrifices are to be performed and certain prayers offered up in their temples: the places of worship are more in number in their towns than, I believe, are to be found in the most populous

[*] I suppose a name of *Bhagavat* or *Crishna*; but *Bhárya* is *Mahadeva*, and *Bajri* or *Vajri* means the *Thunderer*.

and

and most flourishing cities of *Christendom*; many of them are magnificent according to their ideas of architecture, and constructed at a very considerable expence; some of them have four or five square cupolas, and in some of the temples two or three of the extreme cupolas, as well as the doors and windows of them, are decorated with gilt copper.

In the city of *Lelit Pattan* the temple of BAGHERO was contiguous to my habitation, and was more valuable, on account of the gold, silver and jewels it contained, than even the house of the king, besides the large temples there are also many small ones, which have stairs, by which a single person may ascend, on the outside all around them; and some of those small temples have four sides, others six, with small stone or marble pillars polished very smooth, with two or three pyramidal stories, and all their ornaments well gilt, and neatly worked according to their ideas of taste: and I think that, if *Europeans* should ever go into *Népál*, they might take some models from those little temples, especially from the two which are in the great court of *Lelit Pattan* before the royal palace: on the outside of some of their temples there are also great square pillars of single stones from twenty to thirty feet high, upon which they place their

idols

idols superbly gilt. The greatest number of their temples have a good stone staircase in the middle of the four squares, and, at the end of each flight of stairs, there are lines cut out of stone on both sides: around about their temples there are also bells, which the people ring on particular occasions, and when they are at prayers; many cupolas are also quite filled with little bells hanging by cords in the inside about the distance of a foot from each other, which make a great noise on that quarter where the wind conveys the sound. There are not only superb temples in their great cities but also within their castles.

To the eastward of *Cat'hmándú*, at the distance of about two or three miles, there is a place called *Tolu*, by which there flows a small river, the water of which is esteemed holy according to their superstitious ideas, and thither they carry people of high rank, when they are thought to be at the point of death: at this place there is a temple, which is not inferior to the best and richest in any of the capital cities. They also have it on tradition, that, at two or three places in *Nipál*, valuable treasures are concealed under ground: one of those places they believe is *Tolu*, but no one is permitted to make use of them except the king, and that only in cases of necessity. Those treasures,

they

they say, have been accumulated in this manner: when any temple had become very rich from the offerings of the people, it was destroyed, and deep vaults dug under ground one above another, in which the gold, silver, gilt copper, jewels, and every thing of value were deposited. When I was in *Nepâl*, GAINPREJAS, king of *Cat'hmándú*, being in the utmost distress for money to pay his troops, in order to support himself against PRIT'HWI'NA'RA'YAN, ordered search to be made for the treasures of *Tolu*; and, having dug to a considerable depth under ground, they came to the first vault, from which his people took to the value of a lac of rupees in gilt copper, with which GAINPREJAS paid his troops, exclusive of a number of small figures in gold or gilt copper, which the people who had made the search had privately carried off: and this I know very well; because one evening as I was walking in the country alone, a poor man, whom I met on the road, made me an offer of a figure of an idol in gold or copper gilt, which might be five or six sicca weight, and which he cautiously preserved under his arm; but I declined accepting it. The people of GAINPREJAS had not completely emptied the first vault, when the army of PRIT'HWI'NA'RA'YAN arrived at *Tolu*, possessed themselves of the place where the treasure was

was deposited, and closed the door of the vault, having first replaced all the copper there had been on the outside.

To the westward also of the great city of *Lalit Puttan*, at the distance of only three miles, is a castle called *Banga*, in which there is a magnificent temple: no one of the missionaries ever entered into this castle, because the people who have the care of it, have such a scrupulous veneration for this temple, that no person is permitted to enter it with his shoes on; and the missionaries, unwilling to shew such respect to their false deities, never entered it. But when I was at *Népál*, this castle being in the possession of the people of *Górc'ha*, the commandant of the castle and of the two forts which border on the road, being a friend of the missionaries, gave me an invitation to his house, as he had occasion for a little physick for himself and some of his people: I then, under the protection of the commandant, entered the castle several times, and the people durst not oblige me to take off my shoes. One day, when I was at the commandant's house, he had occasion to go into the varanda, which is at the bottom of the great court facing the temple, where all the chiefs dependent upon his orders were assembled, and where also was collected the wealth of the temple; and, withing to speak

speak to me before I went away, he called me into the varanda. From this incident I obtained a sight of the temple, and then passed by the great court which was in front: it is entirely marble almost blue, but interspersed with large flowers of bronze well disposed to form the pavement of the great court-yard, the magnificence of which astonished me, and I do not believe there is another equal to it in *Europe*.

Besides the magnificence of the temples which their cities and towns contain, there are many other rarities. At *Cat'hmandu* on one side of the royal garden there is a large fountain, in which is one of their idols called *Narayan*. This idol is of blue stone, crowned and sleeping on a mattrass also of the same kind of stone, and the idol and the mattrass appear as floating upon the water. This stone machine is very large: I believe it to be eighteen or twenty feet long and broad in proportion, but well worked and in good repair.

In a wall of the royal palace of *Cat'hmandu*, which is built upon the court before the palace, there is a great stone of a single piece, which is about fifteen feet long, and four or five feet thick; on the top of this great stone, there are four square holes at equal distances from each other; in the inside of the wall they pour water into the holes, and in the court side, each

each hole having a clofed canal, every perfon may draw water to drink: at the foot of the ftone is a large ladder, by which people afcend to drink; but the curiofity of the ftone confifts in its being quite covered with characters of different languages cut upon it. Some lines contain the characters of the language of the country; others the characters of *Tibet*, others *Perfian*; others *Greek*, befides feveral others of different nations; and in the middle there is a line of *Roman* characters; which appears in this form, AVTOMNEW INTER LHIVERT; but none of the inhabitants have any knowledge how they came there, nor do they know whether or not any *European* had ever been in *Népál* before the miffionaries, who arrived there only the beginning of the prefent century. They are manifeftly two *French* names of feafons, with an *Englifh* word between them.

There is alfo to the northward of the city of *Cat'hmadù* a hill called *Simbi*, upon which are fome tombs of the *Lamas* of *Tibet*, and other people of high rank of the fame nation: the monuments are conftructed after various forms; two or three of them are pyramidal, very high, and well ornamented; fo that they have a very good appearance, and may be feen at a confiderable diftance: round thefe monuments are remarkable ftones covered with characters, which

which probably are the inscriptions of some of the inhabitants of *Tibet*, whose bones were interred there. The natives of *Népâl* not only look upon the hill as sacred, but imagine it is protected by their idols; and, from this erroneous supposition, never thought of stationing troops there for the defence of it, although it be a post of great importance, and only at a short mile's distance from the city: but during the time of hostilities a party of PRIT'HWI'NA'RA'YAN's troops being pursued by those of GAINPREJAS, the former, to save themselves, fled to this hill, and, apprehending no danger from its guardian idols, they possessed themselves of it and erected a fortification (in their own style) to defend themselves: in digging the ditches round the fort, which were adjoining to the tombs, they found considerable pieces of gold, with a quantity of which metal the corpses of the grandees of *Tibet* are always interred; and when the war was ended, I myself went to see the monuments upon the hills.

I BELIEVE that the kingdom of *Népâl* is very ancient, because it has always preserved its peculiar language and independence; but the cause of its ruin is the dissension which subsists among the three kings. After the death of their sovereign the nobles of *Lalit Pattan* nominated for their king GAINPREJAS, a man

possessed

possessed of the greatest influence in *Népál*; but some years afterwards they removed him from his government, and conferred it upon the king of *Bhatgán*; but he also a short time afterwards was deposed; and, after having put to death another king who succeeded him, they made an offer of the government to PRIT'HWI'NA'RA'YAN, who had already commenced war. PRIT'HWI'NA'RA'YAN deputed one of his brothers, by name DELMERDEN SA'H, to govern the kingdom of *Lelit Pattan*, and he was in the actual government of it when I arrived at *Népál*; but the nobles perceiving that PRIT'HWI'NA'RA'YAN still continued to interrupt the tranquillity of the kingdom, they disclaimed all subjection to him, and acknowledged for their sovereign DELMERDEN SA'H, who continued the war against his brother PRIT'HWI'NA'RA'YAN; but some years afterwards, they even deposed DELMERDEN SA'H, and elected in his room a poor man of *Lelit Pattan*, who was of royal origin.

THE king of *Bhatgán*, in order to wage war with the other kings of *Népál*, had demanded assistance from PRIT'HWI'NA'RA'YAN; but seeing that PRIT'HWI'NA'RA'YAN was possessing himself of the country, he was obliged to desist, and to take measures for the defence of his own possessions; so that the king of *Gorc'hà*, although

although he had been formerly a subject of
GAINRKJAS, taking advantage of the diffensions which prevailed among the other kings
of *Nepâl*, attached to his party many of the
mountain chiefs, promising to keep them in
possession, and also to augment their authority
and importance; and, if any of them were
guilty of a breach of faith, he seized their
country as he had done to the kings of *Marcansis*,
although his relations.

The king of *Gerc'ha* having already possessed himself of all the mountains which surround the plain of *Nepâl*, began to descend into
the flat country, imagining he should be able to
carry on his operations with the same facility and
success as had attended him on the hills; and,
having drawn up his army before a town, containing about eight thousand houses, situate upon a
hill called *Cirtipur*, about a league's distance from
*Cat'hmêndû*, employed his utmost endeavours
to get possession of it: the inhabitants of *Cirtipur*
receiving no support from the king of *Lalit Pattan*, to whom they were subject, applied for assistance to GAINPREJAS, who immediately marched
with his whole army to their relief, gave battle to
the army of the king of *Gerc'ha*, and obtained a
complete victory. A brother of the king of
*Gerc'ha* was killed on the field of battle; and
the king himself, by the assistance of good

bearers,

bearers, narrowly escaped with his life by fleeing into the mountains; after the action, the inhabitants of *Cirtipur* demanded GAIN-PRAJAS for their king, and the nobles of the town went to confer with him on the business; but, being all assembled in the same apartment with the king, they were all surprised and seized by his people. After the seizure of those persons, GAINPRAJAS, perhaps to revenge himself of these nobles for having refused their concurrence to his nomination as king, privately caused some of them to be put to death; another, by name DANUVANTA, was led through the city in a woman's dress, along with several others clothed in a ridiculous and whimsical manner at the expence of the nobles of *Lelit Pattan*. They were then kept in close confinement for a long time: at last, after making certain promises, and interesting all the principal men of the country in their behalf, GAINPRAJAS set them at liberty.

The king of *Gorc'hà*, despairing of his ability to get possession of the plain of *Népál* by strength, hoped to effect his purpose by causing a famine, and with this design stationed troops at all the passes of the mountains to prevent any intercourse with *Népál*; and his orders were most rigorously obeyed, for every person who was found in the road with only a little salt or cotton about him was hung upon a tree; and he caused all the inhabitants of a neighbouring village to be put to death in a most cruel manner: even the women and children did not escape, for having supplied a little cotton to the inhabitants of *Népál*; and when I arrived in that country at the beginning of 1769, it was a most horrid spectacle to behold so many people hanging on trees in the road. However, the king of *Gore'hà* being also disappointed in his expectations of gaining his end by this project, fomented dissentions among the nobles of the three kingdoms of *Népál*, and attached to his party many of the principal ones, by holding forth to them liberal and enticing promises, for which purpose he had about two thousand *Brahmens* in his service. When he thought he had acquired a party sufficiently strong, he advanced a second time with his army to *Cirtipur*, and laid siege to it on the north-west quarter, that he might avoid exposing his army between the two cities of *Cat'hmándù* and *Lelit Pattan*. After a siege of several months, the king of *Gore'hà* demanded the regency of the town of *Cirtipur*, when the commandant of the town, seconded by the approbation of the inhabitants, dispatched to him by an arrow a very impertinent and exasperating answer. The king of *Gore'hà* was so much enraged at this mode of

pro-

proceeding, that he gave immediate orders to all his troops to storm the town on every side: but the inhabitants bravely defended it, so that all the efforts of his men availed him nothing; and, when he saw that his army had failed of gaining the precipice, and that his brother named SURU'PARATNA had fallen wounded by an arrow, he was obliged to raise the siege a second time, and to retreat with his army from *Cirtipur*. The brother of the king was afterwards cured of his wound by our Father MICHAEL ANGELO, who is at present in *Bettia*.

AFTER the action the king of *Gòrc'hà* sent his army against the king of *Lamji*, (one of the twenty-four kings who reign to the westward of *Nèpàl*), bordering upon his own kingdom of *Gòrc'hà*: after many desperate engagements an accommodation took place with the king of *Lamji*; and the king of *Gòrc'hà* collecting all his forces, sent them for the third time to besiege *Cirtipur*, and the army on this expedition was commanded by his brother SURU'PARATNA. The inhabitants of *Cirtipur* defended themselves with their usual bravery, and after a siege of several months, the three kings of *Nèpàl* assembled at *Cat'hmàndù* to march a body of troops to the relief of *Cirtipur*: one day in the afternoon they attacked some of the *Tanas* of the *Gòrc'hians*, but did not succeed in forcing them,

them, because the king of *Gorc'ha*'s party had been reinforced by many of the nobility, who to ruin GAINPREJAS were willing to sacrifice their own lives. The inhabitants of *Cîrtipur* having already sustained six or seven months siege, a noble of *Lalit Pattan* called DANUVANTA fled to the *Gorc'ha* party, and treacherously introduced their army into the town: the inhabitants might still have defended themselves, having many other fortresses in the upper parts of the town to retreat to; but the people at *Gorc'ha* having published a general amnesty, the inhabitants, greatly exhausted by the fatigues of a long siege, surrendered themselves prisoners upon the faith of that promise. In the mean time the men of *Gorc'ha* seized all the gates and fortresses within the town; but two days afterwards PRIT'HWINA'RA'YAN, who was at *Navacota* (a long day's journey distant) issued an order to SURU'PARATNA his brother to put to death some of the principal inhabitants of the town, and to cut off the noses and lips of every one, even the infants who were not found in the arms of their mothers; ordering at the same time all the noses and lips which had been cut off to be preserved, that he might ascertain how many souls there were, and to change the name of the town into *Nyskatipur*, which signifies the *town*

*of*

of *cut-noses*. The order was carried into execution with every mark of horror and cruelty, none escaping but those who could play on wind instruments; although Father MICHAEL ANGELO, who, without knowing that such an inhuman scene was then exhibited, had gone to the house of SURU'PARATNA, interceded much in favour of the poor inhabitants: many of them put an end to their lives in despair; others came in great bodies to us in search of medicines, and it was most shocking to see so many living people with their teeth and noses resembling the skulls of the deceased.

AFTER the capture of *Cirtipar* PRIT'HWI'-NA'RA'YAN dispatched immediately his army to lay siege to the great city of *Lelit Pattan*. The *Gorc'hians* surrounded half the city to the westward with their *Tanas*, and, my house being situated near the gate of that quarter, I was obliged to retire to *Cat'hmandù* to avoid being exposed to the fire of the besiegers. After many engagements between the inhabitants of the town of *Lelit Pattan* and the men of *Gorc'hà*, in which much blood was spilled on both sides, the former were disposed to surrender themselves, from the fear of having their noses cut off, like those at *Cirtipar*, and also their right hands, a barbarity the *Gorc'hians* had threatened them with, unless they would

surrender

surrender within five days. One night all the
Górc'hians quitted the siege of *Lelit Pattan* to
pursue the *English* army, which, under the
command of Captain KINLOCH, had already
taken *Sidúli*, an important fort at the foot of
the *Nipál* hills, which border upon the kingdom of *Tirhút*: but Captain KINLOCH not being able to penetrate the hills, either on the
*Sidúli* quarter or by the pass at *Hareopur*, in the
kingdom of *Macwanpur*, the army of *Górc'hà*
returned to *Nipál* to direct their operations
against the city of *Cat'hmándù*, where GAIN-
PRKJAS was, who had applied for succour to
the *English*. During the siege of *Cat'hmándù*
the *Bráhmens* of *Górc'hà* came almost every
night into the city, to engage the chiefs of the
people on the part of their king; and the more
effectually to impose upon poor GAINPRKJAS,
many of the principal *Bráhmens* went to his
house, and told him to persevere with confidence, that the chiefs of the *Górc'hà* army
were attached to his cause, and that even they
themselves would deliver up their king PRITH'I-
WI'NA'RA'YAN to his hands. Having by these
artifices procured an opportunity of detaching
from his party all his principal subjects, tempt-
ing them with liberal promises, according to
their custom, one night the men of *Górc'hà*
entered the city without opposition, and the
wretched

wretched GAINPRAJAS, perceiving he was betrayed, had scarce time to escape with about three hundred of his best and most faithful *Hindustani* troops towards *Lelit Pattan*, which place however he reached the same night.

THE king of *Gorc'hà* having made himself master of *Cat'hmandù* in the year 1768, persisted in the attempt of possessing himself also of the city of *Lelit Pattan*, promising all the nobles, that he would suffer them to remain in the possession of their property, that he would even augment it; and because the nobles of *Lelit Pattan* placed a reliance on the faith of his promises, he sent his domestick priest to make this protestation, That if he failed to acquit himself of his promise, he should draw curses upon himself and his family even to the fifth past and succeeding generation; so that the unhappy GAINPRAJAS and the king of *Lelit Pattan*, seeing that the nobility were disposed to render themselves subject to the king of *Gorc'hà*, withdrew themselves with their people to the king of *B'hatgàn*. When the city of *Lelit Pattan* became subject to the king of *Gorc'hà*, he continued for some time to treat the nobility with great attention, and proposed to appoint a viceroy of the city from among them. Two or three months afterwards, having appointed the day for making his formal entrance

entrance into the city of *Lelit Pattan*, he made use of innumerable stratagems to get into his possession the persons of the nobility, and in the end succeeded; he had prevailed upon them to permit their sons to remain at court as companions of his son; he had dispatched a noble of each house to *Navacôt*, or *New Fort*, pretending that the apprehensions he entertained of them had prevented his making a publick entrance into the city; and the remaining nobles were seized at the river without the town, where they went to meet him agreeably to a prior engagement. Afterwards he entered the city, made a visit to the temple of BAGHERO adjoining to our habitation, and, passing in triumph through the city amidst immense numbers of soldiers who composed his train, entered the royal palace, which had been prepared for his reception: in the mean time parties of his soldiers broke open the houses of the nobility, seized all their effects, and threw the inhabitants of the city into the utmost consternation: after having caused all the nobles who were in his power to be put to death, or rather their bodies to be mangled in a horrid manner, he departed with a design of besieging *B'batgdn*, and we obtained permission, through the interest of his

son,

son, to retire with all the *Christians* into the possessions of the *English*.

AT the commencement of the year 1769, the king of *Gorc'hà* acquired possession of the city of *B'hatgan*, by the same expedients to which he owed his former successes, and on his entrance with his troops into the city, GAINPREJAS, seeing he had no resource left to save himself, ran courageously with his attendants towards the king of *Gorc'hà*, and, at a small distance from his palanquin, received a wound in his foot, which a few days afterwards occasioned his death. The king of *Lelit Pattan* was confined in irons till his death, and the king of *B'hatgan*, being very far advanced in years, obtained leave to go and die at *Banares*. A short time afterwards the mother of GAINPREJAS also procured the same indulgence, having from old age already lost her eye-sight; but before her departure they took from her a necklace of jewels, as she herself told me, when she arrived at *Patna* with the widow of her grandson; and I could not refrain from tears, when I beheld the misery and disgrace of this blind and unhappy queen.

THE king of *Gorc'hà*, having thus in the space of four years effected the conquest of *Nepàl*, made himself master also of the country of the *Ciratas* to the east of it, and of other kingdoms,

kingdoms, as far as the borders of *Côch Bihâr:* after his decease, his eldest son PRATA'P SINH held the government of the whole country; but scarcely two years after, on PRATA'P SINH's death, a younger brother, by name BAHA'DAR SA'H, who resided then at *Bettia* with his uncle DELMERDEN SA'H, was invited to accept of the government, and the beginning of his government was marked with many massacres. The royal family is in the greatest confusion, because the queen lays claim to the government in the name of her son, whom she had by PRATA'P SINH; and perhaps the oath violated by PRIT'HWINA'RA'YAN will in the progress of time have its effect. Such have been the successors of the kingdoms of *Nepâl,* of which PRIT'HWINA'RA'YAN had thus acquired possession.

ON

ON

# TWO HINDU FESTIVALS,

AND THE

# INDIAN SPHINX.

BY THE LATE COL. PEARSE, MAY 12, 1785.

---

I BEG leave to point out to the Society, that the *Sunday* before last was the Festival of BHAVA'NI', which is annually celebrated by the *Gópas* and all other *Hindus* who keep horned cattle for use or profit: on this feast they visit gardens, erect a pole in the fields, and adorn it with pendants and garlands. The *Sunday* before last was our *first* of *May*, on which the same rites are performed by the same class of people in *England*, where it is well known to be a relique of ancient superstition in that country: it should seem, therefore, that the religion of the East and the old religion of *Britain* had a strong affinity. BHAVA'NI has another festival; but that is not kept by any one set of *Hindus* in particular, and this is appropriated

propriated to one class of people: this is constantly held on the *ninth* of *Baisāc'h*; which does not always fall on our *first* of *May*, as it did this year. Those Members of the Society who are acquainted with the rules which regulate the festivals, may be able to give better information concerning this point: I only mean to point out the resemblance of the rites performed here and in *England*, but must leave abler hands to investigate the matter further, if it should be thought deserving of the trouble. I find, that the festival which I have mentioned, is one of the most ancient among the *Hindus*.

II. DURING the *Hūli*, when mirth and festivity reign among *Hindus* of every class, one subject of diversion is to send people on errands and expeditions that are to end in disappointment, and raise a laugh at the expence of the person sent. The *Hūli* is always in *March*, and the last day is the greatest holiday: all the *Hindus* who are on that day at *Jagannāts'h*, are entitled to certain distinctions, which they hold to be of such importance, that I found it expedient to stay there till the end of the festival; and I am of opinion, and so are the rest of the officers, that I saved above five hundred men by the delay. The origin of the *Hūli*
seems

seems lost in antiquity; and I have not been able to pick up the smallest account of it.

Is the rites of MAYDAY show any affinity between the religion of *England* in times past and that of the *Hindus* in these times, may not the custom of making *April-fools*, on the first of that month, indicate some traces of the *Huli?* I have never yet heard any account of the origin of the *English* custom; but it is unquestionably very ancient, and is still kept up even in great towns, though less in them than in the country: with us it is chiefly confined to the lower classes of people; but in *India* high and low join in it; and the late SHUJA'UL DAULAH, I am told, was very fond of making *Huli-fools*, though he was a *Muselman* of the highest rank. They carry it here so far, as to send letters making appointments in the names of persons, who, it is known, must be absent from their house at the time fixed on; and the laugh is always in proportion to the trouble given.

III. AT *Jagannát'h* I found the *Sphinx* of the *Egyptians*. MURA'RI *Pandit*, who was deputy *Faujdár* of *Balasór*, attended my detachment on the part of the *Mahráttas:* he is now the principal *Faujdár*, and is much of the gentleman, a man of learning, and very intelligent.

telligent. From him I learned, that the *Sphinx*, here called *Singh*, is to appear at the end of the world, and, as soon as he is born, will prey on an elephant: he is, therefore, figured seizing an elephant in his claws; and the elephant is made small, to show that the *Singh*, even a moment after his birth, will be very large in proportion to it.

When I told Mura'ri, that the *Egyptians* worshipped a bull, and chose the God by a black mark on his tongue, and that they adored birds and trees, he immediately exclaimed, "Their religion then was the same with ours; "for we also chuse our *sacred bulls* by the "*same marks*; we reverence the *hansa*, the *ga-* "*rura*, and other birds; we respect the *pippal* "and *vata* among trees, and the *tulasi* among "shrubs; but as for onions, (which I had "mentioned) they are eaten by low men, and "are fitter to be eaten than worshipped."

### REMARK BY THE PRESIDENT.

Without presuming to question the authority of Mura'ri Pandit, I can only say, that several *Bráhmens*, now in *Bengal*, have seen the figure at *Jagannát'h*, where one of the gates is called *Sinhadwár*; and they assure me, that they always considered it as a mere repre-
sentation

fentation of a *Lion* feizing a young elephant; nor do they know, they fay, any fenfe for the word *Sinha* but a *Lion*, fuch as Mr. HASTINGS kept near his garden. The *Hŏlí*, called *Hŏlicà* in the *Védas*, and *P'halgútfava* in common *Sanfcrit* books, is the feftival of the vernal feafon, or *Nawrúz* of the *Perfians*.

A SHORT

# A SHORT DESCRIPTION OF CARNICOBAR,

### BY MR. G. HAMILTON.

#### COMMUNICATED BY MR. ZOFFANY.

---

THE island of which I propose to give a succinct account, is the northernmost of that cluster in the *Bay of Bengal*, which goes by the name of the *Nicobars*. It is low, of a round figure, about forty miles in circumference, and appears at a distance as if entirely covered with trees; however, there are several well-cleared and delightful spots upon it. The soil is a black kind of clay, and marshy. It produces in great abundance, and with little care, most of the tropical fruits, such as pine-apples, plantains, papayas, cocoa-nuts, and areca-nuts; also excellent yams, and a root called *carbu*. The only four-footed animals upon the island are hogs, dogs, large rats, and an animal of the lizard kind, but large, called by by the natives *talonqui*; these frequently carry off fowls and chickens. The only kind of poultry are hens, and those not in great plenty. There are abundance of snakes of many different kinds, and the inhabitants frequently die of their bites. The timber upon the island is of many sorts, in great plenty, and some of it remarkably large, affording excellent materials for building or repairing ships.

The natives are low in stature but very well made, and surprizingly active and strong; they are copper-coloured, and their features have a cast of the *Malay*; quite the reverse of elegant. The women in particular are extremely ugly. The men cut their hair short, and the women have their heads shaved quite bare, and wear no covering but a short petticoat, made of a sort of rush or dry grass, which reaches halfway down the thigh. This grass is not interwoven, but hangs round the person something like the thatching of a house. Such of them as have received presents of cloth petticoats from the ships, commonly tie them round immediately under the arms. The men wear nothing but a narrow strip of cloth about the middle, in which they wrap up their privities so tight that there hardly is any appearance of them. The ears of both sexes are pierced when young, and by squeezing into the holes large plugs of wood, or hanging heavy weights of shells, they contrive to render them wide, and disagreeable to look at. They are naturally disposed to be good-humoured and gay, and are very fond of sitting at table with Europeans, where they eat every thing that is set before them; and they eat most enormously. They do not care much for wine, but will drink bumpers of arrack, as long as they can see. A great part of their time is spent in feasting and dancing. When a feast is held at any village, every one, that chuses, goes uninvited, for they are utter strangers to ceremony. At those feasts they eat immense quantities of pork, which is their favourite food. Their hogs are remarkably fat, being fed upon the cocoa-nut kernel and sea-water; indeed all their domestick animals, fowls, dogs, &c. are fed upon the same. They have likewise plenty of small sea-fish, which they strike very dextrously with lances, wading into the sea about knee deep. They are sure of killing a very small fish at ten or twelve yards distance. They eat the pork almost raw, giving it only a hasty grill over a quick fire. They roast a fowl, by running a piece of wood through it, by way of spit, and holding it over a brisk fire, until the feathers are burnt off, when it is ready for eating, in their

their taste. They never drink water; only cocoa-nut milk and a liquor called *foura*, which oozes from the cocoa-nut-tree after cutting off the young sprouts or flowers. This they suffer to ferment before it is used, and then it is intoxicating, to which quality they add much by their method of drinking it, by sucking it slowly through a small straw. After eating, the young men and women, who are fancifully dress'd with leaves, go to dancing, and the old people surround them smoaking *tobacco* and drinking *foura*. The dancers, while performing, sing some of their tunes, which are far from wanting harmony, and to which they keep exact time. Of musical instruments they have only one kind, and that the simplest. It is a hollow bamboo about two feet and a half long, and three inches in diameter, along the outside of which there is stretched from end to end a single string made of the threads of a split cane, and the place under the string is hollowed a little to prevent it from touching. This instrument is played upon in the same manner as a guitar. It is capable of producing but few notes; the performer makes it speak harmoniously, and generally accompanies it with the voice.

WHAT they know of physick is small and simple. I had once occasion to see an operation in surgery performed on the toe of a young girl,
who

who had been stung by a scorpion or centipes. The wound was attended with a considerable swelling, and the little patient seemed in great pain. One of the natives produced the under jaw of a small fish, which was long, and planted with two rows of teeth as sharp as needles: taking this in one hand, and a small stick by way of hammer in the other, he struck the teeth three or four times into the swelling, and made it bleed freely: the toe was then bound up with certain leaves, and next day the child was running about perfectly well.

Their houses are generally built upon the beach in villages of fifteen or twenty houses each; and each house contains a family of twenty persons and upwards. These habitations are raised upon wooden pillars about ten feet from the ground; they are round, and, having no windows, look like bee-hives covered with thatch. The entry is through a trap-door below, where the family mount by a ladder, which is drawn up at night. This manner of building is intended to secure the houses from being infested with snakes and rats, and for that purpose the pillars are bound round with a smooth kind of leaf, which prevents animals from being able to mount; besides which, each pillar has a broad round flat piece of wood near the top of it, the projecting of which effectually

prevents

prevents the further progress of such vermin as may have passed the leaf. The flooring is made with thin strips of bamboos laid at such distances from one another, as to leave free admission for light and air, and the inside is neatly finished and decorated with fishing lances, nets, &c.

The art of making cloth of any kind is quite unknown to the inhabitants of this island; what they have is got from the ships that come to trade in cocoa-nuts. In exchange for their nuts (which are reckoned the finest in this part of *India*) they will accept of but few articles; what they chiefly wish for is cloth of different colours, hatchets and hanger blades, which they use in cutting down the nuts. Tobacco and arrack they are very fond of, but expect these in presents. They have no money of their own, nor will they allow any value to the coin of other countries, further than as they happen to fancy them for ornaments; the young women sometimes hanging strings of dollars about their necks. However they are good judges of gold and silver, and it is no easy matter to impose baser metals upon them as such.

They purchase a much larger quantity of cloth than is consumed upon their own island. This is intended for the *Choury* market. *Choury* is a small island to the southward of theirs, to which a large fleet of their boats sails every

year

year about the month of *November*, to exchange cloth for *canoes*; for they cannot make these themselves. This voyage they perform by the help of the sun and stars, for they know nothing of the compass.

In their disposition there are two remarkable qualities. One is their entire neglect of compliment and ceremony; and the other, their aversion to dishonesty. A *Carnicobarian* travelling to a distant village upon business or amusement, passes through many towns in his way without perhaps speaking to any one; if he is hungry or tired he goes up into the nearest house, and helps himself to what he wants, and sits till he is rested, without taking the smallest notice of any of the family, unless he has business or news to communicate. Theft or robbery is so very rare amongst them, that a man going out of his house never takes away his ladder, or shuts his door, but leaves it open for anybody to enter that pleases, without the least apprehension of having any thing stolen from him.

Their intercourse with strangers is so frequent, that they have acquired in general the barbarous *Portuguese* so common over *India*. Their own language has a sound quite different from most others, their words being pronounced with a kind of stop, or catch in the throat, at every

every syllable. The few following words will serve to shew those who are acquainted with other *Indian* languages, whether there is any similitude between them.

| | | | |
|---|---|---|---|
| A man, | *Kegonia.* | To eat, | *Gaia.* |
| A woman, | *Kecanna.* | To drink, | *Okk.* |
| A child, | *Chu.* | Yams, | *T'owla.* |
| To laugh, | *Ayehuer.* | To weep, | *Poing.* |
| A canoe, | *App.* | A pine apple, | *Frang.* |
| A house, | *Albanum.* | To sleep, | *Loom loom.* |
| A fowl, | *Hayám.* | A dog, | *Tamam.* |
| A hog, | *Hown,* | Fire, | *Tamia.* |
| Fish, | *Ka.* | Rain, | *Koontra.* |

They have no notion of a God, but they believe firmly in the devil, and worship him from fear. In every village there is a high pole erected with long strings of ground-rattans hanging from it, which, it is said, has the virtue to keep him at a distance. When they see any signs of an approaching storm, they imagine that the devil intends them a visit, upon which many superstitious ceremonies are performed. The people of every village march round their own boundaries, and fix up at different distances small sticks split at the top, into which split they put a piece of cocoa-nut, a wisp of tobacco, and the leaf of a certain plant: whether this is meant as a peace-offering to the devil, or a scarecrow to frighten him away, does not appear.

When a man dies, all his live stock, cloth, hatchet, fishing lances, and in short every moveable thing he possessed is buried with him, and his death is mourned by the whole village. In one view this is an excellent custom, seeing it prevents all disputes about the property of the deceased amongst his relations. His wife must conform to custom by having a joint cut off from one of her fingers; and, if she refuses this, she must submit to have a deep notch cut in one of the pillars of her house.

I was once present at the funeral of an old woman. When we went into the house which had belonged to the deceased, we found it full of her female relations; some of them were employed in wrapping up the corpse in leaves and cloth, and others tearing to pieces all the cloth which had belonged to her. In another house hard by, the men of the village, with a great many others from the neighbouring towns, were sitting drinking *soura* and smoaking tobacco. In the mean time two stout young fellows were busy digging a grave in the sand near the house. When the women had done with the corpse, they set up a most hideous howl, upon which the people began to assemble round

the

the grave, and four men went up into the house to bring down the body: in doing this they were much interrupted by a young man, son to the deceased, who endeavoured with all his might to prevent them; but finding it in vain, he clung round the body, and was carried to the grave along with it: there, after a violent struggle, he was turned away, and conducted back to the house. The corpse being now put into the grave, and the lashings, which bound the legs and arms, cut, all the live stock which had been the property of the deceased, consisting of about half a dozen hogs and as many fowls, was killed, and flung in above it; a man then approached with a bunch of leaves stuck upon the end of a pole, which he swept two or three times gently along the corpse, and then the grave was filled up. During the ceremony the women continued to make the most horrible vocal concert imaginable; the men said nothing. A few days afterwards, a kind of monument was erected over the grave, with a pole upon it, to which long strips of cloth of different colours were hung.

POLYGAMY is not known among them, and their punishment of adultery is not less severe than effectual. They cut, from the man's offending member, a piece of the foreskin proportioned

tioned to the frequent commiſſion or enormity of the crime.

There ſeems to ſubſiſt among them a perfect equality. A few perſons, from their age, have a little more reſpect paid to them; but there is no appearance of authority one over another. Their ſociety ſeems bound rather by mutual obligations continually conferred and received; the ſimpleſt and beſt of all ties.

The inhabitants of the *Andamans* are ſaid to be *Cannibals*. The people of *Carnicobar* have a tradition among them, that ſeveral canoes came from *Andaman* many years ago, and that the crews were all armed, and committed great depredations, and killed ſeveral of the *Nicobarians*. It appears at firſt remarkable, that there ſhould be ſuch a wide difference between the manners of the inhabitants of iſlands ſo near to one another; the *Andamans* being ſavage *Cannibals*; and the others, the moſt harmleſs inoffenſive people poſſible. But it is accounted for by the following hiſtorical anecdote, which I have been aſſured is matter of fact.

Shortly after the *Portugueſe* had diſcovered the paſſage to *India* round the *Cape of Good Hope*, one of their ſhips, on board of which were a number of *Mozambique* negroes, was loſt on the *Andaman* iſlands, which were till then uninhabited. The blacks remained in the iſland and ſettled

it :

it: the *Europeans* made a small shallop in which they sailed to *Pegu*. On the other hand, the *Nicobar* islands were peopled from the opposite main, and the coast of *Pegu*; in proof of which the *Nicobar* and *Pegu* languages are said, by those acquainted with the latter, to have much resemblance.

# ON THE
# CURE
## OF THE
# ELEPHANTIASIS.

BY AT'HAR ALI' KHA'N OF DEHLI.

---

INTRODUCTORY NOTE.

AMONG the afflicting maladies which punish the vices and try the virtues of mankind, there are few disorders of which the consequences are more dreadful or the remedy in general more desperate than the *judhám* of the *Arabs* or *khórah* of the *Indians*: it is also called in *Arabia dáü'lásad*, a name corresponding with the *Leontiasis* of the *Greeks*, and supposed to have been given in allusion to the grim distracted and *lion-like* countenances of the miserable persons who are affected with it. The more common name of the distemper is *Elephantiasis*, or, as LUCRETIUS calls it, *Elephas*, because it renders the skin, like that of of an *Elephant*, uneven and wrinkled, with many tubercles and furrows; but this complaint must not be confounded with the *dtal'fil*, or *swelled legs*, described by the *Arabian* physicians, and very common in this country. It has no fixed name in *English*, tho' HILLARY, in his *Observations on the Diseases of Barbadoes*, calls it the *Leprosy of the Joints*, because it principally affects the extremities, which in the last stage of the malady are distorted, and at length drop off: but, since it is in truth a distemper corrupting the whole mass of blood, and therefore considered by PAUL of *Ægineta* as an *universal ulcer*, it requires a more general appellation, and may properly be named the *Black Leprosy*; which term is in fact adopted by M. BOISSIEU de SAUVAGES and GORRÆUS, in contradistinction to the *White Leprosy*, or the *Beres* of the *Arabs* and *Leucé* of the *Greeks*.

THIS disease, by whatever name we distinguish it, is peculiar to hot climates, and has rarely appeared in *Europe*: the philosophical Poet of *Rome* supposes it confined to *the banks of the Nile*; and it has certainly been imported from *Africa* into the *West-India* Islands by the black slaves, who carried with them their resentment and their revenge; but it has been long known in *Hindustan*, and the writer of the following Dissertation, whose father was Physician to

NA'DIRSHA'H,

NA'DIRSHA'H, and accompanied him from *Perfia* to *Debli*, affures me that it rages with virulence among the native inhabitants of *Calcutta*. His obfervation, that it is frequently a confequence of the *venereal infection*, would lead us to believe, that it might be radically cured by *mercury*; which has, neverthelefs, been found ineffectual, and even hurtful, as HILLARY reports, in the *Weft-Indies*. The juice of *hemlock*, fuggefted by the learned MICHAELIS, and approved by his medical friend ROEDERER, might be very efficacious at the beginning of the diforder, or in the milder forts of it; but, in the cafe of a malignant and inveterate *judhám*, we muft either adminifter a remedy of the higheft power, or, agreeably to the defponding opinion of CELSUS, *leave the patient to his fate, inftead of teazing him with fruitlefs medicines*, and fuffer him, in the forcible words of ARETÆUS, *to fink from inextricable flumber into death*. The life of a man is, however, fo dear to him by nature, and in general fo valuable to fociety, that we fhould never defpond, while a fpark of it remains; and, whatever apprehenfions may be formed of future danger from the diftant effects of *arfenick*, even though it fhould eradicate a prefent malady, yet as no fuch inconvenience has arifen from the ufe of it in *India*, and as experience

muft

muſt ever prevail over theory, I cannot help wiſhing that this ancient *Hindu* medicine may be fully tried under the inſpection of our *European* Surgeons, whoſe minute accuracy and ſteady attention muſt always give them a claim to ſuperiority over the moſt learned natives; but many of our countrymen have aſſured me, that they by no means entertain a contemptuous opinion of the native medicines, eſpecially in diſeaſes of the ſkin. Should it be thought, that the mixture of ſulphur muſt render the poiſon leſs active, it may be adviſeable at firſt to adminiſter orpiment, inſtead of the *cryſtalline arſenick.*

---

*On the* CURE *of the* ELEPHANTIASIS, *and other* DISORDERS *of the* BLOOD.

## God is the all-powerful Healer.

IN the year of the MESSIAH 1783, when the worthy and reſpectable *Maulavi* MI'R MUHAMMED HUSAI'N, who excels in every branch of useful knowledge, accompanied Mr. RICHARD JOHNSON from *Lac'hnau* to *Calcutta,* he viſited the humble writer of this tract, who had long been attached to him with ſincere affection; and, in the courſe of their converſation, "One of the fruits of my late excur-
" ſion," ſaid he, "is a preſent for you, which
" ſuits

"  suits your profession, and will be generally
"  useful to our species : conceiving you to be
"  worthy of it by reason of your assiduity in
"  medical enquiries, I have brought you a pre-
"  scription, the ingredients of which are easily
"  found, but not easily equalled as a powerful
"  remedy against all corruptions of the blood,
"  the *judhám*, and the *Persian Fire*, the re-
"  mains of which are a source of infinite ma-
"  ladies. It is an old secret of the *Hindu* Phy-
"  sicians; who applied it also to the cure of
"  cold and moist distempers, as the palsy, dis-
"  tortions of the face, relaxation of the nerves,
"  and similar diseases : its efficacy too has been
"  proved by long experience; and this is the me-
"  thod of preparing it.

"   TAKE of white *arsenick*, fine and fresh,
"  one *ráti* ; of picked black pepper six times as
"  much : let both be well beaten at intervals
"  for four days successively in an iron mortar,
"  and then reduced to an impalpable powder in
"  one of stone with a stone pestle, and thus
"  completely levigated, a little water being
"  mixed with them. Make pills of them as
"  large as tares or small pulse, and keep them
"  dry in a shady place\*.

ONE

\* The lowest weight in general use among the *Hindus* is
the *ráti*, called in *Sanscrit* either *retica* or *ractica*, indicating
*reddish*, and *trishtamila* from *crishna*, *black* : it is the red and
black

"One of those pills must be swallowed morning and evening with some *betel*-leaf, or, in countries where *betel* is not at hand, with cold water: if the body be cleansed from foulness and obstructions by gentle catharticks and bleeding before the medicine is administered, the remedy will be the speedier."

THE principal ingredient of this medicine is the *arsnick*, which the *Arabs* call *shucc*, the *Persians mergi mūsh*, or *mouse-bane*, and the *Indians, sanc'hyá*; a mineral substance ponderous

*that* seed of the *gunjā*-plant, which is a creeper of the same class and order at least with the *glycyrrhiza*; but I take this from report, having never examined its blossoms. One *rattica* is said to be of equal weight with three barley-corns or four grains of rice in the husk; and eight *retti-weights*, used by jewellers, are equal to seven carats. I have weighed a number of the seeds in diamond-scales, and find the average Apothecary's weight of one seed to be a grain *and five sixteenths*. Now in the *Hindu* medical books *ten* of the *rattica*-seeds are one *mashaca*, and *eight mashaca's* make a *tólaca* or *tola*; but in the law-books of *Bengal* a *mashaca* consists of *sixteen rattica's*, and a *tólaca* of *five mashái's*; and according to some authorities *five ratti's* only go to one *mashni*, *sixteen* of which make a *tólaca*. We may observe, that the silver *retti-weights* used by the goldsmiths at *Banáres*, are *twice* as heavy as the *first*; and thence it is, that eight *retti's* are commonly said to constitute one *masha*, that is, *eight silver weights*, or *sixteen seeds*; *eighty* of which seeds, or *105* grains, constitute the quantity of arsenick in the *Hindu* prescription.

and *cryſtalline*: the *orpiment*, or *yellow* arſenick, is the weaker ſort. It is a deadly poiſon, and ſo ſubtile, that, when mice are killed by it, the very ſmell of the dead will deſtroy the living of that ſpecies: after it has been kept about ſeven years, it loſes much of its force; its colour becomes turbid; and its weight is diminiſhed. This mineral is hot and dry in the fourth degree; it cauſes ſuppuration, diſſolves or unites, according to the quantity given; and is very uſeful in cloſing the lips of wounds, when the pain is too intenſe to be borne. An unguent made of it with oils of any ſort is an effectual remedy for ſome cutaneous diſorders, and, mixed with roſe-water, it is good for cold tumours and for the dropſy; but it muſt never be adminiſtered without the greateſt caution; for ſuch is its power, that the ſmalleſt quantity of it in powder, drawn, like *álcohol*, between the eyelaſhes, would in a ſingle day entirely corrode the coats and humours of the eye; and fourteen *retī's* of it would in the ſame time deſtroy life. The beſt antidote againſt its effects are the ſcrapings of leather reduced to aſhes: if the quantity of arſenick taken be accurately known, four times as much of thoſe aſhes, mixed with water and drunk by the patient, will ſheath and counteract the poiſon.

THE

The writer, conformably to the directions of his learned friend, prepared the medicine; and, in the same year, gave it to numbers, who were reduced by the diseases abovementioned to the point of death: GOD is his witness, that they grew better from day to day, were at last completely cured, and are now living (except one or two, who died of other disorders) to attest the truth of this assertion. One of his first patients was a *Pársí*, named MENU'CHEHR, who had come from *Surat* to this city, and had fixed his abode near the writer's house: he was so cruelly afflicted with a confirmed lues, here called *the Persian Fire*, that his hands and feet were entirely ulcerated and almost corroded, so that he became an object of disgust and abhorrence. This man consulted the writer on his case, the state of which he disclosed without reserve. Some blood was taken from him on the same day, and a cathartick administered on the next. On the third day he began to take the *arsenick-pills*, and, by the blessing of GOD, the virulence of his disorder abated by degrees, until signs of returning health appeared; in a fortnight his recovery was complete, and he was bathed, according to the practice of our Physicians: he seemed to have no virus left in his blood, and none has been since perceived by him.

BUT

But the power of this medicine has chiefly been tried in the cure of the *juzâm*, as the word is pronounced in *India*; a disorder infecting the whole mass of blood, and thence called by some *ṣṣidi koïns*. The former name is derived from an *arabick root*, signifying, in general, *amputation, maiming, excision, and,* particularly, the *truncation* or *erasion* of *the fingers,* which happens in the last stage of the disease. It is extremely contagious, and for that reason the Prophet said; *furrû minâ'lmujdhâmi camâ teferrû minâ'l âsad*, or, "Flee from a person "afflicted with the *judhâm*, as you would flee "from a lion." The author of the *Babhru'l-jawâhir*, or *Sea of Pearls*, ranks it as an infectious malady with the *measles*, the *small-pox*, and the *plague*. It is also *hereditary*, and, in that respect, classed by medical writers with the *gout*, the *consumption*, and the *white leprosy*.

A common cause of this distemper is the unwholesome diet of the natives, many of whom are accustomed, after eating a quantity of *fish*, to swallow copious draughts of *milk*, which fail not to cause an accumulation of yellow and black bile, which mingles itself with the blood and corrupts it; but it has other causes; for a *Brâhmen*, who had never tasted *fish* in his life, applied lately to the composer of this essay, and appeared in the highest degree affected by

a cura corruption of blood; which he might have inherited, or acquired by other means. Those, whose religion permits them to eat beef, are often exposed to the danger of heating their blood intensely through the knavery of the butchers in the *Bázár*, who fatten their calves with *Balúwer*; and those who are are so ill-advised as to take *provocatives*, a folly extremely common in *India*, at first are insenble of the mischief, but, as soon as the increased moisture is dispersed, find their whole mass of blood inflamed and, as it were, adust; whence arises the disorder of which we now are treating. The *Persian*, or venereal, Fire generally ends in this malady; as one DE'VI' PRASA'D, lately in the service of Mr. VANSITTART, and some others, have convinced me by an unreserved account of their several cases.

It may here be worth while to report a remarkable case, which was related to me by a man who had been afflicted with the *juzám* near four years; before which time he had been disordered with the *Persian Fire* and, having closed an ulcer by the means of a strong healing plaister, was attacked by a violent pain in his joints: on this he applied to a *Cabirája*, or *Hindu* Physician, who gave him some pills, with a positive assurance, that the use of them would remove his pain in a few days; and in a few days it was, in fact, wholly removed;

but

but, a very short time after, the symptoms of the *juzám* appeared, which continually increased to such a degree, that his fingers and toes were on the point of dropping off. It was afterwards discovered, that the pills which he had taken were made of cinnabar, a common preparation of the *Hindus*; the heat of which had first stirred the humours, which, on stopping the external discharge, had fallen on the joints, and then had occasioned a quantity of adust bile to mix itself with the blood and infect the whole mass.

Of this dreadful complaint, however caused, the first symptoms are a numbness and redness of the whole body, and principally of the face, an impeded hoarse voice, thin hair, and even baldness, offensive perspiration and breath, and whitlows on the nails. The cure is best begun with copious bleeding, and cooling drink, such as a decoction of the *nilúfer*, or *Nymphæa*, and of violets, with some doses of manna: after which stronger catharticks must be administered. But no remedy has proved so efficacious as the pills composed of arsenick and pepper: one instance of their effect may here be mentioned, and many more may be added, if required.

In the month of *February* in the year just mentioned, one *Shaikh* RAMAZA'NI', who then was an upper-servant to the Board of Revenue, had

had so corrupt a mass of blood, that a black leprosy of his joints was approaching; and most of his limbs began to be ulcerated: in this condition he applied to the writer, and requested immediate assistance. Though the disordered state of his blood was evident on inspection, and required no particular declaration of it, yet many questions were put to him, and it was clear from his answers, that he had a confirmed *juzdm*: he then lost a great deal of blood, and, after due preparation, took the arsenick-pills. After the first week his malady seemed alleviated; in the second it was considerably diminished, and in the third so entirely removed, that the patient went into the bath of health, as a token that he no longer needed a physician.

## ON THE CURE OF PERSONS BITTEN BY SNAKES.

### BY JOHN WILLIAMS, ESQ.

THE following statement of facts relative to the cure of persons bitten by snakes, selected from a number of cases which have come within my own knowledge, require no prefatory introduction: as it points out the means of obtaining the greatest self-gratification the human mind is capable of experiencing—that of the preservation of the life of a fellow-creature, and snatching him from the jaws of death, by a method which every person is capable of availing himself of. Eau de Luce, I learn from many communications which I have received from different parts of the country, answers as well as the pure Caustick Alkali Spirit; and though, from its having some essential oils in its composition, it may not be so powerful, yet, as it must be given with water, it only requires to encrease the dose in proportion; and, so long as it retains its milky white colour, it is sufficiently efficacious.

From the effect of a ligature, applied between the part bitten and the heart, it is evident that the poison diffuses itself over the body by the returning venous blood; destroying the irritability, and rendering the system paralytick. It is therefore probable that the Volatile Caustick Alkali, in resisting the disease of the poison, does not act so much as a specifick in destroying its quality, as by counteracting the effect on the system, by stimulating the fibres, and preserving that irritability which it tends to destroy.

## CASE I.

IN the month of *August* 1780, a servant of mine was bitten in the heel, as he supposed, by a snake; and in a few minutes was in great agony, with convulsions about the throat and jaws, and continual grinding of teeth: having a wish to try the effects of Volatile Alkali in such cases, I gave him about forty drops of Eau de Luce in water, and applied some of it to the part bitten; the dose was repeated every eight or ten minutes, till a small phial-full was expended: it was near two hours before it could
be

be said he was out of danger. A numbness and pricking sensation was perceived extending itself up to the knee; where a ligature was applied so tight as to stop the returning venous blood, which seemingly checked the progress of the deleterious poison. The foot and leg, up to where the ligature was made, were stiff and painful for several days; and, which appeared very singular, were covered with a branny scale.

The above was the first case in which I tried the effects of the Volatile Alkali, and apprehending that the essential oils in the composition of Eau de Luce, though made of the strong Caustick Volatile Spirit, would considerably diminish its powers, I was induced, the next opportunity that offered, to try the effects of pure Volatile Caustick Alkali Spirit, and accordingly prepared some from Quicklime and the Sal Ammoniack of this country.

## CASE II.

In *July* 1782, a woman of the *Bráhmen* cast, who lived in my neighbourhood at *Chunár*, was bitten by a *Cobra de Capello* between the thumb and fore-finger of her right hand: prayers and superstitious incantations were practised by the *Bráhmens* about her till

she

she became speechless and convulsed, with locked jaws, and a profuse discharge of saliva running from her mouth. On being informed of the accident, I immediately sent a servant with a bottle of the Volatile Caustick Alkali Spirit, of which he poured about a tea-spoon-full, mixed with water, down her throat, and applied some of it to the part bitten: the dose was repeated a few minutes after, when she was evidently better, and in about half an hour was perfectly recovered.

This accident happened in a small hut, where I saw the snake, which was a middle-sized *Cobra de Capello*: the *Bráhmens* would not allow it to be killed. In the above case, no other means whatever were used for the recovery of the patient than are here recited.

### CASE III.

A WOMAN-SERVANT in the family of a gentleman at *Benares* was bitten in the foot by a *Cobra de Capello*: the gentleman immediately applied to me for some of the Volatile Caustick Alkali, which I fortunately had by me. I gave her about sixty drops in water, and also applied some of it to the part bitten; in about seven or eight minutes after, she was quite recovered. In the above case, I was not witness to the deleterious effect of the poison on the patient; but saw the snake after it was killed.

## CASE IV.

In *July* 1784, the wife of a servant of mine was bitten by a *Cobra de Capello* on the outside of the little toe of her right foot. In a few minutes she became convulsed, particularly about the jaws and throat, with a continued gnashing of the teeth. She at first complained of a numbness extending from the wound upwards, but no ligature was applied to the limb. About sixty drops of the Volatile Caustick Spirit were given to her in water, by forcing open her mouth, which was strongly convulsed: in about seven minutes the dose was repeated, when the convulsions left her; and in three more she became sensible, and spoke to those who attended her. A few drops of the spirit had also been applied to the wound. The snake was killed and brought to me, which proved to be a *Cobra de Capello*.

## CASE V.

As it is generally believed, that the venom of snakes is more malignant during hot dry weather than at any other season, the following case, which occurred in the month of

*July*

*July* 1788, when the weather was extremely hot, no rain, excepting a slight shower, having fallen for many months, may not be unworthy notice.

A SERVANT belonging to an Officer at *Juanpoor* was bitten by a snake on the leg, about two inches above the outer ancle. As the accident happened in the evening, he could not see what species of snake it was: he immediately tied a ligature above the part bitten, but was in a few minutes in such exquisite torture from pain, which extended up his body and to his head, that he soon became dizzy and senseless. On being informed of the accident, I sent my servant with a phial of the Volatile Caustick Alkali, who found him, when he arrived, quite torpid, with the saliva running out of his mouth, and his jaws so fast locked, as to render it necessary to use an instrument to open them and administer the medicine. About forty drops of the Volatile Caustick Spirit were given to him in water, and applied to the wound; and the same dose repeated a few minutes after. In about half an hour he was perfectly recovered. On examining the part bitten, I could discover the marks of three fangs; two on one side, and one on the other; and, from the distance they were asunder, I should judge it a large snake. More than ten minutes

minutes did not appear to have elapsed from the time of his being bitten till the medicine was administered. The wounds healed immediately, and he was able to attend to his duty the next day. Though the species of snake was not ascertained, yet I judge from the flow of saliva from the mouth, convulsive spasms of the jaws and throat, as well as from the marks of three fangs, that it must have been a *Cobra de Capello*; and, though I have met with five and six fangs of different sizes in snakes of that species, I never observed the marks of more than two having been applied in biting, in any other case which came within my knowledge.

## CASE VI.

In *September* 1786, a servant belonging to Captain S——, who was then at *Benares*, was bitten in the leg by a large *Cobra de Capello*. He saw the snake coming towards him, with his neck spread out in a very tremendous manner, and endeavoured to avoid him; but before he could get out of his way, the snake seized him by the leg, and secured his hold for some time, as if he had not been able to extricate his teeth. Application was immediately made to his master for a remedy, who sent to consult me; but, before I arrived, had given him a quantity of sweet oil, which he drank. So soon as I saw him,

him, I directed the usual dose of Volatile Caustick Alkali to be given, which fortunately brought away the oil from his stomach, or it is probable that the stimulating effect of the Volatile Spirit would have been so much blunted by it as to have become inefficacious: a second dose was immediately administered, and some time after a third. The man recovered in the course of a few hours. As oil is frequently administered as a remedy in the bite of snakes, I think it necessary to caution against the use of it with the Volatile Alkali, as it blunts the stimulating quality of the spirit, and renders it useless.

Of the numerous species of snakes which I have met with, not above six were provided with poisonous fangs; though I have examined many which have been considered by the natives as dangerous, without being able to discover any thing noxious in them.

The following is an instance of the deleterious effect of the bite of a snake called by the natives *Krait*, a species of the *Boa*, which I have frequently met with in this part of the country.

## CASE VII.

On the 16th *September* 1788, a man was brought to me who had been bitten by a snake, with the marks of two fangs on two of his toes; he was said to have been bitten above an hour before I saw him: he was perfectly sensible, but complained of great pain in the parts bitten, with an universal languor. I immediately gave him thirty drops of the Volatile Cauſtick Alkali Spirit in water, and applied ſome of it to the wounds: in a few minutes he became eaſier, and in about half an hour was carried away by his friends, with perfect confidence in his recovery, without having taken a ſecond doſe of the medicine, which indeed did not appear to have been neceſſary: but, whether from the effect of the bite of the ſnake, or the motion of the dooly on which he was carried, I know not; but he became ſick at the ſtomach, threw up the medicine, and died in about a quarter of an hour after. The man ſaid, that the ſnake came up to him while he was ſitting on the ground; and that he put him away with his hand once, but that he turned about and bit him as deſcribed: the ſnake was brought to me, which I examined; it was about two feet and an half long, of a lightiſh brown colour on the back, a white belly, and annulated from end to end, with 208 abdominal, and forty-ſix tail ſcuta. I have met with ſeveral of them from thirteen inches to near three feet in length: it had two poiſonous fangs in the upper jaw,

which

which lay naked, with their points without the upper lip. It does not spread its neck like the *Cobra de Capello*, when enraged; but is very active and quick in its motion.

I HAVE seen instances of persons bitten by snakes, who have been so long without assistance, that when they have been brought to me, they have not been able to swallow, from convulsions of the throat and fauces, which is, I observe, a constant symptom of the bite of the *Cobra de Capello*; and indeed I have had many persons brought to me who had been dead some time; but never knew an instance of the Volatile Caustick Alkali failing in its effect, where the patient has been able to swallow it.

# REMARKS

## ON THE

# CITY OF TAGARA.

### BY LIEUT. FRANCIS WILFORD.

---

THE expedition of ALEXANDER having made the *Greeks* acquainted with the riches of *India*, they soon discovered the way by sea into that country, and having entered into a commercial correspondence with the natives, they found it so beneficial, that they attempted a trade thither.

PTOLEMY PHILADELPHUS, king of *Egypt*, in order to render the means easy to merchants, sent one DIONYSIUS into the Southern parts of *India*, to inquire into the nature of that country, its produce, and manufactures.

IT was then *Tagara* began to be known to the *Greeks*, about two thousand and fifty years years ago.

ARRIAN,

ARRIAN, in his *Periplus Maris Erythræi*, says it was a very large city, and that the produce of the country, at that early period, consisted chiefly of coarse Dungarees *(Othonium vulgare)*, of which vast quantities were exported; Muslins of all sorts *(Sindones omnis generis)*, and a kind of Cotton Stuff dyed of a whitish purple, and very much of the colour of the flowers of Mallows, whence called *Molochyna*.

ALL kinds of mercantile goods, throughout the *Deccan*, were brought to *Tagara*, and from thence conveyed on carts to *Baroach* (*Barygaza*).

ARRIAN informs us, that *Tagara* was about ten days journey to the eastward of another famous Mart, called *Plithana* or *Plithana*.

THAT *Plithana* was twenty days journey to the Southward of *Baroach*; also,

THAT the road was through the *Balagaut* mountains.

AND here we must observe, that the *Latin* translation of the *Periplus* [*] by STUCKIUS is very inaccurate and often erroneous; as, in the following passage, where ARRIAN, speaking of *Tagara* says,

"Παραγίνεται δὲ εἰς αὐτὴν τοιαῦτα ὁμοίως καὶ Πλίθανα γινόμενα εἰς τὸ
"Βαρυγαζα:"

[*] Geographiæ veteris Scriptorum Græci minores, Vol. I.

which

which Stuckius translates thus: "Ex his autem emporiis, *per loca invia et difficillima, res* Barygazam plauftris *convehuntur.*" But it should be, "Ex his autem emporiis, *per maximos ascensus,* res Barygazam *deorsum feruntur.*"

Καταγω signifies *deorsum ferre* (to bring down) not *convehere.*

Ἀναβαι περικας should be translated *per maximos ascensus:* ἀναβα or ἀναβη in this place signifies *an ascent, a road over hills;* and this meaning is plainly pointed out by the words μεγιςτας and περικας.

In short, ἀναβαι περικας is the true translation of the *Hindoo* word *Bala-gaut,* the name of the mountains through which the goods from *Tagara* to *Barzach* used to be conveyed.

This passage in Arrian is the more interesting, as it fixes the time when the *Bala-gaut* mountains were first heard of in *Europe.*

The bearing from *Tagara* to *Pluthana* is expressly mentioned by Arrian (προς ανατολας) but is left out by Stuckius.

Pluthana is an important point to be settled, as it regulates the situation of *Tagara.*

It still exists, and goes nearly by the same name, being called to this day *Pultanah:* it is situated on the Southern bank of the *Godivery,*
about

about two hundred and seventeen *British* miles to the Southward of *Baroach*.

THESE two hundred and seventeen miles, being divided by twenty, the number of days travellers were between *Pultanah* and *Baroach* according to ARRIAN, give nearly eleven miles per day or five cofs, which is the usual rate of travelling with heavy loaded carts.

THE Onyx and several other precious stones are still found in the neighbourhood of *Pultanah*, as related by ARRIAN; being washed down by torrents from the hills, during the rains, according to PLINY.

ARRIAN informs us that the famous town of *Tagara* was about ten days journey to the eastward of *Pultanah*.

ACCORDING to the above proportion, these ten days (or rather somewhat less[*]) are equal to about one hundred *British* miles; and consequently *Tagara*, by its bearing and distance from *Pultanah*, falls at *Deoghir*, a place of great antiquity, and famous through all *India* on account of the *Pagodas* of *Eloura*. It is now called *Doulet-abad*, and about four cofs N. W. of *Aurungabad*.

PTOLEMY agrees very well with ARRIAN, with respect to distances and bearings, if we

[*] Ὀλίγῳ ἐλάσσους δέκα, quasi dies decem.

admit

admit that he has mistaken *Baithana* or *Paithana* for *Plithana*; and this, I am pretty sure, is really the case, and may be easily accounted for, as there is very little difference between ΠΑΙΘΑΝΑ and ΠΑΙΘΑΝΑ in the *Greek* character.

*Paithana*, now *Pattan*\* or *Putten*, is about half way between *Tagara* and *Plithana*.

ACCORDING to PTOLEMY, *Tagara* and *Pattan* were situated to the Northward of the Baund-Ganga (*Bisda* or *Bynda* river) commonly called *Godavery*; and here PTOLEMY is very right.

IN Mr. BUSSY's *marches*, *Pattan* is placed to the Southward of the *Godavery*; but it is a mistake.

IT appears from ARRIAN's *Periplus*, that, on the arrival of the *Greeks* into the *Deccan*, above two thousand years ago, *Tagara* was the *Metropolis* of a large district called *Ariaca*, which comprehended the greatest part of Subah *Aurungabad* and the Southern part of *Concan*; for the northern part of that district, including *Damaun*, *Callian*, the Island of *Salset*, *Bombay*, &c. belonged to the *Rajah* of *Larikeh* or *Lar*, according to ARRIAN and EBN SAID AL MAGREBI.

\* *Patina* Tab. Peutinger. *Patissa* Anonym. Ravenn.

It is necessary to observe here, that though the author of the *Periplus* is supposed to have lived about the year 160 of the present era, yet the materials he made use of in compiling his Directory, are far more ancient; for, in speaking of *Tagara*, he says that the *Greeks* were prohibited from landing at *Callian*, and other harbours on that coast. Now it is well known, that, after the conquest of *Egypt*, the *Romans* had monopolised the whole trade to *India*, and would allow no foreigner to enter the Red Sea; and consequently this passage has reference to an earlier period, previous to the conquest of *Egypt* by the *Romans*.

About the middle of the first century, *Tagara* was no longer the capital of *Ariaca*, Rajah SALBAHAN having removed the seat of the empire to *Pattan*.

PTOLEMY informs us, that *Paithana* or *Pattan* had been the residence of a prince of that country, whose name the *Greeks* have strangely disfigured; we find it variously spelt, in different MSS. of PTOLEMY, *Siripolemæus, Siropolemæus, Siroptolemæus*, &c.

Yet when we consider, that, whenever *Pattan* is mentioned by the Hindoos, they generally add, it was the Residence of

Rajah

*Rajah* SALBAHAN [*], who in the dialect of the *Deccan* is called *Sa'ivanam* or *Salibanam*, I cannot help thinking, that the *Greeks* have disfigured this last word *Salibanum* into *Saripa'am*, from which they have made *Siripolemæus, Siropolemæus*, &c.

BICKERMAJIT ruled for some time over the Northern parts of the *Deccan*: but the *Rajahs*, headed by SALBAHAN, having revolted, they gave him battle, and he was slain. *Tagara* became again the Metropolis of *Ariaca*: at least it was so towards the latter end of the eleventh century, as it appears from a grant of some lands in *Concan*, made by a *Rajah* of *Tagara*: this grant still exists, and was communicated to the ASIATICK SOCIETY by General CARNAC.

WHEN the *Muffulmans* carried their arms into the *Deccan* about the year 1293, *Tagara*, or *Deogbir* was still the residence of a powerful *Rajah*, and remained so till the time of SHAH-JEHAN, when the districts belonging to it became a *Subah* of the *Mogul* Empire. Then *Tagara* was deserted, and *Kerkhi*, four Coss to the South-east of it, became the capital: this place is now called *Aurungabad*.

THUS was destroyed the ancient kingdom or *Rajahship* of *Tagara*, after it had existed, with

[*] (Making use of the very words of PTOLEMY).

little

little interruption, above two thousand years; that is to say, as far as we can trace back its antiquity.

It may appear aftonishing, that though the *Rajah* of *Tagara* was poffeffed of a large tract on the Sea Coaft, yet all the trade was carried on by land.

Formerly it was not fo: on the arrival of the *Greeks* into the *Deccan*, goods were brought to *Callian* near *Bombay*, and then fhipped off. However a *Rajah* of *Larikeh*, or *Lar*, called *Sandanes*, according to Arrian, would no longer allow the *Greeks* to trade either at *Callian* or at the harbours belonging to him on that coaft, except *Baroach*; and, whenever any of them were found at *Callian* or in the neighbourhood, they were confined and fent to *Baroach* under a ftrong guard. Arrian, being a *Greek* himfelf, has not thought proper to inform us, what could induce the *Rajah* to behave in this manner to the *Greeks*; but his filence is a convincing proof that they had behaved amifs; and it is likely enough they had attempted to make a fettlement in the Ifland of *Salfet*, in order to make themfelves independent, and facilitate their conquefts into the *Deccan*.

The fears of the *Rajah* were not groundlefs; for the *Greek* kings of *Bactriana* were poffeffed of the *Punjab Cabul*, &c. in the North of *India*.

There were other harbours, to the South of *Callian*, belonging to the *Rajah* of *Tagara*, but they were not frequented, on account of *Pirates*, who, according to PLINY, ARRIAN, and PTOLEMY, infested these countries, in the very same manner they do now.

# AN INDIAN GRANT OF LAND*

IN Y. C. 1018,

LITERALLY TRANSLATED FROM THE SANSCRIT, AS EXPLAINED BY RA'MALO'CHAN PANDIT.

COMMUNICATED BY GEN. CARNAC.

---

O'M. VICTORY *and* ELEVATION!

*STANZAS.*

MAY He, who in all affairs claims precedence in adoration; may that *Gannávaca*, averting calamity, preserve you from danger!

2. MAY that SIVA constantly preserve you, on whose head shines (GANGA') the daughter of JAHNU resembling-the-pure-crescent-rising-from-the-summit-of-SUME'RU! (*a compound word of sixteen syllables*).

3. MAY that GOD, the cause of success, the cause of felicity, who keeps, placed even by himself on his forehead a section of the-

---

* Found in digging foundations for some new works at the Fort of *Tanna*, the Capital of *Salfit*. The Governor of *Bombay* informed General CARNAC, that none of the *Gujerat Bramins* could explain the inscriptions.

moon-

moon-with-cool-beams, drawn-in-the-form-of-a-line-resembling-that-in-the-infinitely-bright-spike-of-a-fresh-blown-*Cétaca* (who is) adorned-with-a-grove-of-thick-red-locks-tied-with-the-Prince-of-Serpents, be always present and favourable to you!

4. THE son of JI'MU'TACK'TU ever affectionate, named JI'MU'TAVA'HANA, who, surely, preserved (the Serpent) S'ANC'HACHU'DA from *Garúda (the Eagle of* VISHNU), *was* famed in the three worlds, having neglected his own body, as if it had been grass, for the sake of others.

5. *(Two couplets in rhyme.)* In his family was a monarch (*named*) CAPARDIN (or, *with thick hair*, a title of MAHA'DE'VA), chief of the race of SI'LA'RA, repressing the insolence of his foes; and from him came a son, named PULAS'ACTI, equal in encreasing glory to the sun's bright circle.

6. WHEN that son of CAPARDIN was a new-born infant, through fear of him, homage was paid by all his collected enemies, with water held aloft in their hands, to the delight of his realm.

7. FROM him came a son, the only warriour on earth, named SRI'VAPPUVANNA, a Hero in the theatre of battle.

8. His

8. His son, called S'RI' JHANJHA, was highly celebrated, and the preserver *of his country*; he afterwards became the Sovereign of *Gigni*: he had a beautiful form.

8. FROM him *came* a son, whose-renown-was-far-extended-*and-who*-confounded-the-mind-with-his-wonderful-acts, the fortunate BAJJADA DE'VA: he was a monarch, a gem in-the-diadem-of-the-world's-circumference; who used only the forcible weapon of his two arms readily on the plain of combat, and in whose bosom the Fortune of Kings herself amorously played, as *in the bosom* of the foe of MURA (or VISHNU).

9. LIKE JAYANTA, *son* to the foe of VRITTA (or INDRA), like SHANMUC'HA (or CARTICE'YA) *son* to PURA'RI (or MAHA'DE'VA) then sprang from him a fortunate son, with a true heart, invincible;

10. WHO in liberality was CARNA before our eyes, in truth even YUDHISHTHIRA, in glory a blazing Sun, and the rod of CA'LA (or YAMA, *judge of the infernal regions*) to his enemies;

11. BY whom the great counsellors, who were under his protection, *and others* near *him*, are preserved in this world: he is a conqueror, named with propriety S'ARANA'GATA VAJRAPANJARADE'VA.

12. BY

12. By whom when this world was overshadowed with-continual-presents-of-gold, for his liberality he was named JAGADARTHI (or *Enriching the World*) in the midst of the three regions of the universe.

13. THOSE Kings assuredly, whoever they may be, who are endued with minds capable of ruling their respective dominions, praise him for the greatness of his veracity, generosity, and valour; *and to those princes who are deprived of their domains, and seek his protection, he allots a firm settlement: may he*, the Grandfather of the RA'YA, be victorious! *he is* the spiritual guide of *his* counsellors, *and they are* his pupils. Yet farther——

14. HE, by whom the title of GO'MMA'YA was conferred on *a person* who attained the object of his desire; by whom the realm, shaken by a man named E'YAPADE'VA, was even made firm, and by whom, being the prince of *Mamalamburva* (I suppose, *Mambéï*, or *Bombay*) security from fear was given to me broken *with affliction*; He was the King, named S'RI' VIRUDANCA: how can he be otherwise painted? *Here six syllables are effaced in one of the Grants; and this verse is not in the other.*

15. HIS son *was* named BAJJADADL'VA, a gem on the forehead of monarchs, eminently
skilled

skilled in morality; whose deep thoughts all the people, clad in horrid armour, praise even to this day.

16. THEN was born his brother the prince ARICE'SARI' (a lion among his foes), the best of good men; who, by overthrowing the strong mountain of his proud enemies, did the act of a thunder-bolt; having formed great designs even in his childhood, and having seen the Lord of the Moon (MAHA'DE'VA) *standing* before him, he marched by his father's order, attended by his troops, and by valour subdued the world.

YET more——

17. HAVING raised up his slain foe on his sharp sword, he so afflicted the women in the hostile palaces, that their forelocks fell disordered, their garlands of bright flowers dropped from their necks on the vases of their breasts, and the black lustre of their eyes disappeared.

18. A WARRIOUR, the plant of whose fame grows up over the temple of BRAHMAH's Egg (the universe), from-the-repeated-watering-of-it-with-the-drops-that-fell-from-the-eyes-of-the-wives-of-his-slaughtered-foe.

AFTERWARDS by the multitude of his innate virtues (*then follows a compound word of an hundred and fifty-two syllables*) the-fortunate-ARICE'SARI-DE'VARA'JA-Lord-of-the-great-circle-

circle-adorned-with-all-the company-of-princes-
with - VAJRAPANJARA - of - whom - men - seek -
the-protection-an-elephant's-hook-in-the-fore-
head - of - the - world - pleased - with - encreasing -
vice-a - Flamingo - bird - in - the - pool - decked -
with - flowers - like - those-of-paradise-and-with-
A'DITYA - PANDITA - chief - of - the - districts-of-
the-world-through - the - liberality-of - the - lord-
of-the-Western - sea - holder - of - innate - know-
ledge-who-bears-a-golden-eagle - on - his - stand-
ard-descended -from-the-stock-of-JI'MU'TAVA-
HANA-king-of-the-race-of-*Silára*-Sovereign-
of-the-City of-*Tagara* - Supreme - ruler - of - exalted - counsellors - assembled - when - extended -
fame-had-been-attained (*the monarch* thus described) governs - the-whole-region-of-*Cóncana*-
consisting - of - fourteen - hundred - villages-with-
cities-and-other-places-comprehended-in-many-
districts-acquired-by-his-arm. Thus he sup-
ports the burden of thought concerning this
domain. The Chief-Minister s'RI' VA'SAPAIYA
*and* the very-religiously-purified s'RI' VARDHI-
YAPAIYA being at this time present, he, the
fortunate ARTCK'SARIDE'VARA'JA, Sovereign
of the great circle, *thus addresses* even all who
inhabit-the-city-s'RI'-STHA'NACA (*or the Mansion of* LACSHMI'), his-own-kinsmen-and-
others - there - assen bled, princes - counsellors-
priests-ministers-superiors-inferiors- subject - to-
his-

his-commands, alſo the-lords-of-diſtricts,-the-governors-of-towns-chiefs-of-villages-the-maſters-of-families-employed-or-unemployed-ſervants-of-the-King-and-*his*-countrymen. Thus he greets all-the-holy-men-and-others-inhabiting-the-city-of *Hanyamuna:* reverence be to you, as it is becoming, with all the marks of reſpect, ſalutation, and praiſe!

## S T A N Z A.

WEALTH is inconſtant; youth deſtroyed in an inſtant; *and* life placed between the teeth of CRITANTA *(or* YAMA *before mentioned)*.

NEVERTHELESS neglect *is ſhown* to the felicity of departed anceſtors. Oh! how aſtoniſhing are the efforts of men!

AND thus.—Youth is publickly ſwallowed-up-by-the-giantefs Old-Age admitted-into-its-inner-manſion; and the bodily-frame-is-equally-obnoxious-to-the-aſſault-of-death-of-age-and-the-miſery-born-with-man-of-ſeparation-between-united-friends-like-falling-from-heaven-into-the-lower-regions: riches and life are two things more-moveable-than-a-drop-of-water-trembling-on-the-leaf-of-a-lotos-ſhaken-by-the-wind; and the world is like-the-firſt-delicate-foliage-of-a-plantain-tree. Conſidering this in ſecret with a firm diſpaſſionate underſtanding.

derstanding, and also the fruit of liberal donations mentioned *by the wise*, I called to mind these

## STANZAS.

1. In the *Satya*, *Tretâ*, and *Dwâper* Ages, great piety was celebrated: but in this *Calyuga* the *Muni*'s have nothing to commend but liberality.

2. Not so productive of fruit is learning, not so productive is piety, as liberality, say the *Muni*'s, in this *Cali* Age. And thus was it said by the Divine VYA'SA.

3. GOLD was the first offspring of Fire; the Earth *is* the daughter of VISHNU, and kine are the children of the Sun: the three worlds, *therefore*, are assuredly given by him, who makes a gift of Gold, Earth, and Cattle.

4. OUR deceased fathers clap their hands, *our* grandfathers exult: *saying*, "A donor of "land is born in our family: he will re- "deem us."

5. A DONATION of land to good persons, for holy pilgrimages, and on the (five) solemn days of the moon, is the mean of passing over the deep boundless ocean of the world.

6. WHITE parasols and elephants mad with pride (the *insignia* of royalty) *are* the flowers of a grant of land: the fruit *is* INDRA in heaven.

THUS

Thus, confirming the declarations of the ancient *Menu's*-learned-in-the-distinction-between-justice-and-injustice, for the sake of benefit to my mother, my father, and myself, on the fifteenth of the bright moon of *Cártica*, in the middle of the year *Pingala* (perhaps of the *Serpent*), when nine hundred and forty years save one are reckoned as past from the time of King SA'CA, or, in figures, the year 939, of the bright moon of *Cártica* 15 (that is 1708—939—769 years ago from Y. C. 1787) the moon being then full and eclipsed, I having bathed in the opposite sea resembling-the-girdles-round-the-waist-of-the-female-Earth, tinged-with-a-variety-of-rays-like-many-exceedingly-bright-rubies, pearls-*and*-*other*-gems, with-water-whose-mud-was-become-musk-through-the-frequent-bathing-of-the-fragrant-bosom-of-beautiful-Goddesses-rising-up-after-having-dived-in-it; and having offered to the sun, the divine luminary, the-gem-of-one-circle-of-heaven, eye-of-the-three-worlds, Lord of-the-lotos, a dish embellished-with-flowers-of-various-sorts (this dish is filled with the plant *Darbha*, rice in the husk, different flowers, and sandal) have granted to him, who has viewed the preceptor of the Gods and of Demons, who has adored the Sovereign Deity the-husband-of-AMBICA' (or DURGA')

has

has sacrificed, -caused-others-to-sacrifice, -has-read-caused-others-to-read, -and-has-performed-the-rest-of-the-six (Sacerdotal) functions; who-is-eminently-skilled-in-the-whole-business of-performing-sacrifices, who-has-held-up-the-root-and-stalk-of-the-sacred-lotos; who-inhabits-the-city-S'RI'-ST'HA'NACA (*or abode of Fortune*) descended from JAMADAGNI; who-performs-due-rites-in-the-holy-stream; who-distinctly-knows-the-mysterious-branches (of the *Védas*), the domestick priest, the reader, S'RI' TICCAPAIYA, son of S'RI' CHCR'UINTAPAIYA the astronomer, for-the-purpose-of-sacrificing-causing-others-to-sacrifice-reading-causing-others-to-read-and-discharging-the-rest-of-the-six-(Sacerdotal) duties, of performing the (daily service of) *Vaiswadéva* with offerings of rice, milk, and materials of sacrifice, and-of-completing-with-due-solemnity-the-sacrifice-of-fire-of-doing-such-acts-as-must-continually-be-done, and such-as-must-occasionally-be-performed, of paying-due-honours to guests and strangers, and-of-supporting his-own-family, the village of *Chávinúra*-standing-at-the-extremity of-the-territory of *Vatsartja*, and the boundaries of which are, to the East the village of *Púagambú* and a water-fall-from a mountain; to the South the villages of *Núgambú* and *Múládíngarica*; to the West the river *Sámbarapallicá*;

*rapalliea*; to the North the villages of *Sámbrut* and *Cáriyáluca*; and besides this the full *(district)* of *Tícubalá Palliea*, the boundaries of which *are* to the East *Sidábali*; to the South the river *Mót'bala*; to the West *Cúcádwa*, *Hallapallica*, and *Bádaviraca*; to the North *Talávali Pailica*; and also the Village of *Aulaciyá*, the boundaries of which (are) to the East *Tádúga*; to the South *Gévini*; to the West *Charica*; to the North *Calibalá-yacbáli*: (that land) thus surveyed-on-the-four-quarters-and limited-to-its-proper-bounds, with-its-herbage-wood-and-water, and with-power-of-punishing-for-the-ten-crimes, except that before given as the portion of *Déva*, or of *Brahmá*, I have hereby released, and limited-by-the-duration-of-the-sun-the-moon-and-mountains, confirmed with-the-ceremony-of adoration, with a copious effusion of water, and with the highest acts-of-worship; *and the same land* shall be enjoyed by his lineal-and-collateral-heirs, or caused-to-be-enjoyed, nor shall disturbance be given by any person whatever: since it is thus declared by great *Muni's*:

## STANZAS.

1. THE earth is enjoyed by many kings, by SA'GAR, and by others: to whomsoever the soil

soil at any time belongs, to him at that time belong the fruits of it.

2. A SPEEDY gift is attended with no fatigue; a continued support, with great trouble; therefore even the *Rishi's* declare, that a continuance of support is better than a single gift.

3. EXALTED Emperors of good dispositions have given land, as RA'MABHADRA advises again and again: this is the true bridge of justice for sovereigns: from time to time (O kings) that bridge must be repaired by you.

4. THOSE possessions here below, which have been granted in former times by sovereigns, given for - the - sake-of - religion - increase - of - wealth-or-of-fame, are exactly equal to flowers which have been offered to a Deity: what good man would resume *such gifts?*

THUS, confirming the precepts of ancient *Munis*, all future kings must gather the fruit-of-observing-religious-duties; and let not the stain-of- the-crime-of-destroying-this-*grant* be borne henceforth by any-one: since, whatever *prince*, being supplicated, shall, through avarice, having-his-mind-wholly-surrounded-with-the-gloom-of-ignorance -contemptuously - dismiss-the-injured-suppliant; he, being guilty of five great and *five* small crimes, shall long in darkness inhabit *Raurava, Maháraurava, Andha, Támisra,*

*Támisra*, and the other places of punishment. And thus it is declared by the divine VYA'SA:

## STANZAS.

1. HE who seizes land given-by-himself or by-another (sovereign), will rot among worms, himself a worm, in the midst of ordure.

2. THEY who seize granted-land are born again, living with great fear, in dry cavities of trees in the unwatered forests on the *Vindhbian* (mountains).

3. BY seizing one cow, one vesture, or even one nail's breadth of ground, *a king* continues in hell till an universal destruction of the world has happened.

4. BY (a gift of) a thousand gardens, and by (a gift of) a hundred pools of water, by (giving) a hundred *lac* of oxen, a disseisor of (granted) land is not cleared from offence.

5. A GRANTOR of land remains in heaven sixty thousand years; a disseisor, and he who refuses to do justice, continues as many (years) in hell.

AND, agreeably to this, in what is written by the hand of the Secretary, (the King) having ordered it, declares his own intention; as it is written by the command of me, sovereign of
the

the Great Circle, the Fortunate ARICE'SARI DE'VARA'JA, fon of the Sovereign of the Great Circle, the Fortunate, Invincible, DE'VARAJA.

AND this is written, by order of the Fortunate King, by me JO'-UBA, the brother's-fon-of-S'RI' NABĀLAIYA,-the-great-Bard,-dwelling-in-the royal palace; engraved-on-plates-of-copper by VE'DAPAIYA's fon MANA DHA'RA PAIYA. Thus (it ends).

WHATEVER herein (may be) defective in-one-fyllable, or have-one-fyllable-redundant, all that is (neverthelefs) complete evidence (of the grant.) Thus (ends the whole).

A ROYAL.

# A ROYAL GRANT OF LAND,

ENGRAVED ON A COPPER PLATE,
BEARING DATE TWENTY-THREE YEARS BEFORE CHRIST;
AND DISCOVERED AMONG THE RUINS AT

## MONGUEER.

TRANSLATED FROM THE ORIGINAL SANSCRIT
BY CHARLES WILKINS, ESQ. IN 1781.

---

DEB PAUL DEB*.

PROSPERITY!

HIS wishes are accomplished. His heart is stedfast in the cause of others. He walks in the paths of virtue. May the atchievements of this fortunate Prince cause innumerable blessings to his people!

By displaying the strength of his genius, he hath discovered the road to all human acquire-

* In this translation the Sanscrit names are written as they are pronounced in Bengal.

ments;

ments; for being a *Soogut* *, he is Lord of the Universe.

GOPAAL, King of the World, possessed matchless good Fortune; he was Lord of two Brides; the Earth and her Wealth. By comparison of the learned, he was likened unto *Preecut*, *Soger*†, and others, and, it is credited.

WHEN his innumerable army marched, the heavens were so filled with the dust of their feet, that the birds of the air could rest upon it.

---

* *Soogut*—signifies an Atheist, or follower of the *Soogut* a Philosopher, who is said to have flourished at a place called *Keeder* in the province of *Behar*, one thousand years after the commencement of the *Kolee Jug*, or Iron Age; of which this is the 4883d Year. He believed in visible things only, or such as may be deduced from effects the cause of which is known; as, from smoke the existence of fire. He wrote many books to prove the absurdity of the religion of the *Brahmans*, and some upon Astronomy and other sciences, all which are said to be now in being. He further held, that all our actions are attended by their own rewards and punishments in this life; and that all animals having an equal right to existence with Man, they should not be killed either for food or food.

† *Preetu*—was the son of *Been*, and *Rajah* of a place called *Butser* near Lucknow. He flourished in the first Age of the World, and is said to have levelled the earth, and, having prepared it for cultivation, obliged the people to live in society.

‡ *Soger*—the name of a *Rajah* who lived in the second Age at *Oujein*, and is said to have dug the rivers.

HE

He acted according to what is written in the *Shaaſtra* \*, and obliged the different ſects to conform to their proper tenets. He was bleſſed with a ſon, *Dbormo Paal*, when he became independent of his forefathers, who are in heaven.

His elephants moved like walking mountains, and the earth, oppreſſed by their weight and mouldered into duſt, found refuge in the peaceful heavens.

He went to extirpate the wicked and plant the good, and happily his ſalvation was effected at the ſame time: for his ſervants viſited *Kedaar* †, and drank milk according to the law; and they offered up their vows, where the *Ganges* joins the ocean, and at *Gokurnas* ‡, and other places ‖.

\* *Shaaſtra*—book of divine ordinations. The word is derived from a root ſignifying to command.

† *Kedaar*—a famous place, ſituated to the north of *Hindoſtan*, viſited, to this day, on account of its ſuppoſed ſanctity.

‡ *Gokurnas*—a place of religious reſort near *Punjab*.

‖ This and a few other paſſages appear inconſiſtent with the principles of a *Sayed*; to reconcile it therefore, it ſhould be remarked, that as he was iſſuing his orders to ſubjects of a different perſuaſion, it was natural for him to uſe a language the beſt calculated to ſtrike them with awe, and bind them to a performance of his commands. The *Pundit* by whoſe aſſiſtance this tranſlation was made, when he was deſired to explain this ſeeming contradiction, aſked whether we did not, in our courts, ſwear a *Muſſelman* upon the *Koran*, and a *Hindu* by the waters of the *Ganges*, although we ourſelves had not the leaſt faith in either.

WHEN he had completed his conquests, he released all the rebellious Princes he had made captive, and each returning to his own country laden with presents, reflected upon this generous deed, and longed to see him again; as mortals, remembering a pre-existence, wish to return to the realms of light.

THIS Prince took the hand of the daughter of *Porobol*, Raajaa of many countries, whose name was *Raajaa Deber*; and he became ……

THE people, being amazed at her beauty, formed different opinions of her. Some said it was *Lockee* * herself in her shape; others, that the earth had assumed her form; many said it was the Raajaa's fame and reputation; and others, that a houshold goddess had entered his palace. And her wisdom and virtue set her above all the ladies of the court.

THIS virtuous and praise-worthy Princess bore a son *Deb Paal Deb*, as the shell of the ocean produces the pearl: ———

IN whose heart there is no impurity; of few words, and gentle manners; and who peaceably inherited the kingdom of his father, as *Bodheesatwa* † succeeded *Seogot*.

HE who, marching through many countries making conquests, arrived with his elephants

* *Lukee*—the *Hindu* Goddess of Fortune.
† *Deb Paal*—was the son of *Seogot*.

in the forests of the mountains of *Beendbyo*\*, where, seeing again their long-lost families, they mixed their mutual tears; and who going to subdue other Princes, his young horses meeting their females at *Komboge*:†, they mutually neighed for joy.

He who has opened again the road of liberality, which was first marked out in the *Kreeto Joog* ‡ by *Bolee* § ; in which *Bhaargob* ‖ walked in the *Tretaa Joog* ¶; which was cleansed by *Korno* \*\* in the *Dwapor Joog* ††, and was again choked up in the *Kolee Joog* ‡‡, after the death of *Sokodweefee* §§.

\* *Beendbyo*—name of the mountains on the continent near *Ceylon*.

† *Komboge*—now called *Cambay*.

‡ *Kreeto Joog*—the first Age of the World, sometimes called the *Suttee Joog*, or age of purity.

§ *Bulee*—a famous Giant of the first Age who is fabled to have conquered earth, heaven, and hell.

‖ *Bhaargob*—a Brahmen, who, having put to death all the princes of the earth, usurped the government of the whole.

¶ *Tretaa Joog*—the second Age, or of three parts good.

\*\* *Korno*—a famous Hero in the third Age of the World. He was General to *Dorryodon*, whose wars with *Joodhifter* are the subject of the *Mehabharat*, the grand Epick Poem of the *Hindoos*.

†† *Dwapor Joog*—the third Age of the World.

‡‡ *Kolee Joog*—the fourth or present Age of the World, of which 4882 years are elapsed.

§§ *Sokodweefee*—an epithet of *Bickromadetyo*, a famous Rajaa. He succeeded his brother *Sumedetyo*, whom he put to death.

He who conquered the earth from the source of the *Ganges* as far as the well-known bridge which was constructed by the enemy of *Dofaafyo* \*; from the river of *Luckercool* †, as far as the ocean of the habitation of *Boreon* ‡.

At *Mood-go-gheeree* §, where is encamped his victorious army; across whose river a bridge of boats is constructed for a road, which is mistaken for a chain of mountains; where immense herds of elephants, like thick black clouds, so darken the face of day, that people think it the season of the rains; whither the Princes of the North send so many troops of horse, that the dust of their hoofs spreads darkness on all sides; whither so many mighty Chiefs of *Jumboodweep* ‖ resort to pay their respects, that the earth sinks beneath the weight of the feet of their attendants; there *Deb Paal Deb* (who, walking in the footsteps of the mighty Lord of the great *Soogots*, the great Commander, *Raajaa* of *Mehaa Raajaas*, *Dhor-*

\* *Dofaafyo*—one of the names of *Raalen*, whose wars with *Raam* are the subject of a poem called the *Raamayan*.
† *Luckerool*—now called *Lacknipoor*.
‡ *Biran*—God of the Ocean.

According to this account the *Raajaa's Dominions* extended from the Cow's Mouth to Adam's Bridge in *Ceylon*, said to have been built by *Raam* in his wars with *Raaben*; from *La-knpoor* as far as *Gungafet*.

§ *Mood-go-gherree*—now called *Mongurrr*.

‖ *Jumboodweep*—according to the *Hindoo* Geography, implies the habitable part of the Earth.

tho *Paal Deb*, is himself mighty Lord of the
great *Songets*, a great Commander, and *Raajas
of Mohaa Raajaas*) issues his commands.—To
all the inhabitants of the town of *Meseeka*,
situated in *Kreemeelaa*, in the province of *Shee
Nogar* \*, which is my own property, and
which is not divided by any land belonging to
another; to all *Raanok* and *Raaje-pootroo*; to
the † *Omaatyo, Mohaa-kaarttaa-kreeteeko, Mohaa-Dondo-Nayk, Mohaa-Proteehnar, Mohaa-
Saamont Moo, haa-Dow-Saadhon-Saadhoneeko,
Mohaa-Koomaaraa-Matyo*; to the *Promantree*

\* *Sree Nogor*—the ancient name of *Patna*.

† *Omaatyo*—Prime Minifter. *Mohaa-kaarttaa-kreeteeko*,
Chief Investigator of all things. *Mohaa-Dondo-Nayk*,
Chief Officer of Punishments. *Mohaa-Proteehnar*, Chief
Keeper of the Gates. *Mohaa Saamont*, Generaliffimo.
*Mohaa-Dow-Saadhon-Saadhoneeko*, Chief Obviator of Dif-
ficulties. *Mohaa-Koomaaraa-Matyo*, Chief Inftructor of
Children. *Promantree*, Keeper of the Records. *Sorah-
bonge, Patrols. Raajadaarunge*, Vice Roy. *Ooperecti*, Su-
perintendant. *Doofoo-raaddveko*, Invefigator of Crimes.
*Chow-rod-aha-ruverho*, Thief Catcher. *Daan-duks*, Mace-
Bearer, *Dundo-pojorks*, Keeper of the Infruments of Pu-
nifhment. *Soul-kroks*, Collector of Cuftoms. *Gowfureks*,
Commander of a fmall party. *Kystropo*, Supervifor of
Cultivation. *Praoutspoole*, Guard of the Suburbs. *Kothou-
poole*, Commander of a Fort. *Kuendaarohpo*, Guard of the
Wards of the City. *Tadoujooktoko*, Chief Guard of the Wards.
*Beenoejooktoko*, Director of Affairs. *Goodyrofouroko*, Chief
of the Spies. *Gouran-Gomorko, Meffengers. Ohheruors-
means*, Swift Meffengers. *Profopoao*, Governor of a
City. *Torapoloo*, Superintendant of the Rivers. *Twoeko*,
Chief of the Boats.

and *Soroblongo*; to the *Raajoſtaaneeyo*, *Oopo-reeko*, *Dauſusporaadheeko*, *Chowrod dhoroneeko*, *Daundeeko*, *Dondopaaſeeko*, *Sowl-keeko*, *Gowl-meeko*, *Kyotropo*, *Praunlopaálo*, *Kethtopaalo* and *Kaundaarokyo*; to the *Todaajeoktoko* and the *Beeneejooktoko*; to the keeper of the elephants, horses and camels; to the keeper of the mares, colts, cows, buffaloes, sheep, and goats; to the *Dasteprafewryho*, *Gamaa-Gomeeko*, and *Ohherrooromiaano*; to the *Beiſerpotey*, *Toropalee* and *Tereeko*; to the different tribes, *Gowr*, *Maalch*, *Khoſo*, *Hoon*, *Kooleeko*, *Karnaató*, *Laufuato*, and *Bhato*; to all others of our subjects who are not here specified; and to the inhabitants of the neighbouring villages, from the *Brachmen* and fathers of large families, to the tribes of *Medo*, *Ondhoroko*, and *Chondando*.

Be it known, that I have given the above-mentioned town of *Meſeeka*, whose limits include the fields where the cattle graze, above and below the surface, with all the lands belonging to it; together with all the *Maago* and *Modhoo* trees; all its waters and all their tanks and verdure; all its rents and tolls, with all fines for crimes, and rewards for catching thieves. In it there shall be no molestation, no paſſage for troops; nor shall any one take from it the smallest part. I give likewise every thing that has been possessed by the servants of the Raajaa,

Raajaa: 'I give the Earth and Sky, as long as the Sun and Moon shall last, except, however, such lands as have been given to God, and to the *Braahmans*, which they have long possessed and now enjoy. And that the glory of my father and mother and my own fame may be increased, I have caused this *Saasen* \* to be engraved, and granted unto the great *Botho Beebhoraato Meesro*, who has acquired all the wisdom of books and has studied the *Bedds* † under *Oslanyono*; who is descended from *Owpsmonyobo*; who is the son of the learned and immaculate *Botho Boraaboraats*, and whose grandfather was *Botho Eeefworaato*, learned in the *Bedds*, and expert in performing the *Jog* ‡.

Know all the aforesaid, that as bestowing is meritorious, so taking away deserves punishment; wherefore leave it as I have granted it. Let all his neighbours and those who till the land, be obedient to my commands. What you have formerly been accustomed to perform and pay, do it unto him in all things. Dated in the thirty-third *Sombot* ‖ and twenty-first day of the month of *Maarga*.

THUS

\* *Saasen*—signifies an Edict.
† *Bedds*—Hindoo Scriptures.
‡ *Jog*—Sacrifice.
‖ *Sombot*—implies the Æra of *Raajaa Beerzmadittjo*. The *Braahmens*, throughout *Hindystan*, keep time according to the three following Epochas: The *Kisjoekt*, from the flight of *Kreishni*, or commencement of the *Kiee Jug*,

4882

264    A ROYAL GRANT OF LAND,

Thus speak the following *Slokes* * from the *Dhormo Oncofaafon*:

1. "Ram hath required, from time to time of all the Raajaas that may reign, that the bridge of their beneficence be the same, and that they do continually repair it.

2. "Lands have been granted by *Sogor* and many other Raajaas; and the fame of their deeds devolves to their fucceffors.

3. "He who difpoffeffes any one of his property, which I myfelf, or others have given, may he, becoming a worm, grow rotten in orduro with his forefathers.

4. "Riches and the life of man are as tranfient as drops of water upon a leaf of the Lotus. Learning this truth, O man! do not attempt to deprive another of his reputation."

The Raajaah, for the publick good, hath appointed his virtuous fon, *Raajyo Paal*, to the dignity of *Jowbo Raajaa*. He is in both lines of defcent illuftrious, and hath acquired all the knowledge of his father,

4883 years. The _____, from the death of Bntromod____, 1837 years. The _____, from the death of Raajaa ____ 1703.

* *Sloke*—.tanzas, commonly, but erroneoufly, written *Afloquin*.

REMARKS

REMARKS ON THE PRECEDING PAPER,
BY THE PRESIDENT.

SOME doubts having arisen in my mind concerning the preceding translation, I venture to propose them in the form of notes.

P. 255, l. 6. *from bottom. This fortunate Prince*—Is not the first couplet in honour of BUDDHA, one of whose names, in the *Amaracóſh*, is SUGATA? A *follower* of his tenets would have been denominated a *Saugat*, in the derivative form. We must observe, that the *Bauddhas*, or *Saugats*, are called *Atheists* by the *Bráhmans*, whom they opposed; but it is *mere invective*; and this very Grant fully disproves the calumny by admitting a future state of rewards and punishments. SUGAT was a *reformer*; and every reformer must expect to be calumniated.

P. 256. l. 9. *When his innumerable army*) The third stanza in the original is here omitted, either by an oversight, or because the same image of *weeping elephants* occurs afterwards, and might have been thought superfluous in this place: nevertheless, I insert a literal translation of it.

"By whom, having conquered the earth as far as the
"ocean, it was left, as being unprofitably seized; so be
"declared; and his elephants weeping saw again in the
"forests their kindred whose eyes were full of tears."

P. 258. l. 9. *of many countries*) The *Pandits* insist, that *Ráſhtracúta* in the original is the name of a particular country.

P. 263. l. 9. *from bottom. Dated in the 33d Samvat*) That is *year*; for *Samvat* is only an abbreviation of *Samvatsara*. This date, therefore, might only mean the thirty-third *year of the King's reign*; but, since VICRAMÁDITYA was surnamed the *foe of* SACA, and is praised by that *prince* in a preceding stanza, we may safely infer, that the Grant was dated thirty-three years after the *death* of that illustrious Emperor, whom the king of *Gaur*, though a Sovereign Prince, acknowledged as lord paramount of *India*.

MEMO,

# MEMORANDUMS

## CONCERNING

## AN OLD BUILDING,

### IN THE HADJIPORE DISTRICT, NEAR THE GUNDUCK RIVER, &c.

#### BY MR. REUBEN BURROW.

---

THE Pyramids of *Egypt* as well as those lately discovered in *Ireland* (and probably too the *Tower* of BABEL), seem to have been intended for nothing more than images of MAHADEO.

Two of the *Sakkara* Pyramids described by NORDEN, are like many of the small ones usually built of mud in the villages of *Bengal*: one of the Pyramids of *Dusour* drawn by POCOCK, is nearly similar to that I am going to mention, except in the acuteness of the angle: most of the *Pagodas* of the *Carnatic* are either complete or truncated Pyramids; and an old
Stone

Stone Building without any cavity, which I saw in *Yambeab*, near the *Catabeda* river on the *Aracan Coast*, differed so little from a Pyramid that I did not suspect it was meant for the image of SEEVA, till I was told it by the natives.

THE largest building of the kind which I have yet seen in *India*, is about two days journey up the *Ganduck* River near a place called *Kef-fereah*: it goes by the name of " BHEEM " SAIN's DEWRY," but seems evidently intended for the well-known image of MAHADEO; having originally been a cylinder placed upon the frustum of a cone for the purpose of being seen at a distance. It is at present very much decayed, and it is not easy to tell whether the upper part of the cylinder has been globular or conical; a considerable quantity of the outside is fallen down, but it still may be seen a good distance up and down the River.

THE day I went from the River to view it was so uncommonly hot, that the walk and a fever together obliged me to trust to the measurements of a servant. For want of a better instrument, he took the circumference of the cylindrical part in lengths of a spear, and from that as a scale, and a sketch of the building taken at a distance, I deduced the following dimensions; what dependence there may be on

his

his measures I cannot determine; but probably they are not very erroneous.

 Diameter of the Cylindrical part, 64 feet.
 Height of the Cylinder,      65
 Height of the Conic fruſtum on
   which the Cylinder is placed, } 93
 Diameter of the Cone at the baſe, 363

Both the Cone and the Cylinder were of bricks; thoſe of the laſt were of different ſizes, many of them two ſpans long and one broad; others were of the common ſize, but thinner, and they were well burnt though bedded in mortar little better than mud: there did not appear any ſigns of the Cylinder's being hollow: the Conical part was overgrown with jungle, but I broke through it in ſeveral places, and found it every where brick.

I am not recollect whether it be viſible from the ſeite of the antient city where the famous Pillar of *Singeah* ſtands, or not; but have a faint idea that it is. What the intention of theſe extraordinary columns may have been originally, is perhaps not ſo eaſy to tell. At firſt ſight it would ſeem that they were for holding inſcriptions, becauſe thoſe of *Burrah*, *Dehli*, and *Ilahabad*, have inſcriptions (though in a character that has not been yet decyphered); but

            the

the Pillar of *Singreab* seems to have none whatever, for some *Bramins* told me they attended at the time it was dug to the foundation, near twenty feet under ground, by a gentleman of *Patna*, who had hopes to have found some treasures, and that there was not the least vestige of any inscription upon it. Probably those Pillars, CLEOPATRA's Needle, and the *Devil*'s Bolts at *Boroughbridge*, may all have the same religious origin.

PERHAPS the connection of time and place may apologize for the diversity of the subject in mentioning, that while I sat under the shade of a large tree near the Pyramid on account of the sultry heat, some of the people of the adjacent village came and played there with *Cowries* on a diagram, that was formed by placing five points in a circular order, and joining every pair of alternate points by a line, which formed a kind of pentagon. This brought to my recollection a circumstance told me by a gentleman in *England*, that an old piece of silver plate had been dug out of the earth with such a figure upon it. The use of it was totally unknown, as well as the age; and I was desired to find what geometrical properties the figure possessed. One I remember was, that if any number of points whatever were placed in a circular order, and each two alternate points joined,

then

then the sum of all the salient angles of the figure would be equal to two right angles when the number of points was odd; but equal to four right angles when the number was even. EUCLID's properties of the angles of the triangle and trapezium are particular cases of these; but I had no suspicion of the real intention of the figure till I saw the use here made of it. It seems, however, an argument in favour of the identity of the *Druids* and *Bramins*, as well as another well-known diagram usually called the "*Walls of Troy*," which was used originally in the *Hindoo* astrology. These figures, however, appear to have flowed from a much higher source, and to have relation to what LEIBNITZ had a distant idea of, in his Analysis of Situation, EUCLID in his Porisms, and GIRARD perhaps in his restitution of them: in fact, as the modern Algebraists have the advantage of transferring a great part of their labour from the head to the hands, so there is reason to believe that the *Hindoos* had mechanical methods of reasoning geometrically, much more extensive than the elementary methods made use of at present; and that even their games were deduced from, and intended perhaps to be examples of them: but this deserves to be treated more at length elsewhere.

THE same apology may perhaps excuse my mentioning here, that the idea of the *Nile's* deriving

deriving its floods from the melted snows, as well as the *Ganges*, appears to be rather imaginary: they seem to be caused principally by the rains; for the high hills beyond the *Herdwar* apparently retain their snow all the year, and therefore the quantity melted could never produce the enormous swell of the *Ganges*; not to mention that the effect of a thaw seems different from what would arise from the mere difference of heat, and therefore might partly take place in winter and the dry season. That the rains are sufficient for the purpose without recurring to the hypothesis of melted snows, appears from the following fact. A little before I observed the aforesaid Pyramid, I had been a considerable distance up the *Gunduck*: the river was low for the time of the year, and the hills that skirt the borders of *Nepaul* were clear, and apparently not above fifteen cofs distant. Soon after a heavy shower fell upon them for some hours, and the river soon after was filled to the very banks, and continued so for many days, and large trees were torn up by the roots, and came driving down with such force by the torrent, that my boat was often endangered. Now on these hills there was actually no snow whatever; and as the rise was obviously caused by the rains, it may reasonably be concluded that the same effect has the same cause in other places.

## OF THE

# METHOD

## OF

# DISTILLING,

AS PRACTISED BY THE NATIVES AT CHATRA IN RAMGUR, AND IN THE OTHER PROVINCES, PERHAPS WITH BUT LITTLE VARIATION.

BY ARCHIBALD KEIR, ESQ.

---

THE body of the Still they use, is a common, large, unglazed, earthen, water Jar, nearly globular, of about twenty-five inches diameter at the widest part of it, and twenty-two inches deep to the neck, which neck rises two inches more, and is eleven inches wide in the opening. Such, at least, was the size of the one I measured; which they filled about a half with fomented *Móhwah-flowers*, that swam in the liquor to be distilled.

THE Jar they placed in a Furnace, not the most artificial, though seemingly not ill adapted to give a great heat with but a very little fuel. This they made by digging a round hole in the ground, about twenty inches wide, and full three feet deep; cutting an opening in the front, sloping down to the bottom, on the sides perpendicular, of about nine inches wide, and fifteen long, reckoning from the circle where the Jar was to come, to serve to throw in the wood at, and for a passage to the air. On the side top, they cut another small opening, of about four inches by three, the Jar, when placed, forming one side of it, to serve as a chimney for the smoke to go out at. The bottom of the earth was rounded up like a cup. Having then placed the Jar in this, as far as it would go down, they covered it above, all round, with clay, except at the two openings, till within about a fifth of its height; when their furnace was completed.

In this way, I reckon, there was a full third of the surface of the body of the Still or Jar exposed to the flame, when the fire came to be lighted; and its bottom not reaching to within two feet of where the fuel was, left a capacious hollow between them, whence the wood, that was short and dry, when lighted, being mostly converted into flame, and circulating on so great a surface of the Still, gave a much stronger heat than could else have been produced from so very

very little fuel; a consideration well worth the attention of a manufacturer, in our country more especially, where firing is so dear. There indeed, and particularly as coal is used, it would be better, no doubt, to have a grate; and that the air should enter from below. As to the benefit resulting from the body of the Still being of earthen ware, I am not quite so clear in it. Yet, as lighter substances are well known to transmit heat more gradually and slowly than the more solid, such as metals; may not earthen vessels, on this account, be less apt to burn their contents, so as to communicate an empyreumatick taste and smell to the liquor that is distilled, so often, and so justly complained of, with us? At any rate, in this country, where pots are made so cheap, I should think them greatly preferable, as, at least, much less expensive than those which the gentlemen engaged in this manufacture most commonly employ: though of this they are best able to judge.

Having thus made their furnace, and placed the body of the Still in it, as above described, they to this luted on, with moistened clay, to its neck, at the opening, what they here call an *Adkur*; forming with it, at once, a cover for the body of the Still, with a suitable perforation in it to let the vapour rise through; and the under part of the alembick. The *Adkur* was
made

made with two earthen pans, having round holes in their middles, of about four inches diameter; and their bottoms being turned opposite the one to the other, they were cemented together with clay, forming a neck of junction thus, of about three inches, with the small rising on the upper pan. The lowermost of these was more shallow, and about eleven inches wide, so as to cover exactly the opening at the neck of the Jar, to which they luted it on with clay. The upper and opposite of these was about four inches deep, and fourteen inches wide, with a ledge round its perforation in the middle, rising, as is already said, from the inner side of the neck, of about half an inch high, by which a gutter was formed to collect the condensed spirit as it fell down; and from this there was a hole in the pan to let it run off by; to which hole they occasionally luted on a small hollow *Bamboo*, of about two feet and a half in length, to convey it to the receiver below. The upper pan had also another hole in it, of about an inch square, at near a quarter of its circumference from the one below just spoken of, that served to let off the water employed in cooling; as shall be mentioned presently.

Their *Adkur* being thus fitted to the Jar, they completed the alembick by taking a copper pot, such as we use in our kitchens, of about five inches deep, eight wide at the mouth, and

ten

ten at the bottom, which was rather flattish; and turning its mouth downward, over the opening in the *Adkur*, luted it down on the inside of the Jar with clay.

For their cooler they raised a seat, close upon, and at the back part of the furnace, about a foot higher than the bottom of the copper-pot; on this they placed a two or three gallon-pot, with a round hole, of about half an inch, in the side of it; and to this hole, before they lighted their fire, they luted on a short tube of a like bore: placing the pot, and directing its spout so as that, when filled with water, it threw a constant and uniform stream of it, from about a foot high, or near the center of the bottom of the copper-pot: where it was diffused pretty completely over its whole surface; and the water falling down into the upper part of the pan of the *Adkur*, it thence was conveyed through the square hole already mentioned, by a trough luted on to it for that purpose, to a cooling reservoir a few feet from the furnace; from which they took it up again to supply the upper pot as occasion required.

As their stock of water, however, in this sort of circulation was much smaller than it seemingly ought to have been, being scarcely more than six or eight gallons, it too soon became hot; yet in spite of this disadvantage, that so easily might

might have been remedied, and the shortness of the conducting tube, which had nothing but the common air to cool it, there ran a stream of liquor from the Still; and but very little vapour rising from it; beyond any thing I had ever seen from stills of a much larger size, fitted with a worm and cooler. In about three hours time, indeed, from their lighting of the fire, they drew off full fifteen bottles of spirit; which is more, by a great deal, I believe, than could have been done in our way from a still of twice the dimensions.

The conveniences of a worm and cooler, which are no small expence either, I have myself often experienced; and if these could be avoided in so simple a way, that might easily be improved, the hints that are here offered may be of some use. The thin metal head is certainly well adapted, I think, to transmit the heat to the water, which is constantly renewed; and which, if cold, as it ought to be, must absorb the fastest possible: whereas, in our way, the water being confined in a tub, that, from the nature of its porous substance, in a great degree rather retains than lets the heat pass away it soon accumulates in it, and becomes very hot, and, though renewed pretty often, never answers the purpose of cooling the vapour in the worm so expeditiously and effectually

278 METHOD OF DISTILLING

as is done by their more simple and less expensive apparatus. In this country more especially, where labour and earthen wares are so cheap, for as many *rupees* and less, twenty furnaces with stills and every thing belonging to them, independent of the copper-pots, might very well be erected, that would yield above a hundred gallons of spirits a-day; allowing each still to be worked only twice: so very cheap indeed is arrack here, to the great comfort of my miners, and of many thoughtless people beside, that for one single *peyfa*, not two farthings sterling, they can get a whole *Cutcha-feer* of it in the *Bazar*, or above a full *English* pint, and enough to make them completely intoxicated; objects often painful to be seen.

Of the superior excellence of metal in giving out heat from itself, and from vapour contained in it, we have a very clear proof, in what is daily performed on the Cylinder of the steam engine: for cold water being thrown on it when loaded, the contained vapour is constantly condensed; whence, on a vacuum being thus formed, and the weight of the atmosphere acting on the surface of the piston, attached to the arm of the balance, it is made to descend, and to raise the other arm that is fixed to the pump; while this, being somewhat heavier, immediately sinks again, which carries up the piston,

piston, while the Cylinder is again filled: and thus alternately by cooling and filling it, is the machine kept in motion: the power exerted in raising the pump-arm being always in proportion to the Diameter of the Cylinder, or to the surface of the piston, which is exactly fitted to it, and on which the pressure acts.

The contrivance too, of having the under part of the Alembick, where the condensed vapour is collected, or upper part of what they call the *Adkur*, of earthen ware, of so great a thickness, and of course at so great a distance from the heat in the body of the still, is well imagined to keep the spirits the coolest possible when collected and running off.

By thus cooling and condensing the vapour likewise so suddenly as it rises, there is in a great measure a constant vacuum made, or as much as possible can be: but that both steam rises faster, and that water boils with much less heat, when the pressure is taken away from its surface, is an axiom in Chymistry too well known to need any illustration; it boiling in vacuum, when the heat is only ninety or ninety-five by Farenheit's Thermometer; whereas in the open air, under the pressure of the atmosphere, it requires no less than that of two hundred and twelve, ere it can be brought to the boiling point.

I MUST further observe, that the superior excellence of condensing the vapour so effectually and speedily in the Alembick to our method of doing it on a worm and cooler, is greatly on the side of the former; both from the reasons I have already adduced, and because of the small stream of vapour that can be only forced into the worm, where it is condensed gradually as it descends; but above all, from the nature of vapour itself, with respect to the heat contained in it, which of late has been proved by the very ingenious Dr. BLACK to be greater by far than, before his discoveries, was imagined. For vapour he has shewn to be in the state of a new fluid, where water is dissolved by heat; with the assistance perhaps, if I may be allowed a conjecture, of the air which it contains; and all fluids, as he has clearly demonstrated, on their becoming such, absorb a certain quantity of heat, which becomes what he very properly calls latent heat, it being heat not appearing either to the senses or to the Thermometer, while they remain in that liquid state; but showing itself immediately by its effects on whatever is near it, upon their changing their form from fluid to solid; as on water becoming ice, or metals fixing, and the like. In the solution of Salts also, there is an absorption of heat, as we daily experience in

the

the cooling of our liquors by dissolving Saltpetre in water; and this he has found to be the case with water itself, and other fluids, when passing into a state of vapour by boiling. From the most accurate and judicious experiments, indeed, he infers, and with the greatest appearance of truth, that the heat thus concealed in vapour raised by boiling, from any given bulk of water, would be fully sufficient, if collected in a piece of iron of the like size, to make it perfectly red-hot. What then must be the effect of so much heat, communicated in our way of distilling to the worm, and to the water in the tub, will be sufficiently evident from what has been said, to prove I think that we have hitherto employed a worse and more defective method than we might have done with respect to cooling at least, both in the making of spirits, and in other distillations of the like kind, where a similar mode is adopted.

THE poor ignorant *Indian* indeed, while he with wonder surveys the vast apparatus of *European* distillers, in their immense large stills, worms, tubs, and expensive furnaces, and finds that spirits thus made by them are more valued, and sell much dearer than his own, may very naturally conclude, and will have his competitors join with him in opinion, that

this

this must alone surely be owing to their better and more judicious manner of distilling with all those ingenious and expensive contrivances, which he can no wise emulate: but in this, it would appear, they are both equally mistaken; imputing the effects, which need not be controverted perhaps, to a cause from which they by no means proceed: the superiority of their spirits not at all arising from the superior excellence of these stills and furnaces, nor from their better mode of conducting the distillation, in any respect; but chiefly rather from their greater skill and care in the right choice, and proper management, of the materials they employ in fermentation; and above all, as I apprehend, from the vast convenience they have in casks, by which, and from their abilities in point of stock, they are enabled, and do in fact, in general keep their spirits for a certain time, whence they are mellowed and improved surprizingly both in taste and salubrity.

With respect to the latter improvement, I mention it more particularly here, and the more willingly also, as in general it seems to have been but too little attended to where a due attention to it might be of the greatest use. For of all things that have been found grateful to the human palate, there was none ever used, I believe, more hurtful to the body, and to the

nerves

nerves especially, than fresh drawn ardent spirits: and this owing evidently to the principle of inflammability, of which with water they are mostly made up, being then in a more loose and detached state, less assimilated with the other principles than it afterwards becomes with time. By time indeed, it is gradually not only more assimilated, but at length changes its nature altogether; so as to become, what was at first so pernicious, a benign, cooling liquor: when the spirit is strong, the change, it is true, goes on more slow and imperceptibly; yet as a partial alteration is only wanted to mellow it for use, a few years keeping would be sufficient to answer the purpose here; and whether or no it could be possible to prevent any other from being sold than that which had been kept a certain time, is well worth the consideration of the Legislature.

That the great noxious quality of fresh drawn spirits, is chiefly owing to the cause I have assigned, a little attention, and comparing of the effects that are uniformly produced by the principle of inflammability, wherever it is met with in a loose and weakly combined state, as it is in them, will easily convince us of: whereas, when fully assimilated either in spirits, or with any other body, it becomes entirely inert, and useful, more or less, either for food

or

or physick, according to what it happens to be united with. Thus we find it in putrid animal substances, where it lately formed part of a healthy body, being now detached, or but weakly united with air, exhibiting a most offensive, and pernicious poison: though this absorbed again by a living plant is presently changed into good and wholesome nourishment; to the vegetable immediately, and to any animal who may afterwards choose to eat it. In like manner Sulphur, which is a compound of this principle alone, united to a pure acid, the most destructive to all animal and vegetable substances, yet it being here perfectly inert also, may be taken into the body with safety; when, if loosened either by heat or by an alkaline salt uniting with the acid, its noxious quality is presently made perceivable to whoever comes within its reach.

MANY other instances of a like nature might easily be added, and some too more apposite perhaps than those I have here mentioned; but every one's own experience, with what I have already said, will sufficiently evince the propriety and utility of putting an entire stop, if possible, to the sale of what ought to be so justly prohibited; and this, in its consequences, may even help to lead to other more effectual means of correcting, in a great measure, the cruel abuse

abuse of spirits in general, that has been long so loudly and so justly complained of, amongst the soldiers, lower *Europeans*, and our servants in this country; where the very worst and indeed poisonous sort of them is daily sold at so very cheap a rate.

ALL I need further add with respect to distillation, and on the superior advantages in the mode of conducting it here to that we have been in use to employ, for the raising of spirits, simple waters, and the like, is only to observe, I have no sort of doubt but that the intelligent Chymical Operators at home, if ever they should get a hint of it, will make no manner of scruple to use it also, and to improve upon it greatly by a few ingenious contrivances, which their knowledge and experience will so easily suggest. The principles on which it seems founded indeed, especially with regard to their way of cooling, are so striking and just, that in many other distillations besides those of spirits and waters, they may be employed, I apprehend, with very great profit and advantage. I shall now, however, confine myself to mention only the benefit that may result from a like process in the raising of the finer Aromaticks, while the heat contrived, as in our way, besides impeding the distillation, must from its long action on such subtile bodies, probably injure them greatly

greatly in the essential quality on which their excellence depends; and upon this very account I am apt to imagine that the greater quantity obtained, and the superior quality of the *Oil* of *Roses* made in this country, to that made from *Roses* with us, is owing chiefly, if not entirely, to their better and more judicious manner of extracting it here. For, with us, the Still being made of metal, may in the first instance, impart too great and too sudden a degree of heat; and next, the *Oil* continuing so long in the vapour, and that much compressed, may, in so delicate a subject, not only entirely almost unite it with the water, so as to render the separation impracticable, but may at the same time alter its essence so completely, as that it can no longer appear in the state it otherwise might have been found in, had the operation been better conducted, or in the way they do here. A very few trials however would much better certify this than all I can possibly say on the subject, or in fact than all the reasoning in the world. Therefore, as to my own particular opinion of the flavour and quality of the *Roses* at home being equal if not superior to that of those in this country, I may be entirely silent; the rules and reasoning in Chymistry, though serving greatly to enlarge and improve our understanding, being what of themselves

can

can never be depended upon till confirmed by facts and experiments; where many things often turn out very different from what, from our best and most plausible arguments, we had the greatest reason to expect. Or, if it should be found to be really true, what I have often heard asserted, by those however who had it only from others, but not of their own particular knowledge, that, in distilling their *Oil* of *Roses* at the places where they make it the best, they use also with their *Roses Sandal-wood*, and some other Aromaticks, no *Roses* whatsoever, it is plain, could ever of themselves be made to afford a like *Oil*; nor without such an addition as they employ. A circumstance, by the bye, that might possibly easily be certified by some one of the many ingenious correspondents of the Society, who may happen to reside where it is made; and a knowlege of the real truth of it would certainly be of use.

*Chatra*, Dec. 24. 1786.

## ON THE
# PANGOLIN
## OF
# BAHAR.

SENT BY MATTHEW LESLIE, ESQ.

---

THE singular animal which M. BUFFON describes by the name of *Pangolin*, is well-known in *Europe* since the publication of his Natural History and GOLDSMITH's elegant abridgement of it; but if the figure exhibited by BUFFON was accurately delineated from the three animals the spoils of which he had examined, we must consider that which has been lately brought from *Caracdiab* to *Chitra*, and sent thence to the Presidency, as a remarkable variety, if not a different species, of the *Pangolin*: ours has hardly any neck, and though some filaments are discernible between the scales, they can scarce be called bristles; but the principal difference is in the tail; that of BUFFON's animal being long, and tapering almost to a point, while that of ours is much shorter, ends obtusely, and resembles in form and flexibility the tail of a lobster. In other respects, as far as we can judge from the dead subject, it has all the characters of BUFFON's *Pangolin*; a name derived from that by which the animal is distinguished in *Java*, and consequently preferable to *Manis* or *Pholidotus*, or any other appellation deduced from an *European* language. As to the *scaly Lizard* the *scaled Armadillo*, and the *five-nailed Ant-eater*, they are manifestly improper designations of this animal; which is neither a *Lizard* nor an *Armadillo* in the common acceptation; and, though it be an *Ant-eater*, yet it essentially differs from the *hairy* quadruped usually known by that general description. We are told, that the *Malabar* name of this animal is *Alungu*: the natives of *Babár* call it *Bajrá-cít*, or, as they explain the word, *Stone-vermin*; and in the stomach of the animal before us was found about a teacupful of small *stones*, which had probably been swallowed for the purpose of facilitating digestion; but the name alludes, I believe, to the *hardness* of the scales; for *Vajracita* means in *Sanscrit* the *Diamond*, or *Thunderbolt*, reptile, and *Vajra* is a common figure in the *Indian* poetry for any thing excessively *hard*. The *Vajracita* is believed by the *Pandits* to be the animal which gnaws their *sacred stone*, called *Sálgrámattá*;

*músili*; but the *Pangolin* has apparently no teeth, and the *Sálgrams*, many of which look as if they had been worm-eaten, are perhaps only decayed in part by exposure to the air.

THIS animal had a long tongue shaped like that of a cameleon; and, if it was nearly adult, as we may conclude from the young one found in it, the dimensions of it were much less than those which BUFFON assigns *generally* to his *Pangolin*; for he describes its length as six, seven, or eight feet including the tail, which is almost, he says, as long as the body, when it has attained its full growth; whereas ours is but thirty-four inches long from the extremity of the tail to the point of the snout, and the length of the tail is fourteen inches; but, exclusively of the head, which is five inches long, the tail and body are, indeed, nearly of the same length; and the small difference between them may show, if BUFFON be correct in this point, that the animal was young: the circumference of its body in the thickest part is twenty inches, and that of the tail only twelve.

WE cannot venture to say more of this extraordinary creature, which seems to constitute the first step from the quadruped to the reptile, until we have examined it alive, and observed its different instincts; but as we are assured, that it is common in the country round *Khispúr*, and at *Chátigám*, where the native *Muselmans*

mans call it the *Land-carp*, we shall possibly be able to give on some future occasion a fuller account of it. There are in our *Indian* provinces many animals, and many hundreds of medicinal plants, which have either not been described at all, or, what is worse, ill described by the naturalists of *Europe*; and to procure perfect descriptions of them from actual examination, with accounts of their several *uses* in medicine, diet, or manufactures, appears to be one of the most important objects of our institution.

---

ON THE

## DISSECTION OF THE PANGOLIN,

IN A

LETTER TO GEN. CARNAC FROM ADAM BURT, Esq.

COMMUNICATED BY GEN. CARNAC.

SIR,

IN compliance with your desire, I most willingly do myself the honour to present to you my observations and reflections on the dissection of the *Pangolin*, an animal which is distinguished in the FIRST VOLUME of the TRANSACTIONS of the ASIATICK SOCIETY, by a name a name which I do not at present remember; but probably the animal is of the same genus with the *Manis*, as described in the former edition of the ENCYCLOPÆDIA BRITANNICA, or, perhaps, not different from the *Pangolin* of BUFFON.

THERE are on each foot five claws, of which the outer and inner are small when compared with the other three. There are no distinct toes; but each nail is moveable by a joint at its root. This creature is extremely inoffensive. It has no teeth; and its feet are unable to grasp. Hence it would appear, that nature, having furnished it with a coat of mail for its protection, has, with some regard to justice, denied it the powers of acting with hostility against its fellow-creatures. The nails are well adapted for digging in the ground; and the animal is so dexterous in eluding its enemies by concealing itself in holes and among rocks, that it is extremely difficult to procure one.

THE upperjaw is covered with a cross cartilaginous ridge, which, though apparently not at all suited to any purposes of mastication, may, by encreasing the surface of the palate, extend the sense of taste. The œsophagus admitted my forefinger with ease. The tongue at the bottom of the mouth is nearly about the size of the little finger, from whence it tapers to a point.

point. The animal at pleasure protrudes this member a great way from the mouth. The tongue arises from the ensiform cartilage, and the contiguous muscles of the belly, and passes in form of a round distinct muscle from over the stomach, through the thorax, immediately under the sternum; and interior to the windpipe in the throat. When dissected out, the tongue could be easily elongated so as to reach more than the length of the animal exclusive of its tail. There is a cluster of salivary glands seated around the tongue as it enters the mouth. These will necessarily be compressed by the action of the tongue; so as occasionally to supply a plentiful flow of their secretion.

THE stomach is *cartilaginous*, and analogous to that of the gallinaceous tribe of birds. It was filled with small stones and gravel, which in this part of the country are almost universally calcareous. The inner surface of the stomach was rough to the feel, and formed into folds, the interstices of which were filled with a frothy secretion. The guts were filled with a sandy pulp, in which, however, were interspersed a few distinct small stones. No vestiges of any animal or vegetable food could be traced in the whole *primæ viæ*. The gall-bladder was distended with a fluid resembling in colour and consistence the dregs of beer.

The subject was a female: its dugs were two, seated on the breast. The uterus and organs of generation were evidently those of a viviparous animal.

FORCIBLY struck with the phenomena which this quadruped exhibited, my imagination at once overleaped the boundaries by which science endeavours to circumscribe the productions and the ways of Nature; and believing with BUFFON, *que tout ce qui peut être est*, I did not hesitate to conjecture, that this animal might possibly derive its nourishment from mineral substances. This idea I accordingly hazarded in an address to Colonel KYD: the spirit of inquiry natural to that gentleman could be ill satisfied by ideas thrown out apparently at random; and he soon called on me to explain my opinion, and its foundation.

THOUGH we have perhaps no clear idea of the manner in which vegetables extract their nourishment from earth, yet the fact being so, it may not be unreasonable to suppose, that some animal may derive nutriment by a process somewhat similar. It appears to me, that facts produced by SPALLANZANI directly invalidate the experiments from which he has drawn the inference, that fowls swallow stones merely from stupidity; and that such substances are altogether unnecessary to those animals. He reared fowls, without permitting

mitting them ever to swallow sand or stones; but he also established the fact, that carnivorous animals may become frugivorous, and herbivorous animals may come to live on flesh. A wood-pidgeon he brought to thrive on putrid meat. The experiment on fowls, then, only corroborates the proof, that we have it in our power by habits to alter the natural constitution of animals. Again, that eminent investigator of truth found, that fowls died when fed on stones alone; but surely that fact is far short of proving, that such substances are not agreeable to the original purposes of nature in the digestive process of these animals. When other substances shall have been detected in the stomach of this animal, my inference from what I have seen, must necessary fall to the ground. But if, like other animals with muscular and cartilaginous stomachs, this singular quadruped confume grain, it must be surprizing that no vestige of such food was found present in the whole alimentary canal, since in that thinly inhabited country the wild animals are free to feed without intrusion from man. Nor can it be inferred from the structure of the stomach, that this animal lives on ants or on insects. Animals devoured as food, though of considerable size and solidity, with a proportionally small extent of surface to be acted on by the

gastric

gastric juice and the action of the stomach, are readily dissolved and digested by animals possessing not a cartilaginous, but a membranaceous, stomach, as for instance, a frog in that of a snake.

In the stomach many minerals are soluble, and the most active things which we can swallow. Calcareous substances are readily acted on. Dr. Priestley has asked, "May not phlogistic matter be the most essential part of the food and support of both vegetable and animal bodies?" I confess, that Dr. Priestley's finding cause to propose the question, inclines me to suppose, that the affirmative to it may be true. Earth seems to be the basis of all animal matter. The growth of the bones must be attended with a constant supply, and in the human species there is a copious discharge of calcareous matter thrown out by the kidneys and salivary glands. May not the quadruped in question derive phlogiston from earth; salt, from mineral substances? And as it is not deprived of the power of drinking water, what else is necessary to the subsistence of his corporeal machine?

Considering the scaly covering of this animal, we may conceive, that it may be at least necessary for its existence, on that account, to imbibe a greater proportion of earth than is necessary to other animals. It may deserve

serve consideration, that birds are covered with feathers, which in their constituent principles approach to the nature of horn and bone. Of these animals the gallinaceous tribe swallow stones; and the carnivorous take in the feathers and bones of their prey: the latter article is known to be soluble in the membranaceous stomachs; and hence is a copious supply of the earthy principles. In truth, I do not know that any thing is soluble in the stomach of animals, which may not be thence absorbed into their circulating system, and nothing can be so absorbed without affecting the whole constitution.

WHAT I have here stated is all that I could advance to the Colonel; but my opinion has been since not a little confirmed by observing the report of experiments by M. BRUGNATELLI of *Pavia*, on the authority of M. CRELL, by which we learn, that some birds have so great a dissolvent power in the gastric juice as to dissolve in their stomachs flints, rock crystal, calcareous stones and shells.

I BEG only farther to observe, that some things in BUFFON's description of the *Pangolin*, not apparently quite applicable to this animal, might have been owing to his description being only from the view of a dried preparation, in which the organs of generation would be obliterated, and the dugs shrivelled away so as

to

to be imperceptible: elfe that elegant philofopher could not have afferted, that " *tous les animaux quadrupedes qui font couverts d'écailles, font ovipares.*"

Excuse my prolixity, which is only in me the neceffary attendant of my fuperficial knowledge of things. In ingenuoufnefs, however, I hope that I am not inferior to any man: and I am proud to fubfcribe myfelf,

SIR,

Your moft obedient and humble fervant,

ADAM BURT.

Gya, *Sept.* 14, 1789.

# DESCRIPTION OF THE LA'CSHA, OR LAC INSECT*.

BY MR. W. ROXBURGH, SURGEON ON THE MADRAS ESTABLISHMENT.

COMMUNICATED BY DR. JAMES ANDERSON.

---

*Jan. 2, 1790.*

SOME pieces of very fresh-looking Lac, adhering to small branches of *Mimosa Cinerea*, were brought me from the mountains on the 20th of last month. I kept them carefully, and to-day, the 4th of *December*, fourteen days from the time they came from the hills, myriads of exceedingly minute animals were observed creeping about the Lac, and branches it adhered to, and more still issuing from small holes over the surface of the cells: other small and perforated excrescences were observed with a glass amongst the perforations, from which the minute insects issued, regularly two to each hole, and crowned with some very fine

---

* This discovery of Mr. ROXBURGH will bring LAC a Genus into the Class *Hemiptera* of LINNÆUS.

white

white hairs. When the hairs were rubbed off, two white spots appeared. The animals, when single, ran about pretty briskly, but in general they were so numerous as to be crowded over one another. The body is oblong, tapering most towards the tail, below plain, above convex, with a double, or flat margin: laterally on the back part of the thorax are two small tubercles, which may be the eyes: the body behind the thorax is crossed with twelve rings: legs six: feelers (antennæ) half the length of the body, jointed, hairy, each ending in two hairs as long as the antennæ: rump, a white point between two terminal hairs, which are as long as the body of the animal. The mouth I could not see. On opening the cells, the substance that they were formed of cannot be better described, with respect to appearance, than by saying it is like the transparent amber that beads are made of: the external covering of the cells may be about half a line thick, is remarkably strong, and able to resist injuries: the partitions are much thinner: the cells are in general irregular squares, pentagons, and hexagons, about an eighth of an inch in diameter, and one quarter deep: they have no communication with each other: all those I opened during the time the animals were issuing, contained in one half, a small bag filled with a thick red jelly-like liquor replete with

what

what I take to be eggs; these bags, or utriculi, adhere to the bottom of the cells, and have each two necks, which pass through perforations in the external coat of the cells, forming the forementioned excrescences, and ending in some very fine hairs. The other half of the cells have a distinct opening, and contain a white substance, like some few filaments of cotton rolled together, and numbers of the insects themselves ready to make their exit: several of the same insects I observed to have drawn up their legs and to lie flat: they did not move on being touched, nor did they show any signs of life with the greatest irritation.

*December 5.* The same minute hexapedes continue issuing from their cells in numbers; they are more lively, of a deepened red colour, and fewer of the motionless sort. To-day I saw the mouth: it is a flattened point about the middle of the breast, which the little animal projects on being compressed.

*December 6.* The male insects I have found to-day: a few of them are constantly running among the females most actively: as yet they are scarce more, I imagine, than one to 5000 females, but twice their size. The head is obtuse; eyes black, very large; antennæ clavated, feathered, about ⅟₇ the length of the body: below the middle an articulation, such as those in the legs: colour between the eyes a beautiful shining

shining green: neck very short: body oval, brown: abdomen oblong, the length of body and head: legs six: wings membranaceous, four, longer than the body, fixed to the sides of the thorax, narrow at their insertions, growing broader for ¼ of their length, then rounded: the anterior pair is twice the size of the posterior: a strong fibre runs along their anterior margins: they lie flat like the wings of a common fly, when it walks or rests: no hairs from the rump: it springs most actively to a considerable distance on being touched: mouth in the under part of the head: maxillæ transverse. To-day the female insects continue issuing in great numbers, and move about as on the 4th.

*December 7.* The small red insects still more numerous, and move about as before: winged insects, still very few, continue active. There have been fresh leaves and bits of the branches of both *Mimosa Cinerea* and *Cerinda* put into the wide mouthed bottle with them: they walk over them indifferently without showing any preference nor inclination to work nor copulate. I opened a cell whence I thought the winged flies had come, and found several, eight or ten, more in it, struggling to shake off their incumbrances: they were in one of those utriculi mentioned on the 4th, which ends in two mouths,

mouths, shut up with fine white hairs, but one of them was open for the exit of the flies; the other would no doubt have opened in due time: this utriculus I found now perfectly dry, and divided into cells by exceeding thin partitions. I imagine, before any of the flies made their escape, it might have contained about twenty. In these minute cells with the living flies, or whence they had made their escape, were small dry dark-coloured compressed grains, which may be the dried excrements of the flies.

### NOTE BY THE PRESIDENT.

THE *Hindus* have six names for *Lac*; but they generally call it *Lácshá* from the multitude of small insects, who, as they believe, discharge it from their stomachs, and at length destroy the tree on which they form their colonies: a fine *Pippala* near *Crishnanagar* is now almost wholly destroyed by them.

# TRANSLATION

## OF A

## SANSCRIT INSCRIPTION,
COPIED FROM A STONE AT BOODDHA-GAYA.
BY MR. WILMOT, 1785.

TRANSLATED BY CHARLES WILKINS, ESQ.

---

IN the midst of a wild and dreadful forest, flourishing with trees of sweet-scented flowers, and abounding in fruits and roots; infested with Lions and Tigers; destitute of human society, and frequented by the *Moonees*, resided *Bood-dha* the Author of Happiness, and a portion of *Narayan*. This Deity *Haree*, who is the Lord *Hareesa*, the possessor of all, appeared in this ocean of natural Beings at the close of the *Devapara*, and beginning of the *Kalee Yoog:* he who is omnipresent and everlastingly to be contemplated, the Supreme Being, the Eternal One, the Divinity worthy to be adored by the most praise-worthy of mankind, appeared here with a portion of his divine nature.

ONCE

ONCE upon a time the illustrious *Amara*, renowned amongst men, coming here, discovered the place of the Supreme Being, *Bood-dha*, in the great forest. The wise *Amara* endeavoured to render the God *Bood-dha* propitious by superior service; and he remained in the forest for the space of twelve years, feeding upon roots and fruits, and sleeping upon the bare earth; and he performed the vow of a *Moonee*, and was without transgression. He performed acts of severe mortification, for he was a man of infinite resolution, with a compassionate heart. One night he had a vision and heard a voice saying, "Name whatever boon "thou wantest." *Amara Deva* having heard this, was astonished, and with due reverence replied, "First, give me a visitation, and then grant "me such a boon." He had another dream in the night, and the voice said, "How can "there be an apparition in the *Kalee-Yoog?* "The same reward may be obtained from the "sight of an Image, or from the worship of an "Image, as may be derived from the immediate visitation of a Deity." Having heard this, he caused an Image of the Supreme Spirit *Bood-dha* to be made, and he worshipped it, according to the law, with perfumes, incenses, and the like; and he thus glorified the name

of that Supreme Being, the Incarnation of a portion of *Veeſhnoo*: " Reverence be unto thee in
" the form of *Bood-dha!* Reverence be unto
" the Lord of the Earth! Reverence be unto
" thee, an incarnation of the Deity and the
" Eternal One! Reverence be unto thee, O
" God, in the form of the God of Mercy;—
" the diſpeller of pain and trouble, the Lord of
" all things, the Deity who overcometh the
" ſins of the *Kalee-Yoog*, the Guardian of the
" Univerſe, the Emblem of Mercy towards
" thoſe who ſerve thee—*OM!* the poſſeſſor of
" all things in vital form! Thou art *Brahma,*
" *Veeſhnoo*, and *Maheſa!* Thou art Lord of the
" Univerſe! Thou art, under the proper form
" of all things moveable and immoveable, the
" poſſeſſor of the whole! and thus I adore
" thee. Reverence be unto the beſtower of
" ſalvation, and *Reſheekéſa*, the ruler of the
" faculties! Reverence be unto thee *(Kéſavah),*
" the deſtroyer of the evil Spirit *Kéſee!* O
" *Damordara*, ſhew me favour! Thou art he
" who reſteth upon the face of the milky
" ocean, and who lyeth upon the ſerpent *Séſa*.
" Thou art *Treevikrama* (who at three ſtrides
" encompaſſed the earth)! I adore thee, who
" art celebrated by a thouſand names, and
" under various forms, in the ſhape of *Bood-dha*,
" the God of Mercy! Be propitious, O Moſt
" High God!"

HAVING

HAVING thus worshipped the Guardian of mankind, he became like one of the just. He joyfully caused a holy Temple to be built of a wonderful construction, and therein were set up the divine foot of *Veeshnoo*, for ever Purifier of the sins of mankind, the images of the *Pandoos*, and of the descents of *Veeshnoo*, and in like manner of *Brahma*, and the rest of the Divinities.

THIS place is renowned; and it is celebrated by the name of *Bood-dha-Gaya*. The fore-fathers of him who shall perform the ceremony of the *Sradha* at this place shall obtain salvation. The great virtue of the *Sradha* performed here, is to be found in the book called *Vayoo-poorana*; an Epitome of which hath by me been engraved upon stone.

VEEKRAMADEETYA was certainly a king renowned in the world. So in his court there were nine learned men, celebrated under the epithet of the *Nava-ratnanee*, or nine Jewels; one of whom was *Amara Déva*, who was the King's Chief Counsellor, a man of great genius and profound learning, and the greatest favourite of his Prince. He it certainly was who built the holy temple which destroyeth sin, in a place in *Jamboodweep*, where, the mind being steady, it obtains its wishes, and in a place where it may obtain salvation, reputation, and enjoyment, even in the country of *Bharata*, and the province

vince of *Kerkata*, where the place of *Beed-dhu*, Purifier of the sinful, is renowned. A crime of an hundred fold shall undoubtedly be expiated from a sight thereof, of a thousand fold from a touch thereof, and of a hundred thousand fold from worshipping thereof. But where is the use of saying so much of the great virtues of this place? Even the Hosts of Heaven worship with joyful service both day and night.

THAT it may be known to learned men, that he verily erected the house of *Beed-dha*, I have recorded, upon a stone, the authority of the place, as a self-evident testimony, on Friday the fourth day of the new moon in the month of *Madhoo*, when in the seventh or mansion of *Ganisa*, and in the year of the Era of *Veckramadeetya* 1005.

THE

# AN INSCRIPTION ON A PILLAR NEAR BUDDAL.

TRANSLATED FROM THE SANSCRIT,

BY CHARLES WILKINS, ESQ.

---

SOME time in the month of *November*, in the year 1780, I discovered, in the vicinity of the town of *Buddal*, near which the Company have a Factory, and which at that time was under my charge, a decapitated monumental column, which at a little distance has very much the appearance of the trunk of a cocoa-nut tree broken off in the middle. It stands in a swamp overgrown with weeds, near a small temple dedicated to *Hargouree*, whose image it contains.

It is formed of a single stone of a dirty grey complexion; and it has lost by accident a considerable part of its original height. I was told upon the spot, that it had, in the course of time, sunk considerably in the ground; but upon my digging about the foundation I found this was not the case. At a few feet above the ground is an Inscription engraved in the stone, from which I took two reversed impressions with printer's ink. I have lately been so fortunate as to decypher the character; and I have the honour to lay before the Society a translation of it.

The original character of this Inscription is very different from the modern form; but it so much resembles that on the plate found by Colonel WATSON at *Mongueer*, that I am induced to conclude it to be a work of the same period. The language is *Sanskreet*, and the whole is comprised in twenty-eight metrical verses of various measures.

CHARLES WILKINS.

*July* 14, 1785.

## I.

PROSPERITY!

VEERA DEV was of the *Sandeelya* race.*; from him was descended *Panchal*; of whose generation, and of whom, was *Garga* born.

## II.

He, another *Sakra*†, was ruler but of one quarter, and had no authority in other regions. He, too, was defeated by *Ditya* ‡ chiefs; but being a virtuous prince, he became supreme over every country without reserve; and his conduct was such, that he laughed *Vreehaspatee* § to scorn.

## III.

Etcha ‖ was his wife; and, like love, she was the mistress of his heart. She was admired for the native purity of her mind, and her beauty was like the light of the moon.

* A tribe of *Brahmans* still extant.
† Eendra, the God of the Heavens, who is supposed to be the Guardian of the East.
‡ Evil Spirits. Eendra is said to have lost his kingdom, for a while, to the Assers or Evil Spirits.
§ The Tutor of the Good Spirits and the Planet Jupiter.
‖ Love, Desire.

## IV.

In his countenance, which was like the flower of the waters *, were to be traced the lines of four sciences †. The three worlds were held in subjection by his hereditary high rank.

From these two was descended a *Brahman* like *Kamalayonee* ‡, and he took unto himself the name of *Sree Darbha-panee*:

Whose country (extending to *Reva-Janak* §; to the father of *Gowree* ||, whose piles of rocks reek with the juice exuding from the heads of intoxicated elephants, and whose snow-white mountains are brightened by the sun's rays; to the two oceans;—to that whence *Aroon* ¶ riseth from its bed, and to that wherein the sun sinketh in the west) the Prince

---
\* The Lotus.
† Arms, Music, Mechanics, Physics.
‡ *Brahma.*
§ Perhaps the *Nerbudda.*
¶ The snowy Mountains that part *India* from *Tartary.* Gowree, one of the names of the *Parvati*, the consort of *Seev.*
¶ The Charioteer of the Sun—the Aurora of the *Hindoos.*

*Sree*

Sree Deo-Pal P; by his policy, rendered tributary;

VI.

At whose gates (although the prospect, hidden by the dust arising from the multitude of marching force, was rendered clear from the earth being watered by constant and abundant streams flowing from the heads of lustful elephants of various breeds), stood, scarce visible, amongst the vast concourse of nobles flocking to his standard from every quarter, Sree Deo Pal in expectation of his submission.

VII.

Whose throne that Prince (who was the image of Eendra, and the dust of whose feet was impressed with the diadems of sundry potentates) himself ascended with a flash of glory, although he had formerly been wont to offer him large sums of Pertas † bright as the lunar rays.

VIII.

To him was born of the Princess Barkara, the Brahman Someswar, who was like Som ‡

* If this be the Prince mentioned in the Copper-plate found by Col. Watson, he reigned at Monguer above 1800 years ago.
† A square Coin.
‡ The Moon.

the offspring of *Atree*, and a favourite of the Most High.

### IX.

He adopted the manners of *Dhananjay*\*, and did not exult over the ignorant and ill-favoured. He spent his riches amongst the needy. He neither vainly accepted adulation, nor uttered honey-words. His attendants were attached by his bounty; and because of his vast talents, which the whole universe could not equal, he was the wonder of all good men.

### X.

Anxious for a home and an asylum, he took the hand of *Ranna* †, a Princess of his own likeness, according to the law, even as *Seev* the hand of *Seeva* ‡—even as *Haree* § the hand of *Lakshmee*.

### XI.

From this pair proceeded into life, bursting forth like *Gooba* ‖ with a countenance of a

\* One of the sons of *Pandoo*, commonly called *Arjoon*.
† A Princess of this name is also mentioned in Colonel Watson's Plate.
‡ *Seev* is the feminine of *Seev*.
§ *Haree*, a name of *Veeshnoo*.
‖ *Gooba*, a name of *Kartick*.

golden

golden hue, the fortunate *Kedara Meefra*, whofe actions rendered him the favourite of heaven. —The lofty diadem which he had attained fhone with faultlefs fplendour, kiffing the vaft circumference of the earth. His extenfive power was hard to be limited; and he was renowned for boundlefs knowledge raifed from his own internal fource.

### XII.

THE ocean of the four fciences, which had been at a fingle draught drunk up, he brought forth again, and laughed at the power of *Agaftya* \*.

### XIII.

TRUSTING to his wifdom, the king of *Gowr* † for a long time enjoyed the country of the eradicated race of *Ootkal* ‡, of the *Hoons* § of humbled pride, of the kings of *Draver* ‖ and *Goorjar* ¶, whofe glory was reduced, and the univerfal fea-girt throne.

\* Who is faid to have drunk up the ocean.
† The kingdom of *Gowr* anciently included all the countries which now form the kingdom of *Bengal* on this fide the *Brahmapootra*, except *Mongheer*.
‡ Orixa.
§ *Huns*.
‖ A country to the fouth of the Carnatick.
¶ *Guzarrat*.

XIV. He

## XIV.

He considered his own acquired wealth the property of the needy, and his mind made no distinction between the friend and the foe. He was both afraid and ashamed of those offences which condemn the soul to sink again into the ocean of mortal birth; and he despised the pleasures of this life, because he delighted in a supreme abode.

## XV.

To him, emblem of *Vreehaspatee*,\* and to his religious rites, the Prince *Sree Soora Pál* (who was a second *Eendra*, and whose soldiers were fond of wounds) went repeatedly; and that long and happy companion of the world, which is girt with several oceans as with a belt, was wont, with a soul purified at the fountain of faith, and his head humbly bowed down, to bear pure water before him.

## XVI.

VANWA, of celestial birth, was his consort, with whom neither the fickle *Lukshmee*, nor *Savee* † constant to her lord, were to be compared.

\* The Preceptor of the Good Spirits, and the Planet *Jupiter*.
† The Consort of *Seev*.

XVII. SHE,

## XVII.

Sam, like another *Dewaka* *, bore unto him a son of high renown, who resembled the adopted of *Yasodha* † and husband of *Lakshmee* ‡.

## XVIII.

This youth, by name *Sree Gourava Misra*, was acquainted with all the constellations. He resembled *Ram*, the son of *Jamadagnee* §. He was another *Ram*.

## XIX.

His abilities were so great, that he was solicitous to discover the essence of things, wherefore he was greatly respected by the Prince *Sree Narayan Pal*. What other honour was necessary?

## XX.

His policy (who was of no mean capacity, and of a reputation not to be conceived), fol-

* The real mother of *Kreeshna*.
† The foster-mother of *Kreeshna*.
‡ *Reekmenee*, the Consort of *Kreeshna*. She is here called *Lakshmee*, in compliance with the idea of her being a descent of that Goddess.
§ This is neither the conqueror of *Loke*, nor the brother of *Kreeshna*.

lowing

lowing the sense of the *Veds*, was of boundless splendour, and, as it were, a descent of *Dharma*, the Genius of Justice. It was regulated by the example of those who trust in the power of speech over things future, who stand upon the connexion of family, who are in the exercise of paying due praise to the virtues of great men, and who believe in the purity of *Astrology*.

### XXI.

In him was united a lovely pair, *Lakshmee* and *Saraswatee*, the disposer of fortune, and the Goddess of Science, who seemed to have forsaken their natural enmity, and to stand together pointing at friendship.

### XXII.

He laughed to scorn him who, in the assemblies of the learned, was intoxicated with the love of argument, and confounded him with profound and elegant discourses framed according to the doctrine of the *Sastras*; and he spared not the man who, because of his boundless power and riches, was overwhelmed with the pride of victory over his enemy in the field.

### XXIII.

He had a womb, but it obstinately bore him no fruit. One like him can have no great relish

for

for the enjoyments of life! He never was blessed with that giver of delight, by obtaining which a man goeth unto another almoner *.

## XXIV.

He who was, as it were, another *Valmeekee* † born in this dark age of impiety, amongst a dreadful and a cruel race of mortals, was a devout man who displayed the learning of the *Veds* in books of moral tales.

## XXV.

His profound and pleasing language, like *Ganga*, flowing in a triple course ‡ and constant stream, purifieth and delighteth.

## XXVI.

He to whom, and to those of whose generation, men were wont to resort as it were to *Brahma*, waited so long in expectation of being a father, that, at length, he himself arrived at the state of a child.

---

* He had no issue to perform the *Sradh* for the release of his soul from the bonds of sin. By *another almoner* is meant the Deity.

† The first Poet of the *Hindoos*, and supposed author of the *Ramayan*.

‡ He is supposed to have written in three languages.

XXVII. By

## XXVII.

By him was recorded here, upon this lasting column, the superior beauty of whose shaft catcheth the eye of the beholder, whose aspiring height is as boundless as his own ideas, which is, as it were, a stake planted in the breast of *Kalee* \*, and on whose top sits *Tarkshya* †, the foe of serpents and favourite bird of *Haree*, the line of his own descent.

## XXVIII.

GAROOR, like his fame, having wandered to the extremity of the world, and descended even unto its foundation, was exalted here with a serpent in his mouth.

This Work was executed by the Artist BEENDOO BHADRA.

\* Time.
† Otherwise called *Garur*.

---

### REMARKS ON THE PRECEDING PAPER.
### BY THE PRESIDENT.

VERSE II. *a virtuous prince.*—). Many stanzas in this Inscription prove that the *Shadiba* family were not *Princes*, but that some of them were Prime *Ministers* to the kings of *Gaur*, or *Bengal*, according to this comparative Genealogy:
Kings.

|  Kings.           |  Ministers*.   |
|-------------------|----------------|
| GO'PA'LA.         | PA'NCHA-LA.    |
| DHERMAPA'LA.      | GARDA.         |
| DE'VAPA'LA. B. C. 23. | *DERBHAPA'NI. |
| RA'JYAPA'LA.      | SOME'SWARA.    |
| S'URAPA'LA.       | * CE'DA'RAMIS'RA. |
| NA'RA'YANAPA'LA. A. C. 67. | * GURAVAMIS'RA. |

So that reckoning thirty years to a generation, we may date the pillar of GURAVAMIS'RA in the sixty-seventh year *after* CHRIST. A *Pandit*, named RA'DHA'CA'NTA, with whom I read the original, appeared struck with my remark on the two families, and adopted it without hesitation; but, if it be just, the second stanza must be differently interpreted. I suspect *Dharma*, the Genius of *Justice* or *Virtue*, to be the true reading instead of *dharmya*, or *virtuous*, and have no doubt, that *part* must be substituted for *parà*: the sense will then be, that INDRA was ruler in *the East* only, and, though valiant, had been defeated even there by the *Daityas* or *Titans*, but that DHARMA was made sovereign over him in all quarters.

VERSE V. Whose country). The original is:

á révájanascánmatangajamadastimyachcheb'hilásanghateh,
á gauriśipituriswariṇdraciransaihpuśhyatsitimaógireh,
mártan'dāstameyódayáruṇ'ajaláś śrás'irásádwayàt,
nityá yaśya bhuwan chacára caradán ari dévapalo nripah.

The father of *Revà* is the *Mahendra* mountain in the south, in which that river has its source; as the father of GAURI is the *Himàlaya* in the north, where IS'WARA, who has a moon on his forehead, is believed often to reside: hence RA'DHA'CA'NTA proposed a conjectural emendation, which would have done honour to SCALIGER or BENTLEY. Instead of *Indra*, which is a name of the *sun*, he reads *indu*, or the *moon*, by changing only a small straight line into a small curve; and then the stanza will run thus:

By whose policy the great Prince DE'VAPA'LA made the earth tributary, from the father of *Revà*, whose-piles-of-rocks-are-moist-with-juice-from-the-heads-of-lascivious-elephants, to the father of GAURI, whose-white-mountains-are-brightened-with-beams-from-the-moon-of-ISWARA;—*and* as far as the-two-oceans-whose-waters-are-red-with-the-rising-and-with-the-setting-Sun.

The words connected by hyphens are compounds in *Sanscrit*.

VERSE VI. (submission). I understand *avasara* in this place to mean the *leisure* of the Minister from publick affairs, for which even the King waited at the head of his army.

VERSE VII. (urn of Picchi). The common sense of *pit'ha* is a *chair*, *foot*, or *throne*; and in this sense it occurs in the thirteenth verse. *Udupachch'habipit'ham*, or *with-a-foot-bright-as-the-moon*, appears to be the compound epithet of *asanam*, or *chair of state*, which though the King had often given to his Minister, yet, abashed by his wisdom, and apprehensive of his popularity, he had himself ascended his throne *with fear*.

VERSE X. The tenth stanza is extremely difficult, as it contains many words with two meanings, applied in one sense to the Minister CE'DA'RA MIS'RA, but, in another, to CA'RTICE'YA, the *Indian* MARS: thus, in the first hemistich, *pic'hin* means *fire* or a *peacock*; *sichà*, a *bright flame*, or a *crest*, and *sacti*, either *power* or a *spear*. As the verse is differently understood, it may be a description of the *Bráhmen* or of the Deity.

VERSE XII. The *Bráhmens* of this province insist, that by the four *Vidyà's*, or *branches of knowledge*, are meant the four *Vèda's*, not the *Upavèda's*, or *Medicine*, *Archery*, *Musick*, and *Mechanicks*; and they cite two distichs from the *Agnipurána*, in which *eighteen Vidyà's* are enumerated, and, among them, the *four Vèdas*; *three* only of which are mentioned in the *Amercósh* and in several older books. In this

this verse also RA'DHA'CA'NT has displayed his critical sagacity: instead of *ahla* he reads *bála*, and, if his conjecture be right, we must add, "*even when he was a boy.*"

VERSE XVI. constant to her lord]. RA'DHA'CA'NT reads *anapatyayá*, or *childless*, for *anupatyayá*; SATI' having borne *no children*, till she became regenerate in the person of PA'RVATI'.

VERSE XXIII. it obstinately bore him no fruit). The original stanza is uncommonly obscure: it begins with the words *yáirbabhúva*, the two first syllables of which certainly mean *a womb*; but several *Pandits*, who were consulted apart, are of opinion, that *yé* is the relative, of which some word in the masculine gender, signifying *speech*, is the antecedent, though not expressed: they explain the whole stanza thus—" *That speech*, which came " forth (*nirbabhúva*) inconsiderately, of which *there was* " no fruit, *he was a man* who spoke nothing of that kind " for his own gratification: *he was a man* also, by whom " *no present*-of-playthings was ever *given*, which the sup- " pliant having received goes to another *more beautiful* " giver." If the relative had been *yen* in the *neuter* gender, I should have acquiesced in the translation offered by the *Pandits*; but the suppression of so material a word as *speech*, which, indeed, is commonly *feminine* in *Sanscrit*, appears unwarrantably harsh according to *European* ideas of construction.

VERSE XXVI. If the preceding interpretation be just, the object of the Pillar was to perpetuate the names of GURAVA MIS'RA and his ancestors; and this verse must imply, that *he expected to receive from his own sons the pious offices which he had performed to his forefathers.*

A

DESCRIPTION

OF A

CAVE NEAR GYA'.

BY JOHN HERBERT HARRINGTON, ESQ.

A KNOWLEDGE of the antiquities of *Hindoſtan* forming one of the several objects proposed by the institution of our Society, with the hope of communicating something acceptable on this head, I took the opportunity of a late excursion up the country to see the *Cave* which Mr. HODGKIS a few years since attempted to visit, at the desire, I believe, of the late Governor-General, but was assassinated in his way to it by the followers of one of the rebellious Allies of CHYT SING. On my describing it to the President, whom I had the pleasure to accompany, I was encouraged by him to think that a particular account of it would be curious and useful; and in consequence made a second visit to it from *Gyá*, when I

took

took the following measurements, and, by the means of my *Moonshee*, a copy of the Inscription on it, which I had despaired of presenting to you, but in its original language (a *Pandit* at *Benáres* having attempted in vain to get it read, during these last three months), till the kind assistance of Mr. WILKINS enabled me to add the accompanying translation and remarks to what would otherwise have given little satisfaction.

The hill, or rather rock, from which the cavern is dug, lies about fourteen miles North of the ancient city of *Gyâ*, and seems to be one of the south eastern hills of the chain of mountains called by RENNEL *Caramnshab*, both being a short distance to the west of the *Pónzá*.

It is now distinguished by the name of *Nágarjunee*; but this may perhaps be a modern appellation; no mention of it being made in the Inscription. Its texture is a kind of Granite, called by the MOHUMMEDAN natives *Sung Kháreb*, which composes the whole rock, of a moderate height, very craggy and uneven, and steep in its ascent.

The *Cave* is situated on the southern declivity, about two thirds from the summit: a tree immediately before it prevents its being seen from the bottom. It has only one narrow entrance, from the south, two feet and a half in breadth, six feet high, and of thickness exactly equal. This leads to a room of an oval form, with a vaulted roof, which I measured twice, and found to be forty-four feet in length from east to west, eighteen feet and an half in breadth, and ten feet and a quarter in height at the centre. This immense cavity is dug entirely out of the solid rock, and is exceedingly well polished, but without any ornament. The same stone extends much farther than the excavated part, on each side of it, and is altogether, I imagine, full a hundred feet in length. The inhabitants near know nothing of its history or age, but I learnt from the Chief of a neighbouring village, that a tradition is extant of a MOHUMMEDAN, named MINHA'J-U-DEEN, having performed his *Cheeleh*, or forty days devotion, in this cavern; and that he was cotemporary with MUKHDOOM SHERF-U-DEEN, a venerable *Welee*, who died in *Behár* in the 500th year of the *Hijree*; and he even went so far as to aver that he himself was descended from MINHA'J-U-DEEN, and had records at *Patna* of his family's genealogy to the present time. What credit is due to this I will not pretend to say; but the room is certainly now frequented by MOHUMMEDANS, and has been for some time, as there are the remains of an old mosque close before it, and within a raised terrace, such as the MOHUMMEDAN devotees are used to construct for their religious retirement. There are two Inscriptions, one on each side of the interior part of the entrance: the impressions of both which my *Moonshee* took off in the course of three days, with much trouble, and sufficient accuracy to enable Mr. WILKINS to understand and explain the whole of one, though many *Pandits*, I was informed, who had seen the original engraving, had attempted in vain to decypher it. The other, which consists of one line only, is unfortunately of a different character, and remains still unintelligible.

THE following letter and remarks, which Mr. WILKINS has favoured me with, make it unnecessary for me to say any thing of the contents of the Inscription: I can only regret with him that the date is yet undiscovered; as what is now but a gratification of curiosity might then have been a valuable clue to the illustration of obscure events in ancient history. There are, however, several other *Caves* in the adjoining hills, which I likewise visited, but had not time to take the Inscriptions: and from these, I hope a date will be discovered.

WERE any other testimony besides the Inscription wanted to shew that these Caves were religious temples, the remains of three defaced images near another which I visited, called

*Curram*

*Curram Choffar*, would be sufficient proof of it. A third, the name of which I could not learn, has its entrance very curiously wrought with Elephants and other ornaments, of which, I hope, in a short time to present a drawing to the Society.

---

A
LETTER
FROM
CHARLES WILKINS, ESQ.
TO THE SECRETARY.

DEAR SIR,

HAVING been so fortunate as to make out the whole of the very curious Inscription you were so obliging as to lend me, I herewith return it, and also a copy of my translation, which is as literal as the idioms would admit it to be.

The first lines of the first verse allude to the story of *Bhimasen*'s killing the evil spirit *Mabeshasoor*, who in the disguise of a Buffalo, as the name imports, had fought with *Eendra*, and his celestial bands, for a hundred years, defeated him, and usurped his throne. The story is

is to be found at large in a little book called *Chandee*. The vanquished spirits, being banished the Heavens and doomed to wander the Earth, after a while assemble, with their Chief *Eendra* at their head, and resolve to lay their grievances before *Veeshnoo* and *Seev*. Conducted by *Brahma*, they repair into the presence of those Deities, who heard their complaints with compassion; and their anger was so violent against *Maheeshasoor*, that a kind of flame issued from their mouths, and from the mouths of the rest of the principal Gods, of which was formed a Goddess of inexpressible beauty with ten arms, and each hand holding a different weapon. This was a transfiguration of *Bhawanee* the consort of *Seev*, under which she is generally called *Doorga*. She is sent against the usurper. She mounts her lion, the gift of the mountain *Heemalay* (snowy), and attacks the Monster, who shifts his form repeatedly; till at length the Goddess *planteth her foot upon his head*, and cuts it off with a single stroke of her sword. Immediately the upper part of a human body issues through the neck of the headless Buffalo and aims a stroke, which being warded off by the lion with his right paw, *Doorga* puts an end to the combat by piercing him through the heart with a spear. I have in my possession a statue of the Goddess with one
foot

foot on her lion, and the other on the Monster, in the attitude here lastly described.

The want of a date disappointed my expectations. I had some hopes that it was contained in the single line, which you informed me was taken from another part of the *Cave*; but, although I have not yet succeeded in making out the whole, I have discovered enough to convince me that it contains nothing but an invocation. If you should be so fortunate as to obtain correct copies of the rest of the Inscriptions that are to be found in the *Caves* of those mountains, I make no doubt but that we shall meet with some circumstance or other, that will guide us to a discovery of their antiquity.

I have the pleasure to subscribe myself,

DEAR SIR,

Your very sincere friend,
And obedient humble servant,
CHARLES WILKINS.

*Calcutta*, 17th *March* 1785.

[ 531 ]

A

TRANSLATION

OF A

SANSCRIPT INSCRIPTION,

WHEN the foot of the Goddess * was, with its tinkling ornaments, planted upon the head of *Maheeshasoor* †, all the bloom of the new-blown flower of the fountain ‡ was dispersed with disgrace, by its superior beauty. May that foot, radiant with a fringe of refulgent beams issuing from its pure bright nails, endue you with a steady and an unexampled devotion, offered up with fruits, and shew you the way to dignity and wealth!

The illustrious *Yagna Varma* was a Prince whose greatness consisted in free-will offerings. His reputation was as unsullied as the Moon. He was renowned amongst the Martial Tribes; and although he was, by descent, by wisdom,

* *Bhawanee*, the wife of *Seev*.
† The name of an Evil Spirit.
‡ Epithet of the Lotus.

courage,

courage, charity, and other qualities, the fore-leader of the royal line; yet, from the natural humility of his temper, he disturbed not the powerful ocean.

His auspicious son, *Sardoola Varma*, a Prince whose magnificence flowed, as it were, from the tree of imagination \*, displayed the ensign of royalty in sacrifices, and the world was subdued by his infinite renown. He gratified the hopes of relations, friends, and dependants; and honour was achieved from the deed of death † near the uprising ocean.

By his pious son, called *Ananta Varma* because of his infinite renown, the holy abode of us contemplative men, who are always studious for his good and employed in his service, hath been increased and rendered famous as long as the earth, the sun and moon, and starry heaven shall endure; and *Katayanee* ‡ having taken sanctuary, and being placed, in this cavern of the wonderful *Veendya* § mountains,

The holy Prince gave unto *Bhavianee*, in perpetuity, the village ———— ‖ and its hilly

\* In the original *Kalpa-taru*, a fabulous tree which yielded every thing that was demanded.

† He was probably carried to *Ganga-Sagar* to die.

‡ One of the names of *Durga* or *Bowanee*.

§ The name of the chain of mountains which commences at *Chunar*.

‖ The name, which consisted of two long syllables, is wanting in the original.

lands,

lands, by whose lofty mountain-tops the sunny beams are cast in shade; its filth and impurities are washed away by the precious stores of the *Mahanada* \*, and it is refreshed by the breezes from the waving *Preeyangoos* † and *Bakoolas* ‡ of its groves.

\* Probably the river called the *Mahanab* in RENNEL's Map of South *Bahar*.
† Probably the *Champa*.
‡ *Moulsree*.

TWO

# TWO INSCRIPTIONS

## FROM THE

# VINDHYA MOUNTAINS,

TRANSLATED FROM THE SANSCRIT,

BY CHARLES WILKINS, ESQ.

---

FIRST INSCRIPTION, IN A CAVERN, CALLED THE GROT OF THE SEVEN RISHI's' NEAR GAYA.

1. ANANTA VARMA, master of the hearts of the people, who was the good son of *Sree* SARDOOLA, by his own birth and great virtues classed amongst the principal rulers of the earth, gladly caused this statue of KREESHNA of unsullied renown, confirmed in the world like his own reputation, and the image of KANTEEMATEE * to be deposited in this great mountain-cave.

2. SREE SARDOOLA, of established fame, jewel of the diadems of kings, emblem of time to the martial possessors of the earth, to the sub-

* RADHA, the favourite Mistress of KREESHNA.

missive

missive the tree of the fruit of desire, a light to the Military Order, whose glory was not founded upon the feats of a single battle, the ravisher of female hearts, and the image of SMARA * became the ruler of the land.

3. WHEREVER *Sree* SARDOOLA is wont to cast his own discordant sight towards a foe, and the fortunate star, his broad eye, is enflamed with anger between its expanded lids, *there* falleth a shower of arrows from the ear-drawn string of the bow of his son, the renowned ANANTA VARMA, the bestower of infinite happiness.

---

SECOND INSCRIPTION, IN A CAVE BEHIND NAGARJENI.

1. THE auspicious *Sree* YAJNA VARMA, whose movement was as the sportive elephants in the season of lust, was, like MANOO †, the appointer of the military station of all the chiefs of the earth.—By whose divine offerings, the GOD with a thousand eyes ‡ being constantly invited, the emaciated *Powloma* §, for

---

* KAMA DEVA the *Cupid* of the *Hindus*.
† The first legislator of the *Hindus*.
‡ *Eendra*, a deification of the Heavens.
§ The wife of *Eendra*.

a long

a long time fullied the beauty of her cheeks with falling tears.

2. ANANTA VARMA by name, the friend of strangers; renowned in the world in the character of valour; by nature immaculate as the lunar beams, and who is the offspring of *Sree* SARDOOLA:—By him this wonderful statue of BHOOTAPATEE and of DEVEE*, the maker of all things visible and invisible, and the granter of boons, which hath taken sanctuary in this cave, was caused to be made. May it protect the universe!

3. THE string of his expanded bow, charged with arrows, and drawn to the extremity of the shoulder, bursteth the circle's centre. Of spacious brow, propitious distinction, and surpassing beauty, he is the image of the moon with an undiminished countenance. ANANTA VARMA to tho end! Of form like SMARA † in existence, he is seen with the constant and affectionate standing with their tender and fascinated eyes constantly fixed upon him.

4. FROM the machine his bow, reproacher of the crying *Koorara* ‡, bent to the extreme, he is endued with force; from his expanded

* *Seeva*, or *Mahadeva*, and his consort in one image, as a type of the deities, *Genitor* and *Genitrix*.
† The *Hindoo Cupid*.
‡ A bird that is constantly making a noise before rain.

virtue

virtue he is a provoker; by his good conduct his renown reacheth to afar; he is a hero by whose coursing steeds the elephant is disturbed, and a youth who is the seat of sorrow to the women of his foes. He is the director, and his name is ANANTA *.

* This word signifies Eternal or Infinite.

[ 338 ]

# THE
## TRANSLATION OF AN INSCRIPTION
### IN THE
## MAGA LANGUAGE,
ENGRAVED ON A SILVER PLATE FOUND IN A CAVE NEAR ISLA'MABA'D.

COMMUNICATED BY JOHN SHORE, ESQ.

---

ON the 14th of *Mágha* 904, *Chándi Láh Rája* \*, by the advice of *Bowangari Rauli*, who was the director of his studies and devotions, and in conformity to the sentiments of twenty-eight other *Raulis*, formed the design of establishing a place of religious worship; for which purpose a cave was dug, and paved with bricks, three cubits in depth, and three cubits also in diameter, in which were deposited one hundred and twenty brazen images of small dimensions, denominated *Tabmúdas*; also, twenty brazen images larger than the former, denominated *Lángúda*; there was likewise a large image of stone called *Lingudagári*,

\* Perhaps, *Sándilyah*.

with

with a vessel of brass in which were deposited two of the bones of T*hākur*: on a silver plate were inscribed the *Hawca*, or the mandates of the Deity; with that also styled *Tasmah Chuckforma Tahma*, to the study of which twenty-eight *Raulis* devote their time and attention; who, having celebrated the present work of devotion with festivals and rejoicings, erected over the cave a place of religious worship for the *Magas* in honour of the Deity.

God sent into the world Buddha Avatá'r to instruct and direct the steps of angels and of men; of whose birth and origin the following is a relation: When Buddha Avatá'r descended from the region of souls in the month of *Mágh*, and entered the body of Mahá'mà'yá', the wife of Sootah Dannah, *Rájá* of *Cailàs*, her womb suddenly assumed the appearance of clear transparent crystal, in which Buddha appeared, beautiful as a flower, kneeling and reclining on his hands. After ten months and ten days of her pregnancy had elapsed, Mahá'má'yá' solicited permission from her husband the *Rájá* to visit her father, in conformity to which the roads were directed to be repaired and made clear for her journey; fruit-trees were planted; water-vessels placed on the road-side; and great illuminations prepared for the occasion. Mahá'má'yá' then
commenced

commenced her journey, and arrived at a garden adjoining to the road, where inclination led her to walk and gather flowers: at this time, being fuddenly attacked with the pains of childbirth, fhe laid hold on the trees for fupport, which declined their boughs at the inftant, for the purpofe of concealing her perfon, while fhe was delivered of the child; at which juncture BRAHMA' himfelf attended with a golden veffel in his hand, on which he laid the child, and delivered it to INDRA, by whom it was committed to the charge of a female attendant; upon which the child alighting from her arms, walked feven paces, whence it was taken up by MAHA'MA'YA' and carried to her houfe; and on the enfuing morning news were circulated of a child being born in the *Rájá*'s family. At this time TAPASWI *Muni*, who, refiding in the woods, devoted his time to the worfhip of the Deity, learned by infpiration that BUDDHA was come to life in the *Rájá*'s palace: he flew through the air to the *Rájá*'s refidence, where, fitting on a throne, he faid, " I have repaired " hither for the purpofe of vifiting the child." BUDDHA was accordingly brought into his prefence: the *Muni* obferved two feet fixed on his head, and, divining fomething both of good and bad import, began to weep and to laugh alternately. The *Rájá* then queftioned him with

regard

regard to his present impulse, to whom he answered, "I must not reside in the same place with BUDDHA, when he shall arrive at the rank of *Avatàr*: this is the cause of my present affliction, but I am even now affected with gladness by his presence, as I am hereby absolved from all my transgressions." The *Muni* then departed; and, after five days had elapsed, he assembled four *Pandits* for the purpose of calculating the destiny of the child; three of whom divined, that as he had marks on his hands resembling a wheel, he would at length become a *Rájà Chacravertì*; another divined, that he would arrive at the dignity of *Avatàr*.

THE boy was now named SA'CYA, and had attained the age of sixteen years; at which period it happened, that the *Rájà* CHUHIDAN had a daughter named VASUTA'RA', whom he had engaged not to give in marriage to any one till such time as a suitor should be found who could brace a certain bow in his possession, which hitherto many *Rájà*'s had attempted to accomplish without effect. SA'CYA now succeeded in the attempt, and accordingly obtained the *Rájà*'s daughter in marriage, with whom he repaired to his own place of residence.

ONE day, as certain mysteries were revealed to him, he formed the design of relinquishing

his

his dominion; at which time a son was born in his house whose name was RAGHU. SA'CYA then left his palace with only one attendant and a horse, and, having crossed the river GANGA', arrived at *Balichli*, where, having directed his servant to leave him and carry away his horse, he laid aside his armour.

WHEN the world was created, there appeared five flowers, which BRAHMA' deposited in a place of safety: three of them were afterwards delivered to the three S'ikhers, and one was presented to SA'CYA, who discovered, that it contained some pieces of wearing apparel, in which he clothed himself, and adopted the manners and life of a mendicant. A traveller one day passed by him with eight bundles of grass on his shoulders, and addressing him, saying: "A long period of time has elapsed since "I have seen the *T'hécur*; but now since I "have the happiness to meet him, I beg to pre- "sent him an offering consisting of these bundles "of grass." SA'CYA accordingly accepted of the grass, and reposed on it. At that time there suddenly appeared a golden temple containing a chair of wrought gold, and the height of the temple was thirty cubits, upon which BRAHMA' alighted, and held a canopy over the head of SA'CYA: at the same time INDRA descended with a large fan in his hand, and NA'GA,

the

the *Rájá* of serpents, with shoes in his hand, together with the four tutelar deities of the four corners of the universe; who all attended to do him service and reverence. At this time likewise the chief of *Asurs* with his forces arrived, riding on an elephant, to give battle to SA'CYA, upon which BRAHMA', INDRA, and the other deities, deserted him and vanished. SA'CYA, observing that he was left alone, invoked the assistance of the Earth; who, attending at his summons, brought an inundation over all the ground, whereby the *Asur* and his forces were vanquished, and compelled to retire.

AT this time five holy scriptures descended from above, and SA'CYA was dignified with the title of BUDDHA *Avatár*. The scriptures confer powers of knowledge and retrospection, the ability of accomplishing the impulses of the heart, and of carrying into effect the words of the mouth. SA'CYA resided here, without breaking his fast, twenty-one days, and then returned to his own country, where he presides over *Rájá's*, governing them with care and equity.

WHOEVER reads the *Ciric*, his body, apparel, and the place of his devotions, must be purified; he shall be thereby delivered from the evil machinations of demons and of his enemies; and the ways of redemption shall be open to him. BUDDHA *Avatár* instructed a certain *Rauli* by name ANGULI MA'LA in the writings of the *Cáric*, saying, " Whoever shall read and study " them, his soul shall not undergo a transmi- " gration," and the scriptures were thence called *Anguli Málá*. There were likewise five other books of the *Cáric* denominated *Vachanam*, which if one peruse, he shall thereby be exempted from poverty and the machinations of his enemies; he shall also be exalted to dignity and honours, and the length of his days shall be protracted: the study of the *Cáric* heals afflictions and pains of the body, and whoever shall have faith therein, heaven and bliss shall be the reward of his piety.

# APPENDIX;

### CONTAINING

A HYMN TO CAMDEO. By SIR WILLIAM JONES.

A HYMN TO NARAYENA. BY THE SAME.

AN ACCOUNT OF EMBASSIES AND LETTERS BETWEEN THE EMPEROR OF CHINA, AND SULTAN SHAHROKH. TRANSLATED BY SIR WILLIAM CHAMBERS.

A SHORT ACCOUNT OF THE MARRATTA STATE, THE PRODUCTIONS AND PECULIARITIES OF THE COUNTRY; AND OF THE CUSTOMS AND MANNERS OF THE MARRATTAS. BY THE SAME:

### SELECTED FROM THE

*ASIATIC MISCELLANY.*

# APPENDIX.

## A HYMN TO CAMDEO.

### BY SIR WILLIAM JONES.

#### THE ARGUMENT.

THE *Hindú* God to whom the following poem is addressed, appears evidently the same with the *Grecian* EROS and the *Roman* CUPIDO; but the *Indian* description of his person and arms, his family, attendants, and attributes, has new and peculiar beauties.

ACCORDING to the mythology of *Hindustán*, he was the son of MAYA, or the general *attracting power*, and married to RETTY or *Affection*; and his bosom friend is BESSENT or *Spring*: he is represented as a beautiful youth, sometimes conversing with his mother and consort in the midst of his gardens and temples; sometimes riding by moon-light on a parrot or lory, and attended by dancing-girls or nymphs, the foremost of whom bears his colours, which are a *fish* on a red ground. His favourite place of resort is a large tract of country round AGRA, and principally the plains of *Matra*, where KRISHEN also and the nine GOPIA, who are clearly the *Apollo* and *Muses* of the *Greeks*, usually spend the night with musick and dance. His bow of sugar-cane or flowers, with a string of bees, and his five arrows, each pointed with an *Indian* blossom of a heating quality, are allegories equally new and beautiful. He has at least twenty-three names, most of which are introduced in the Hymn: that of *Cám* or *Cáma* signifies *desire*, a sense which it also bears in ancient and modern *Persian*; and it is possible, that the words *Dipuc* and *Cupid*, which have the same signification,

## A HYMN TO CAMDEO.

signification, may have the same origin; since we know that the old Etrurians, from whom great part of the Roman language and religion was derived, and whose system had a near affinity with that of the Persians and Indians, used to write their lines alternately forwards and backwards, as furrows are made by the plough; and though the two last letters of *Cupido* may be only the grammatical termination, as in *libido* and *cupiedo*, yet the primary root of *cupio* is contained in the three first letters. The seventh stanza alludes to the bold attempt of this deity to wound the great God *Mahadeo*, for which he was punished by a flame consuming his corporeal nature and reducing him to a mental essence; and hence his chief dominion is over the minds of mortals, or such deities as he is permitted to subdue.

WHAT potent God from AGRA's orient bow'rs
  Floats through the lucid air, whilst living flow'rs
With sunny twine the vocal arbours wreathe,
And gales enamour'd heav'nly fragrance breathe?
  Hail pow'r unknown! for at thy back
  Vales and groves their bosoms deck,
  And ev'ry laughing blossom dresses
  With gems of dew his musky tresses.
I feel, I feel thy genial flame divine,
And hallow thee and kiss thy shrine.

" Know'st thou not me?" Celestial sounds I hear!
" Know'st thou not me?" Ah, spare a mortal ear!
" Behold"—My swimming eyes entranc'd I raise,
But oh! they shrink before th' excessive blaze.
  Yes, son of MAYA, yes, I know
  Thy bloomy shafts and easy bow,
  Cheeks with youthful glory beaming,
  Locks in braids ethereal streaming,
Thy scaly standard, thy mysterious arms,
And all thy pains and all thy charms.

God

## A HYMN TO CAMDEO

God of each lovely sight, each lovely sound,
Soul-kindling, world-inflaming, starry-crown'd,
Eternal CAMA! Or doth SMARA bright,
Or proud ANANGA give thee more delight?
    Whate'er thy seat, whate'er thy name,
    Seas, earth, and air thy reign proclaim:
    Wreathy smiles and roseate pleasures
    Are thy richest, sweetest treasures.
All animals to thee their tribute bring,
And hail thee universal king.

Thy consort mild, AFFECTION ever true,
Graces thy side, her veil of glowing hue,
And in her train twelve blooming girls advance,
Touch golden strings and knit the mirthful dance.
    Thy dreadful implements they bear,
    And wave them in the frantic air,
    Each with pearls her neck adorning,
    Brighter than the tears of morning.
Thy crimson ensign, which before them flies,
Decks with new stars the sapphire skies.

God of the flow'ry shafts and flow'ry bow,
Delight of all above and all below!
Thy lov'd companion, constant from his birth,
In heav'n clep'd BESSENT, and gay SPRING on earth,
    Weaves thy green robe and flaunting bow'rs,
    And from thy clouds draws balmy show'rs,
    He with fresh arrows fills thy quiver
    (Sweet the gift and sweet the giver).
And bids the many-plum'd warbling throng
Burst the pent blossoms with their song.

He bends the luscious cane, and twists the string
With bees how sweet! but ah, how keen their sting!
He with five flow'rets tips thy ruthless darts,
Which through five senses pierce enraptur'd hearts:

                                  Strong

Strong CHUMPA, rich in od'rous gold,
Warm AMER, nurs'd in heav'nly mould,
Dry NAGKESER in silver smiling,
Hot KITICUM our sense beguiling,
And last, to kindle fierce the scorching flame,
LOVESHAFT, which Gods bright BELA name.

Can men resist thy pow'r, when KRISHEN yields,
KRISHEN, who still in MATRA's holy fields
Tunes harps immortal, and to strains divine
Dances by moon-light with the GOPIA nine?
But, when thy daring arm untam'd
At MAHADEO a love-shaft aim'd,
Heav'n shook; earth sunk with flowy wonder,
Told his deep dread in bursts of thunder;
Whilst on thy beauteous limbs an azure fire
Blaz'd forth, which never must expire.

O thou for ages born, yet ever young,
For ages may thy BRAMIN's lay be sung!
And when thy Lory spreads his em'rald wings
To waft thee high above the tow'r of Kings,
  Whilst o'er thy throne the moon's pale light
  Pours her soft radiance through the night,
  And to each floating cloud discovers
  The haunts of blest or joyless lovers,
Thy mildest influence to thy Bard impart,
To warm, but not consume his heart.

A HYMN

# A HYMN TO NARAYENA;

## BY SIR WILLIAM JONES.

### THE ARGUMENT.

A COMPLETE introduction to the following Ode would be no less than a full comment on the VAYDS and PURANS of the HINDUS, the remains of *Egyptian* and *Persian* theology, and the tenets of the *Ionick* and *Italick* schools; but this is not the place for so vast a disquisition. It will be sufficient here to premise, that the inextricable difficulty attending the *vulgar notion of material substances*, concerning which

"We know this only, that we nothing know,"

induced many of the wisest among the ancients, and some of the most enlightened among the moderns, to believe, that the whole Creation was rather an *energy* than a *work*, by which the Infinite Being who is present at all times and in all places, exhibits to the minds of his creatures a set of perceptions, like a wonderful picture or piece of musick, always varied, yet always uniform; so that all bodies and their qualities exist, indeed, to every wise and useful purpose, but exist only as far as they are *perceived*; a theory no less pious than sublime, and as different from any principle of Atheism, as the brightest sunshine differs from the blackest midnight. This illusive operation of the Deity the *Hindu* Philosophers call MAYA, or *Deception*; and the word occurs in this sense more than once in the commentary on the *Rig Veda*, by the great VASISHTHA, of which Mr. HALHED has given us an admirable Specimen.

THE *first* stanza of the Hymn represents the sublimest attributes of the Supreme Being, and the three forms in which they most clearly appear to us, *Power*, *Wisdom*, and *Goodness*, or, in the language of ORPHEUS and his disciples, *Love*. THE *second* comprises the *Indian* and *Egyptian* doctrine of the Divine Essence and Archetypal Ideas; for a distinct account of which the reader must be referred to a noble description

description in the Sixth Book of PLATO's *Republick*; and the fine explanation of that passage in an elegant discourse by the Author of CYRUS, from whose learned work a hint has been borrowed for the conclusion of this piece. The *third* and *fourth* are taken from the Institutes of MENU, and the eighteenth *Parva* of VYASA, entitled *Srey Bhagawat*, part of which has been translated into *Persian*, not without elegance, but rather too paraphrastically. From BRAHME, or the Great Being, in the *neuter* gender, is formed BRAHMA, in the *masculine*; and the second word is appropriated to the Creative Power of the Divinity.

THE Spirit of God, called NARAYENA, or *Moving on the Water*, has a multiplicity of other epithets in *Sanscrit*, the principal of which are introduced, expressly or by allusion, in the *fifth* stanza; and two of them contain the names of the Evil Beings who are feigned to have sprung from the ears of VISHNU; for thus the Divine Spirit is intitled, when considered as the Preserving Power; the *earth* ascribes the perception of *secondary qualities* by our *senses* to the immediate influence of *Maya*, with the *Powers* [illegible] the *primary* qualities of Extension and Solidity.

## THE HYMN.

SPIRIT of Spirits, who, through ev'ry part
 Of space expanded and of endless time,
 Beyond the stretch of lab'ring thought sublime,
 Bad'st uproar into beauteous order start,
  Before Heaven was, Thou art:
Ere spheres beneath us roll'd or spheres above,
 Ere earth in firmamental ether hung,
 Thou sat'st alone; till, through thy myſtick Love,
 Things unexiſting to exiſtence ſprung,
  And grateful deſcant ſung.
What firſt impell'd thee to exert thy might?
 Goodneſs unlimited. What glorious light
 Thy pow'r directed? Wiſdom without bound.
 What prov'd it firſt? Oh! guide my fancy right;
  Oh! raiſe from cumbrous ground
  My ſoul in rapture drown'd,

That

That fearless it may soar on wings of fire;
For Thou, who only know'st, Thou only canst inspire.

Wrapt in eternal solitary shade,
 Th' impenetrable gloom of light intense,
 Impervious, inaccessible, immense,
Ere spirits were infus'd or forms display'd,
BREHM his own mind survey'd,
As mortal eyes (thus finite we compare
 With infinite) in smoothest mirrors gaze:
 Swift, at his look, a shape supremely fair
Leap'd into being with a boundless blaze,
 That fifty suns might daze.
Primeval, MAYA was the Goddess nam'd,
 Who to her sire, with Love divine inflam'd,
 A casket gave with rich Ideas fill'd,
From which this gorgeous Universe he fram'd;
 For, when th' Almighty will'd
 Unnumber'd worlds to build,
From Unity diversified he sprang,
While gay Creation laugh'd, and procreant Nature rang.

First an all-potent all-pervading sound
 Bade flow the waters—and the waters flow'd,
 Exulting in their measureless abode,
 Diffusive, multitudinous, profound,
 Above, beneath, around:
Then o'er the vast expanse primordial wind
 Breath'd gently till a lucid bubble rose,
 Which grew in perfect shape an Egg refin'd:
 Created substance no such lustre shows,
 Earth no such beauty knows.
Above the warring waves it danc'd elate,
 Till from its bursting shell with lovely state
 A form cærulean flutter'd o'er the deep,
 Brightest of beings, greatest of the great:

VOL. II.            A a            Who

  Who not as mortals sleep
  Their eyes in dewy sleep,
 But heav'nly-pensive on the Lotos lay,
That blossom'd at his touch and shed a golden ray.

Hail, primal blossom! hail empyreal gem!
 KEMEL, or PEDMA, or whate'er high name
 Delight thee, say, what four-form'd Godhead came,
  With graceful stole and beamy diadem,
   Forth from thy verdant stem?
Full-gifted BRAHMA! Rapt in solemn thought
 He stood, and round his eyes fire-darting threw:
 But, whilst his viewless origin he sought,
 One plain he saw of living waters blue,
  Their spring nor saw nor knew.
Then, in his parent stalk again retir'd,
 With restless pain for ages he inquir'd
 What were his pow'rs, by whom, and why conferr'd:
With doubts perplex'd, with keen impatience fir'd,
  He rose, and rising heard
  Th' unknown all-knowing Word,
 "BRAHMA! no more in vain research persist:
"My veil thou canst not move—Go; bid all worlds exist."

Hail, self-existent, in celestial speech
 NARAYEN, from thy watry cradle, nam'd:
Or VENAMALY may I sing unblam'd,
 With flow'ry braids, that to thy sandals reach,
  Whose beauties who can teach?
Or high PEITAMBER clad in yellow robes
 Than sun-beams brighter in meridian glow,
That weave their heav'n-spun light o'er circling globes?
Unwearied, lotos-eyed, with dreadful bow,
  Dire Evil's constant foe!
Great PEDMANABHA, o'er thy cherish'd world
 The pointed Chacra, by thy fingers whirl'd,

          Fierce

Fierce KYTABH shall destroy and MEDHU grim,
  To black despair and deep destruction hurl'd.
    Such views my senses dim,
    My eyes in darkness swim:
  What eye can bear thy blaze, what utt'rance tell
Thy deeds with silver trump or many-wreathed shell!

Omniscient Spirit, whose all-ruling pow'r
  Bids from each sense bright emanations beam;
  Glows in the rainbow, sparkles in the stream,
  Smiles in the bud, and glistens in the flow'r
    That crowns each vernal bow'r,
Sighs in the gale, and warbles in the throat
  Of ev'ry bird that hails the bloomy spring,
  Or tells his love in many a liquid note,
  Whilst envious artists touch the rival string,
    Till rocks and forests ring;
Breathes in rich fragrance from the sandal grove,
  Or where the precious musk-deer playful rove:
  In dulcet juice from clust'ring fruit distills,
  And burns salubrious in the tasteful clove:
    Soft banks and verd'rous hills
    Thy present influence fills;
In air, in floods, in caverns, woods, and plains,
Thy will inspirits all, thy sov'reign MAYA reigns.

Blue crystal vault, and elemental fires,
  That in th' ethereal fluid blaze and breathe;
  Thou, tossing main, whose snaky branches wreathe
  This pensile orb with intertwisting gyres;
    Mountains, whose radiant spires
Presumptuous rear their summits to the skies,
  And blend their emerald hue with sapphire light;
  Smooth meads and lawns, that glow with varying dyes
  Of dew-bespangled leaves and blossoms bright,
    Hence! vanish from my sight:

Delusive pictures! unsubstantial shows!
  My soul absorb'd One only Being knows,
  Of all perceptions One abundant source,
  Whence ev'ry object ev'ry moment flows:
    Suns hence derive their force,
    Hence planets learn their course;
  But suns and fading worlds I view no more:
God only I perceive; God only I adore.

# AN ACCOUNT OF EMBASSIES AND LETTERS

THAT PASSED BETWEEN THE EMPEROR OF CHINA AND SULTAN SHAHROKH, SON OF AMIR TIMUR.

EXTRACTED FROM THE MATLA US SADEIN OF ABDUR REZAK,

AND TRANSLATED BY

WILLIAM CHAMBERS, ESQ.*

---

## THE TRANSLATOR's PREFACE.

THE ensuing Extracts are made from a work which is not entirely unknown in Europe. M. D'HERBELOT makes particular mention of it under the article *Schahrokh*, and expresses a hope of seeing it one day translated by M. GALLAND; but no such translation has ever appeared. The following account taken from the HABIB US SIER of *Khondemir*, shows in what degree of esteem the Author and his work have been held in *Asia*.

" KAMAL UD DIN ABDUL REZAK was a son of JELAL UD
" DIN ISHAK of *Samarcand*, and was born at *Herat* on
" the 12th of *Shaban* 816 or (6th November, A. D. 1413).
" His father ISHAK resided at the court of Sultan SHAH-
" ROKH, in quality of Kazy and Imam, and was some-

* Now SIR WILLIAM CHAMBERS.

times

"times confulted on points of law, and defired to read
"*learned* * treatifes in his Majefty's prefence. ABDUR
"REZAK, after his father's death, in the year 841
"(A. D. 1437), wrote a comment on AZD UD DIN
"YAHIA's Treatife of *Arabic* prepofitions and pronouns,
"and dedicated it to Sultan Shahrokh; on occafion of
"which he had the honour to kifs his Majefty's hand. In
"the latter part of that prince's reign, he went as his
"ambaffador to the King of *Bijanagur* (*Vifapour*), and
"experienced various extraordinary incidents and viciffi-
"tudes on that journey; but at length returned to *Khora-*
"*fan* in fafety. After the death of Sultan SHAHROKH,
"he was fuccefsively admitted to the prefence of MIRZA
"ABDUL LATIF, MIRZA ABDULLAH, and MIRZA
"ABUL KASIM; and in the firft *Jumad* of 877 (or Oc-
"tober 1472), under the reign of Sultan ABU SAID, he
"was appointed Superintendant of the *Khankah* of
"MIRZA SHAHROKH, where he continued to the time
"of his death, which happened in the latter *Jumad* of the
"year 877 (anfwering to part of *July* and *Auguft* 1482).
"AMONG the excellent productions of his pen is that ufeful
"work the *Matla us Sadein*, which is in every one's
"hand, and is univerfally known, where he has given a
"general hiftory of events from the time of Sultan ABU
"SAID BAHADAR KHAN, down to the affaffination of
"MIRZA SULTAN ABU SAID GURKAN."

ABU SAID BAHADAR KHAN was the ninth in fucceffion from CHENGEZ KHAN, of thofe that reigned over *Perfia* at large. His death happened in the year of the *Hijerah* 736, or A. D. 1335; and MIRZA SULTAN ABU SAID GURKAN was killed in the *Hijerah* year 873, or A. D. 1468: fo that this hiftory takes in a period of more than 130 folar years, of which the laft fifty were in the life-time of the author. And as his father held an eminent

* This word, and others thus diftinguifhed in the following Extracts, are fuch as are fupplied but not expreffed in the Original.

ftation

station at court before him; it is plain he had the best means of information respecting events for several years preceding; which gives sufficient weight to what he says on the subject of these Embassies. This testimony is also confirmed by that of a cotemporary writer, SHERF UD DIN ALY YEZDY, who, in his *Supplement to the Zaffer-Namah* \*, mentions most of these Embassies, and gives us all the Letters, except the first from the Emperor of China, which, as it assumes a stile of superiority that could not be agreeable to SHAHROKH MIRZA, SHERF UD DIN, who wrote his book under the auspices of that Prince, and dedicated it to him, might have his reasons for omitting.

BUT, apart from the authenticity of the history, the Letters themselves seem to have strong marks of being genuine, both in the matter they contain, and in the stile in which they are written. Of the first every one may form his opinion; the latter must be submitted to the judgment of those who peruse them in the original language. They will perceive, that while those from Sultan SHAHROKH are penned with that purity and propriety of diction which might be expected from a *Persian* Monarch, those from the Emperor of *China* are expressed in such quaint and awkward terms, as might be supposed to come from a *Mogul* Interpreter translating each word of a *Chinese* letter at the peril of his life. But the simplicity and unaffected brevity of the *Chinese* original, seems to have been such as could not suffer any material injury from a servile translation, and much of the national character is visible in these productions.

IT may be proper to mention here, who the two monarchs were that carried on this correspondence.

SULTAN SHAHROKH, or, as he is commonly called by the historians, SHAHROKH MIRZA, was the fourth son of the famous TIMUR, and youngest of the two that sur-

\* A work of which Monſ. de la Croix translated a part, but not the Supplement.

vived

vived him. At the time of his father's death, which happened on the 17th *Shaban* 807 (or 17th *February* 1405), he was at *Herat*, the capital of *Khorasan*; to the government of which he had been appointed nine years before. Finding, on that event, that the people of that extensive province were strongly attached to him, he was solemnly inaugurated, and founded a new kingdom at that city in the succeeding month. Before two years were expired, he added the rich province of *Mazinderan* to that of *Khorasan*; and in two years more the impolitic conduct of his nephew, KHALIL SULTAN, put him in peaceable possession of the capital city of *Samarcand*, and all the countries north of the *Oxus* that were then subject to it. Within the two years next following he subdued all countries southward on the side of *Sistan* or *Sijistan*, of which he visited the principal strong-holds in person; and this was the expedition from which he was just returned when the first embassy arrived. In 816 of the *Hidjerah* (or A. D. 1413), he added *Farsistan* to his former acquisitions; and in the *Hidjerah* year 819 (or A. D. 1416), he possessed himself of *Kerman*. His only opponents after that were, KARA YUSUF the TURKUMAN, and his sons, the last of whom he vanquished in a pitched battle on the plains of *Salmass*, in *Azerbaijan* (*Aderbaitzan*), in 832 (A. D. 1428); which event left him the undisturbed possession of an empire composed of the following extensive territories;—*Khorasan*, the center of his dominions; *Mawerannaher* and *Turkistan*, north of the *Oxus*; *Balkh* and *Badakshan*, to the north-east; *Zabulistan* to the south-east; *Sistan*, *Kerman*, and *Farsistan* to the south; and *Irak*, *Mazenderan* and *Azerbaijan* to the west. All which he continued to govern with great reputation till his death, which happened in the month of *Zilhidjah* 850, (or *February* 1447), after he had lived 71, and reigned 43 lunar years.

THE *Chinese* Emperor, who in these Extracts calls himself DAY-MING, was the third prince of the dynasty of *Ming*, and ascended the throne in the year 1403, five years before

the

the first of these Embassies. It was the founder of this dynasty, the father of this prince, that drove the *Tartars* of the race of CHENGIZ KHAN entirely out of *China*, after which he kept his court at *Nanking*, where he first established himself; but the above Emperor, his son, removed it back to *Peking*, in the seventh year of his reign. He is said to have been generous, and an encourager of learning; but was dreaded on account of some cruelties with which he began his reign. He died A.D. 1426, after he had governed China 23 years.

# AN ACCOUNT OF EMBASSIES, LETTERS, &c.

**FROM THE ANNALS OF THE HIDJERAH YEAR 811. (COMMENCING 26TH MAY, A.D. 1408.)**

WHEN the King (*i. e.* SHAHROKH MIRZA) returned from his expedition to *Seistan*, ambassadors, who had been sent by the Emperor of *China* to condole with him *on the death of his father*, arrived with a variety of presents, and represented what they had to say on the part of their monarch. The King, after shewing them many favours and civilities, gave them their dismission.

**FROM THE ANNALS OF THE HIDJFRAH YEAR 815 (COMMENCING 12TH MAY, A.D. 1412).**

ABOUT this time ambassadors from DAY-MING KHAN, Emperor of *Chin* and *Machin*, and

and all those countries, arrived at *Herat*. His
Majesty (*i. e.* SHAHROKH MIRZA) issued orders
on this occasion, that the city and the bazars
should be decorated, and that the merchants
should adorn their shops with all possible art
and elegance. The Lords *of the Court also* went
out to meet them, to signify that they regarded
their coming as an auspicious event, and conducted them into the city with the utmost honour and ceremony. It was a time of rejoicing, like the day of youth, and of gaiety
as on a night of nuptial festivity. His Majesty
ordered the royal gardens to be bedecked like
the gardens of Paradise, and sent his martial
and lion-like yesàvals to assign every one his
proper mansion. After which his Majesty
himself, irradiated with a splendour like the
sun, ascended his throne as that glorious luminary when in the zenith of his course, and bestowed upon the chief of his lords, and on the
ambassadors, the happiness of kissing his hand.
The latter, after offering him their presents,
delivered their message. The purport of what
they said on that occasion, and the letter they
brought from the Emperor of *China*, was as
follows:

LETTER

### LETTER FROM THE EMPEROR OF CHINA.

"The great Emperor DAY-MING sends
this letter to the country of *Samarcand* to
SHAHROKH BAHADUR.

"As we consider that the Most High God
has created all things that are in heaven and
earth, to the end that all his creatures may
be happy, and that it is in consequence of
his sovereign decree that we are become
Lords of the face of the earth, we therefore
endeavour to exercise rule, in obedience to
his commands; and for this reason we make
no partial distinctions between those that are
near, and those that are afar off, but regard
them all with an eye of equal benevolence.

"We have heard, before this, that thou art
a wise and an excellent man, highly distinguished above others, that thou art obedient to the commands of the Most High
God, that thou art a father to thy people
and thy troops, and art good and beneficent
towards all; which has given us much satisfaction. But it was with singular pleasure
we observed, that when we sent an ambassador with Kimkhâs, and Torkos, and a dress,
thou didst pay all due honour to our command, and didst make a proper display of
the favour thou hadst received, insomuch
"that

" that small and great rejoiced at it. Thou
" didst also forthwith dispatch an ambassador
" to do us homage, and to present us the ra-
" rities, horses, and choice manufactures of
" that country. So that with the strictest re-
" gard to truth we can declare, that we have
" deemed thee worthy of praise and of dis-
" tinction.

" The government of the *Moguls* was some
" time ago extinct, but thy father Timur
" Fuma was obedient to the commands of the
" Most High God, and did homage to our great
" Emperor Tay Zuy, nor did he omit to
" send ambassadors with presents. He *(the
" emperor)* for this reason granted protection
" to the men of that country, and enriched
" them all. We have now seen that thou art
" a worthy follower of thy father, in his
" noble spirit, and in his measures; we have
" therefore sent Duji-chun-batay-kasay,
" and Harara Suchu, and Dan-ching Sada-
" Sun Kunchi, with congratulations, and a
" dress, and Kimkhàs, and Torkos, &c. that
" the truth may be known. We shall here-
" after send persons whose office it will be to
" go and return successively, in order to keep
" open a free communication, that merchants
" may traffick and carry on their business to
" their wish.

" Khalil

"KHALIL SULTAN is thy brother's son; it is necessary that thou treat him with kindness, in consideration of his rights as being the son of so near a relation. We trust that thou wilt pay attention to our sincerity and to our advice in these matters. This is what we make known to thee!"

Another letter was sent with the presents, and contained a particular account of them; besides one calculated to serve as a pass, which was to remain with the ambassadors. Each was written in the *Persian* language and character, as well as in the *Turkish* language with the *Mogul* character, and likewise in the language and character of *China*.

His Majesty attended to the letter, and apprehended its meaning with his usual penetration; and after he had understood the objects of the embassy, gave his assent to them all, and then gave orders that the lords should entertain the ambassadors.

When the affairs of the *Chinese* ambassadors were settled, they had an audience of leave, and set out on their return. Sheikh Mohammed Bakshy accompanied them as Envoy on the part of his Majesty; and as the Emperor of *China* had not yet assented to the *Mussulman* Faith, nor regulated his conduct by the law of the *Koran*, his Majesty, from motives of friendship,

ship, sent him a letter of good advice in *Arabic* and *Persian*, conceiving, that perhaps the Emperor might be prevailed upon to embrace the faith.

### THE ARABIC LETTER.

#### IN THE NAME OF THE MOST MERCIFUL GOD.

"THERE is no GOD but GOD, and MOHAMMED is his Apostle."

"MOHAMMED, the Apostle of GOD, hath said, "As long as ever there shall remain a people of mine that are steady in keeping the commandments of GOD, the man that persecutes them shall not prosper, nor shall their enemy prevail against them, until the day of judgment."

"WHEN the Most High GOD proposed to create ADAM and his race, he said, "I have been a treasure concealed, but I chuse now to be known. I therefore create human creatures, that I may be known." It is then evident from hence, that the wisdom of the *Supreme Being*, whose power is glorious, and whose word is sublime, in the creation of the human species, was this, That the knowledge of him and of the true faith might shine forth and be propagated. For this purpose also he sent his Apostle to direct men in the way, and teach them the true religion, that it might be exalted

"above

" above all others, notwithstanding the oppofi-
" tion of the Affociaters; and that the law and
" the commandments, and the rites concerning
" clean and unclean, might be known. And he
" granted us the fublime and miraculous *Koran*
" to filence the unbelievers, and cut fhort their
" tongues when they difpute and oppofe the
" truth; and it will remain by his fovereign fa-
" vour and farextending grace unto the laft day.

" He hath alfo eftablifhed by his power in
" every age and period puiffant fovereigns, and
" mafters of numerous armies, in all parts of the
" world from eaft to weft, to adminifter juftice
" and exercife clemency, and to fpread over the
" nations the wings of fecurity and peace; to
" direct them to obey the obvious commands of
" God, and to avoid the evils and exceffes
" which he has forbidden; to raife high among
" them the ftandards of the glorious law, and to
" take away heathenifm and infidelity from the
" midft of them, by promoting the belief of
" the unity.

" The Moft High God, therefore, conftrains
" us, by his paft mercies and prefent bounties,
" to labour for the eftablifhment of the rules of
" his righteous and indifpenfable law; and
" commands us, under a fenfe of thankfulnefs
" to him, to adminifter juftice and mercy to
" our fubjects in all cafes, agreeably to the
" prophetic code and the precepts of MUSTAFA.
" He

"He requires us also to found mosques and
"colleges, alms-houses, and places of worship,
"in all parts of our dominions, that the study
"of the sciences and of the laws, and the mo-
"ral practice which is the result of those stu-
"dies, may not be discontinued.

"Seeing then that the permanence of tem-
"poral prosperity, and of dominion in this
"lower world, depends on an adherence to
"truth and goodness, and on the extirpation of
"heathenism and infidelity from the earth,
"with a view to future retribution, I cherish
"the hope that your Majesty and the nobles
"of your realm will unite with us in these
"matters, and will join us in establishing the
"institutions of the sacred law. I trust also
"that your Majesty will continue to send hither
"ambassadors, and express messengers, and will
"strengthen the foundations of affection and
"friendship, by keeping open a free communi-
"cation between the two empires; that travel-
"lers and merchants may pass to and fro un-
"molested, our subjects in all our cities may
"be refreshed with the fruits of this com-
"merce, and that means of support may abound
"among all ranks of people.

"Peace be to him that follows the right
"path, for God is ever gracious to those that
"serve him!"

### THE PERSIAN LETTER.

" To the Emperor DAY-MING, the Sultan
" SHAHROKH sends boundless peace!

" THE Most High God having, in the
" depth of his wisdom, and in the perfection
" of his power, created ADAM, was pleased *in
" succeeding times* to make of his sons prophets
" and apostles, whom he sent among men to
" summon them to obey the truth. To some
" of these prophets also, as to ABRAHAM,
" MOSES, DAVID, and his Disciples, he gave
" *particular* books, and taught *each of them*
" a law commanding the people of the time in
" which they lived, to obey that law, and to
" remain in the faith of each respectively. All
" these Apostles *of God*, called upon men to
" embrace the religion of the unity, and the
" worship of the true GOD, and forbade the
" adoration of the sun, moon, and stars, of
" kings and idols; and though each of them
" had a special *and distinct* dispensation, they
" were nevertheless all agreed in the doctrine
" of the unity of the Supreme Being. At
" length, when the apostleship and prophetick
" office devolved on our Apostle MOHAMMED
" MUSTAFA (on whom be mercy and peace
" from God), the other systems were abolished,
" and he became the apostle and prophet of
" the latter time. It behoves all the world,
" therefore,

"therefore, lords, kings, and viziers, rich and
"poor, small and great, to embrace this reli-
"gion, and forsake the systems and persua-
"sions of past ages. This is the true and the
"right faith, and this is *Islamism*.

"SOME years before the present period,
"CHENGEZ KHAN sallied forth, and sent his
"sons into different countries and kingdoms.
"He sent JOJY KHAN into the parts about
"*Saray, Krim* (or *Crimea*, and the *Desht*
"*Kafchak*, where some of the Kings his suc-
"cessors, such as UZBEK, and JANI KHAN and
"URUS KHAN, professed the *Mussalman* faith,
"and regulated their conduct by the law of
"MOHAMMED. HULAKU KHAN was appointed
"to preside over the cities of *Khorasan* and
"*Irak*, and the parts adjacent, and some of his
"sons who succeeded to the government of
"those countries, having admitted the light of
"the *Mohammedan* faith into their hearts, be-
"came in like manner professors of *Islamism*,
"and were so happy as to be converted to it
"before they died. Among these were the
"King GAZAN, so remarkable for the sincerity
"of his character, ALJAY-TU-SULTAN also,
"and the fortunate monarch ABU-SAID BAHA-
"DUR, till at length the sovereignty devolved
"on my father AMIR TIMUR (whose dust
"I venerate *). He throughout his empire

* Literally, " May his grave be perfumed."

" made

"made the religion of MOHAMMED the stan-
"dard of all his measures, so that in the times
"of his government the professors of Islamism
"were in the most prosperous condition. And
"now that by the goodness and favour of Di-
"vine Providence, the kingdoms of Kharasan,
"Irák, and Maweralnaher, are come into my
"possession, I govern according to the dictates
"of the holy law of the Prophet, and its positive
"and negative precepts; and the Yergu and
"institutions of Gengyz Khan are abolished.

"As then it is sure and certain that salvation
"and deliverance in eternity, and sovereignty
"and prosperity in the world, are the effect of
"faith and Islamism, and the favour of the
"Most High, it is our duty to conduct ourselves
"with justice and equity towards our subjects;
"and I have hope that by the goodness and
"favour of GOD, your Majesty also will in those
"countries make the law of MOHAMMED, the
"Apostle of GOD, the rule of your administra-
"tion, and thereby strengthen the cause of
"Islamism; that this world's few days of so-
"vereignty may in the end be exchanged for
"an eternal kingdom, and the old adage be
"verified, "May thy latter end be better than
"thy beginning!"

"AMBASSADORS from those parts, lately
"arrived here, have delivered us your Majesty's
"presents, and brought us news of your wel-
"fare,

"fare, and of the flourishing state of your do-
"minions. The affection and friendship which
"subsisted between our respective fathers, is re-
"vived by this circumstance; as indeed it is
"proverbial, that "a mutual friendship of fa-
"thers creates a relationship between their
"sons." In return, we have dispatched
"MOHAMMED BAKSHY as our ambassador
"from hence, to acquaint your Majesty with
"our welfare. And we are persuaded that
"henceforward a free communication will be
"maintained between the two countries, that
"merchants may pass and repass in security,
"which, at the same time that it contributes
"to the prosperity of kingdoms, is what raises
"the character of princes both in a political and
"in a religious view. May the grace of cha-
"rity, and the practice of the duties of amity,
"ever accompany those who profess to walk in
"the right path! FINIS."

---

FROM THE ANNALS OF THE HIDJERAH YEAR
820 (COMMENCING 17. FEB. A. D. 1417.)

DAY-MING KHAN, Emperor of *China*, having again sent ambassadors to his Majesty, they
arrived in the month of *Rabia ul Avvul* (*May*
1417): the chief of them were BIDACHIN, and
TUFA-CHIN, and JAT-BACHIN, who came attended by three hundred horse, and brought
with them an abundance of rarities and presents,

sents, such as Shonkars, Damasks, Kimkhástuffs, vessels of China-ware, &c. They also brought royal presents for each of the Princes and the Agas. With them came a letter, the contents of which consisted generally of an enumeration of past favours and civilities, and of expressions of confidence in the future continuance of his Majesty's friendship. The points more particularly insisted on were, that both parties should strive to remove all constraints arising from distance of place, and a diversity of manners, and to open wide the doors of agreement and union, that the subjects and merchants of both kingdoms might enjoy a free and unrestrained intercourse with each other, and the roads be kept open and unmolested. Moreover, as, on occasion of the first embassy from *China*, the AMIR SEYYID AHMED IEKKHAN had sent the Emperor a white horse, that animal had, it seems, proved particularly agreeable to him, and he now sent that Lord a number of things in return, together with a picture of the horse drawn by *Chinese* painters, with a groom on each side holding his bridle. The ambassadors were handsomely entertained, and at length, as on former occasions, received their dismission, when the King sent ARDASHER TAVACHY back with them to *China*.

FROM

FROM THE ANNALS OF THE HIDJERAH YEAR
822 (COMMENCING 27. JANUARY 1419).

In the annals of the year 820 it was mentioned that DAY-MING KHAN, Emperor of *China*, sent ambassadors *that year* to the Court of his Majesty at his capital of *Herât*, who dispatched ARDASHER TAVACHY with them *when they went back to China*. ARDASHER at this time returned from thence, and gave his Majesty an account of that country, and of the approach of a new embassy. About the end of *Ramzun* (*October* 1419), the ambassadors BIMA-CHIN and JAN-MACHIN arrived at *Herât*, and presented to the King the presents and rarities they had brought, and a letter from the Emperor of *China*, a copy of which is here subjoined, written in their manner, which is this: they write the name of their monarch on the first line, and begin the others at some distance below, and when, in the course of the letter, they come to the name of GOD, they leave off and begin a new line with that, and they follow the same method in writing the name of a sovereign prince. The letter, therefore, which was sent on the present occasion is here inserted, having been copied word for word *from the original* in the manner above described.

## AN EXACT COPY OF THE LETTER FROM CHINA.

"The great Emperor DAY-MING sends
"this letter to——
"——SULTAN SHAHROKH. We conceive
"that——
"——The Most High has made you know-
"ing and wise, and perfect, that the kingdom
"of the *Iſlamites* may be well governed, and it
"is owing to this, that the men of that king-
"dom are become prosperous.
"Your Majesty is of an enlightened mind,
"skilful, accomplished, and judicious, and fu-
"perior to all the *Iſlamites*. You honour and
"obey the commands of——
"——The Most High, and you reverence
"the things that relate to him, which is the
"way to enjoy his protection.
"We, on a former occasion, sent AMIR
"SEYRA-LIDA with others as our ambassadors,
"who arrived at——
"——Your Majesty's Court, and you were
"pleased to receive them with much honour
"and ceremony, which LIDA and the rest re-
"prefented to us, so that it has all been made
"clear and manifeſt, and fully known to us.
"Your ambaſſadors BEG BUKA and the others
"alſo arrived here with LIDA and the rest, on
"their

" their return, and delivered at this Court all
" the presents of tigers, *Arabian* horses, lynxes,
" and other things which you sent to us. We
" viewed them all. You have on this occasion
" displayed the sincerity of your affection, and
" we are exceedingly sensible *of your kindness.*
" The western country, which is the seat of
" *Islamism*, has from old time *been famous for*
" *producing* wise and good men, but it is pro-
" bable that none have been superior to——

" ——Your Majesty. Well may we afford
" protection and encouragement to the men
" of that country, for we deem it consonant to
" the will of Heaven that we should do so.
" Indeed, how should not——

" ——The Most High be well pleased with
" those men who practise mutual affection,
" where one heart reflects the sentiments of
" another, as mirrour opposed to mirrour, and
" that though at a distance! In the eye of
" friendship, generosity and civility are pre-
" cious above all things, but even in these also
" there is somewhat more particularly so. We
" now send Uchangku and others in company
" with your ambassadors Beg-Buka and the
" rest, who will deliver to——.

" ——Your Majesty our presents, consist-
" ing of seven Sùngkûrs, each of which we have
" flown with our own hands, and Kimkhâs, &c.

" Though

"Though Sūngkūrs are not produced in this
"our Empire of *China*, they are constantly
"brought us as rarities from the sea-coasts, so
"that we have always enow; but in that
"country of yours, *it seems*, they are scarce.
"We have sent you choice ones, such as might
"be deemed worthy the great soul of——

"——Your Majesty. In themselves, to
"be sure, they are of little value, but as they
"are tokens of our affection, we trust they
~~will~~

"——Your Majesty. Henceforth, it is re-
"quisite that the sincerity of our friendship be
"increased, and that ambassadors and mer-
"chants be always passing and repassing *be-
"tween us* without interruption, to the end that
"our subjects may all live in plenty, ease and
"security. *We may then* assuredly *hope that*——

"——The Most High will make us expe-
"rience more of his goodness and mercy.

"This is what we have thought proper
"to write to you."

Each time that letters *from the Emperor of China* were thus brought to his Majesty, there were three; and each was written in three different sorts of character; *that is to say*, first, in the vulgar character in which we now write, and in the *Persian* language; secondly, in the *Mogul* character, which is that of the *Vigûrs*,

and

and in the *Turkish* language; and thirdly, in the *Chinese* character and language: but the purport was exactly the same in all. There was another, which contained a particular account of the things sent, whether living creatures or other rarities, and was written in like manner in these three languages and characters. And there was likewise a letter to answer the purpose of a pass, which was written like the rest in these three languages and characters. The dates of months and years inserted in each were those of the Emperor's reign.

A SHORT

# A SHORT ACCOUNT OF THE M'ARRATTA STATE,

WRITTEN IN PERSIAN BY A MUNSHY, WHO ACCOM-
PANIED COLONEL UPTON ON HIS EMBASSY TO
POONAH.

TRANSLATED BY W. CHAMBERS, ESQ.
CHIEF JUSTICE OF THE SUPREME COURT OF JUDI-
CATURE AT FORT WILLIAM IN BENGAL.

---

THE first person who appears to have sig-
nalized himself at the head of this State
was SEVA or SEVAJEE, the son of SAMBHA,
who was a descendant of the Rajah RANACE of
*Oodeipoor*. He maintained a long war with
AURENGZEBE, who having, with great difficulty,
overcome him, and seized his person, carried
him with him to *Dehly*, and there had him
closely confined; but SEVAJEE, by procuring
the intercession of one of the Begums, who was
of the *Oodeipoor* family, found means, after

some

some time, to have the severity of his confinement relaxed, and then, having watched his opportunity, made his escape in the dress of a *Savajee Fakeer*, and travelled undetected in a large company of that profession into the province of *Bengal*. His escape being known, orders were issued throughout all parts of the kingdom to apprehend him; and a Nazerbauz, or Emissary, having introduced himself into this body of *Fakeers* with that view, actually discovered SEVAJEE among them; but instead of keeping his own counsel, called out, with an air of triumph, "I am sure SEVAJEE is amongst "you." Ere the Nazim of *Bengal*, however, could be apprized of the discovery, and issue the warrants for his arrest, SEVA took care to move off in the night, and reached the territories of the *Decan* in safety. There by his Vackeels, whom he still contrived to maintain at the court of TANAH SHAH, he made himself known to that Prince, was sent for by him immediately, and loaded with civilities and compliments: this was in the day-time, and SEVAJEE retired to his lodging. But at night, when TANAH SHAH sent for him again, SEVAJEE returned him for answer, "That in " all *Hindostan* he had seen three special Block-" heads:—First, AURENGZEBE, that with so " much labour and pains had secured his per-
" son,

"son, and could not keep him when he had
"him: Secondly, The emissary in *Bengal*
"who discovered him, and yet failed in appre-
"hending him; and, Thirdly, The Shah him-
"self, into whose presence Seva observed, his
"own feet had carried him this morning, and
"yet he had not the sense to secure him. And
"now," continued he, "think not that a bird
"that has flown out of the cage will be so
"easily caught again, or that I too am a fool
"to fall into the snare you have laid for me."
He fled from *Heiderabad* the same moment, and
made his way good to *Sattarah*, where he collected his scattered forces, prepared himself for
war, and set on foot the same disturbances in
the empire *that had cost* Aurengzebe *so much
to suppress before.* It is said, that when he left
*Heiderabad*, he had nothing of value about him
but a ring, worth about two rupees and a half;
and that having sold it, he continued to live
upon the amount till he reached *Sattarah*,
where he entered on the possession of a kingdom. Aurengzebe was now obliged to march
into the *Decan* a second time; and, after long
wars and much stratagem, he at length got
Seva into his power again: but Aurengzebe
was then become old and infirm, and the Begum
who was the patroness of Sevajee interceded
for him with such success, that she not only
procured

procured him pardon, for all his past offences, but got him reinstated in his kingdom, with a Firmaun to collect the *Chouth* on the *Decan*, and other provinces over which he should prevail. This Firmaun of AURENGZEBE the *Marrattas* say they are still possessed of, and that the *Chouth* allowed them in it is at the rate of ten *per cent.* on the revenue.

WHEN Rajah SEVA died, his son Rajah SAHOO succeeded him in his kingdom, and enlarged it by considerable conquests. The declining state of the empire during the reign of MOHAMMED SHAH, gave him an opportunity of levying the *Chouth* on several provinces; and the extraordinary aggrandizement of his power has rendered his name famous to this day. When he grew old, he summoned before him all his principal chiefs and generals, in order to ascertain their abilities and prowess; for among his own relations he saw none that he thought worthy to succeed him in the full exercise of that power which he possessed. Amidst all those, therefore, that came before him on this occasion, the person that appeared most eminent in worth and dignity was BAUJEE Row, a Bramin, and native of the province of *Goknn*. On being questioned by Rajah SAHOO concerning the power and influence he possessed

in

in the realm, BAUJEE ROW * told him, that he had 25,000 horse then actually ready for the field, and could raise as many more in a very short space of time. Rajah SAHOO, therefore, selected him from among the rest, invested him with the office and title of PAISHWAH, or Leader of all the *Marratta* Chiefs, and granted him an allowance of ten *per cent.* on all the *Marratta* revenue, as well as ten *per cent.* on all the *Chouth* that should be collected, for his own private expences, besides what he was to receive for the pay of the troops, &c. in token of which elevation he girt him round with a golden sash, and ordered all the other generals to be obedient to his orders and authority.

The *Marrattas*, then, consider Rajah SAHOO as having been a sharer with the Emperor of *Dehly* in the whole kingdom of *Hindostan*, and therefore of imperial dignity. The Paishwah they consider as a Viceroy, or Regent, with unlimited powers, and the Ministers of the Paishwah as the Viziers or Prime Minister of other kingdoms.

AT present RAM Rajah is a prisoner at large in the fort of *Sattarah*. He is descended from

* The writer seems here to have mistaken the name of the son for that of the father. The person here described must have been BISSONAUTH BALAUJEE, whose eldest son was called BAUJEE ROW, as indeed is mentioned by this writer himself in the sequel.

the

the brother of Rajah Sahoo, and the *Marratta* Chiefs account him the proper master of the *Kingdom*, without which no Paishwah can be appointed; and his name is also inserted in the Paishwah's seal.

BAUJEE ROW and CHEMNAUJEE APPAH were the sons of BISSONAUTH*. CHEMNAUJEE APPAH had one son, whose name was SADASHEVAM; but he has been *more commonly* called BHAW SAHAB. He was killed in the battle with the *Abdaulees*, but his wife still lives; her name is PARABATTY BAEE, and she has a great share in the politics of the Paishwah's court.

BAUJEE Row had three sons, viz. BAULAUJEE PUNDET, vulgarly called NANNAH, RAGONAUTH Row, and SHAMSHAIR BEHAUDER †, who was born of MUSSAMMAH MASTAUNY.

BAULAUJEE PUNDET had three sons: BISSWASS Row, the eldest, was killed in the battle with the *Abdaulees*; the second was MAUDHEVROW, who governed as Paishwah for twelve years, and died. He was an excellent Chief. The third was NARRAYEN Row, who was assassinated by means of the intrigues

---

* This is plainly the BISSONAUTH BALAUJEE mentioned in the preceding note, and confirms what is there observed.

† He was also called JANNOBAH.

VOL. II.   C c   of

of RAGONAUTH ROW, and by the hands of SHEIKH YUSUPH GARDIA, SOMAIR SING, &c. MANDHEVEROW, the son of NARRAYEN ROW, a child of two years, is now on the Musnud as Paishwah.

---

### ACCOUNT OF THE ASSASSINATION OF NARRAYEN ROW, AND THE FIRST RISE OF THE DISTURBANCES BETWEEN RAGONAUTH ROW AND HIS OPPONENTS.

MAUDHEVEROW, the elder brother of NARRAYEN ROW, governed as Paishwah twelve years, and by his amiable conduct gave universal satisfaction to those under his authority. Even his uncle RAGONAUTH ROW he took care to sooth and pacify, though at the same time he kept him a kind of prisoner at large in the castle [*]. But NARRAYEN ROW, who was then only nineteen years old, had no sooner been seated on the Musnud, than he ordered RAGONAUTH ROW into strict confinement [†], spoke of him privately in insulting and

---

[*] By the castle he means the palace of the Paishwah at Poonah.

[†] His confinement in NARRAYEN ROW's time was, if any thing, more easy, which indeed may be presumed from his

and injurious terms; and used all means to mortify and humble him.—RAGONAUTH Row, no longer able to bear such treatment, concerted measures with SOMAIR SING JEMATDAR and YUSUPH KHAN GARDIR, men not of the *Marratta* nation, and who had been raised and patronized by former Paishwahs. As there had hitherto been no instance of treasons or conspiracies in the *Marratta* state, the palace of the Paishwah was not at all secured, either by watchmen, guards, or any force. SOMAIR SING and YUSUPH KHAN therefore, with their respective corps, entered the castle on pretence of coming to demand their pay *, and surrounded the palace of NARRAYEN ROW; after which, entering the house, they came to the apartment where RAGONAUTH ROW † and the young prince were together, and immediately prepared themselves to assassinate the latter. NARRAYEN ROW, *seeing the situation he was in*, threw himself in tears at the feet of his

his negociations with the murderers of that prince; for if it had been *strict*, in the sense here intended, such people could not have found means to concert these measures with him.

* On pretence of going to real calling. SOMAIR SING and KNEREG SING were two officers that had the charge of the palace itself.

† RAGONAUTH ROW was in the palace, but in an apartment of his own; and NARRAYEN ROW, on the alarm, ran thither to him.

uncle,

uncle, crying out, in the most affecting manner, "I seek no greatness; I want no government: you are my father's brother, and I your brother's son; grant me but my life, and be yourself Paishwah." Upon this RAGONAUTH Row apparently said a great deal to forbid them: but they *, not crediting the sincerity of his commands, proceeded to their work, and killed NARRAYEN ROW. They afterwards beset RAGONAUTH Row for two days in the castle for the four lacks of rupees he had engaged to give them: but at length MOOROOBAH PHER NEVEIS †, a man of great distinction at *Poonah*, and the son of the secretary of the civil department, paid them two lacks in ready money, out of his own private purse, and having settled the mode of payment of the rest, delivered RAGONAUTH Row from this dilemma. There was then a general meeting of the *Marratta* Chiefs, to appoint a successor to NARRAYEN Row; and as there was no one left of the family of BAULAJEE Row, except RAGONAUTH Row, they found

* TULAUJEE, a Khidmatdar of NARRAYEN Row, was the person that killed him.

† PHER, or PHED NEVEIS, is the Chief Secretary of the Civil Department. The word *Phed* is a *Marratta* word signifying a Durbar, or Cutchery, the place where all the business of the civil department is transacted; and *Neveis* is a *Persian* word signifying *Secretary*.

themselves

themselves under a necessity, without farther consideration, of placing him upon the Musnid. Some time after this he assembled all his forces, and marched to make war on the NAVAUB NIZAM ALY KHAN. SAKHARAM BAUBOO and BAULAUJEE PUNDRT took leave of him on the march, and returned to the city of *Poonah* to carry on the affairs of government, while the other Chiefs accompanied RAGONAUTH Row on his expedition. At the expiration of eight months, GANGAW BAUEE, the widow of NARRAYEN ROW, who was pregnant at the time of her husband's death, was delivered of a son. Upon this event\*, SAKHARAM BAUBOO (who had formerly served RAGONAUTH ROW as his Dewan, and is a subtle old politician), BAULAJEE PHER NEVEES, and others, amounting in all to twelve of the principal men in the government, consulted together; and having taken her and her child, MAUDHEVEROW, into the fort of *Poorendher*, which is nine cofs † distant from *Poonah*, with a sufficient stock of

---

\* The writer is here mistaken in the order of events. GANGAW BAUEE was not delivered till after the revolution, though, being in the third month of her pregnancy, they secured her, and took RAM RAJA out of his confinement at *Sattarah*, to serve as a state-engine, till her delivery should afford them another.

† It is eleven cols distant from *Poonah*.

necessaries,

necessaries, they there secured themselves. The fortress of *Poorendher* is seated on a rock two miles high, and is exceedingly strong. The names of these twelve Chiefs, who are famous for the appellation of the Twelve Brothers, are as follow :

1. SAKHARAM BAUBOO.
2. BAULAUJEE PUNDET, vulg. NANAB PHER NEVEES.
3. MOOROOBAH PHER NEVEES, first cousin to BAULAUJEE PUNDET.
4. TRIMBEC MAMAH, called so because he was mamoo, or uncle by the mother's side, of BHAW SAHAB, alias SADASHEVAH ROW, alias SUDABAH.
5. SAUBAUJEE BHONSALAH, son of RAGHOJEE BHONSALAH.
6. MEER MOOSAH KHAN\*, Dewan to the NAVAUB NIZAM ALY KHAN.
7. HARREE PUNDET PHADKIAH (from PHADKAY, a family name).
8. VAUMAN ROW, the brother of GOWPAWL ROW.
9. MALHAR ROW RASTAH, *of the cast of the Shroffs*†; he was uncle of NABRAYEN ROW by the mother's side.
10. BHOWN ROW PRITTEE NIDHEE, chief Pridhaun, or Vizier.

---
\* Called also RUKKUN UD DOWLAH.
† This is a mistake, he is a *Braman*.

11. NAVROQ

11. NAUROO APPAH, the Soubahdar of the city of Poonah and its dependencies.

12. NAUROO BAUBJEE*, who has the superintendance of all the forts.

THESE Chiefs, after consulting together, agreed in opinion, that RAGONAUTH ROW, in the murder of his nephew, had been guilty of such an act of treachery as had not its equal in all the *Marratta* history; and that as there was a son of NARRAYEN ROW surviving †, he alone had the proper title to the Paishwahshi This point once settled, they wrote letters to the Chiefs that had accompanied RAGONAUTH ROW on his expedition; and this measure had such an effect, that most of them withdrew from him by degrees, a part retiring to their own governments, and the rest joining the standard of the son of NARRAYEN ROW. RAGONAUTH ROW, on seeing the ruin that

---

* He has the superintendance of three or four forts.—The *Marrattas* have hundreds of forts in their possession which were never placed under the inspection of one officer. He is also called NARUO PUNDET.

† Here the writer has been misinformed; for this son was not born when they plotted the revolution. They consulted the astrologers, and were assured by them that GANOAW BAUFE would have a son; and their dependence on that promise was so firm, that they proceeded as they would have done if a son had actually been born.

hung

hung over him, ceased from his hostilities* against NIZAM ALY KHAN, and betook himself to TUKKOJEE HOLKAR, MAHADAJEE SENDHBEAH, and the other Chiefs who reside at their jagheers in *Udgein*, and the neighbouring districts. His fortune, however, had now forsaken him, and they refused him their assistance, alledging, that though they professed an absolute subjection to the authority of the Paishwah, yet as his family was now immersed in feuds and dissensions, they would by no means interfere by lending their aid to either party, but would sit neuter till the quarrel should be decided, and would then pay homage to him who should be fixed on the Musnud of the Paishwahship.

The country of *Udgein* lies to the north-east of *Poonah*, at the distance of an hundred and thirty *kerray cols* †.

RAGONAUTH ROW, unable to prevail, returned from thence, had an engagement with TRIMBEC ROW MAMAH ‡, in which the lat-

* The fact is, that he had already made peace with the Nizam, and was within five days march of the Carnatic when the news of the revolution reached his camp.

† A *kerray col* is equal to two of the common measure.

‡ The writer mistakes the order of the events: RAGONAUTH ROW first conquered TRIMBEC, and then proceeded to *Udgein*.

ter was slain, and then went to *Surat*, where he solicited succours from the *English*. The gentlemen there being under the orders of the Governor and Council of *Bombay*, consulted them on the occasion, and they both determined to assist RAGONAUTH ROW with three battalions of sepoys, and a train of artillery. At that time the *Marratta* Chiefs that were on the side of RAGONAUTH ROW were, MANAU-JEE PHANKERAH\*, GOVENDEROW KÁYEK-VAUR (the brother of FATEH SING KAYEK-VAUR, who was with the other party), and some other Chiefs of inferior note. Those of the other side were, HARREE PUNDET PHAD-KIAH, BALWANT APPAH †, &c. with their quotas, making in all a body of about 25,000 horse. Both armies met on the north side the *Narbadah*, within thirty cofs of *Surat*, and had a severe engagement; but the loss on both sides was about equal. When, however, letters of prohibition were received from the Governor-General and Council of *Bengal*, both parties ceased from hostilities, and remained inactive.—And now that Colonel JOHN UPTON has

---

\* His name is MANAJEE SAINDHEEAH; but they give him the title of PHANKERAH, which is equivalent to FEARNOUGHT in *English*.

† His name is KRISHNA ROW. His father's name was BALWANT.

concluded

concluded a peace with the Ministers of MAUD-HUYROW, the son of the deceased NARRA-YEN Row, the gentlemen of *Bombay* have re-manded their troops from succouring RAGO-NAUTH ROW; but RAGONAUTH ROW, on the other hand, refuses to trust himself in the *Marratta* countries, as he thinks his life would be in danger if he should do so. He wishes rather to go to *Calcutta*, or *Benares*; and in his last letter to the Colonel he says he will go to *Europe*.

### PARTICULARS RELATIVE TO RAGONAUTH ROW.

RAGONAUTH ROW (who is commonly called RAGNOBAH) is a Chieftain of great eminence, and the only survivor of note in the family of BAUJER Row. He formerly sig-nalized himself by very confiderable military achievements; for it was he that wrested the half of *Guzerat* from the hands of DAUMAU-JEE KATEKVAUR, and that afforded such im-portant affiftance to the NAVAUB GAUZY UD DEEN KHAN in the war with the *Jauts*, in the time of AHMED SHAH. It was he, too, that marched at the head of 100,000 horse against the fon of ABDAULEE SHAW, drove him from
*Lahore*,

*Lahore*, and planted the *Marratta* standards as far as the shore of the *Attock*. The ABDAULEE SHAW was then engaged in a war on the side of *Khorasan*; but the year following he entered *Hindostan* with a large army to chastise the *Marrattas*, at a time when the NAVAUB GAUZY UD DEEN KHAN was in the country of the *Jauts*, and under their protection. On receiving news of this event, the Paishwah, BAULAUJEE PUNDET, told his son *, RAGONAUTH ROW, that he expected he would take upon him the charge of this expedition also against the *Abdaulees*; to which RAGONAUTH ROW replied, that he was not averse to it if he would grant him a supply of twenty Lack † of Rupees for the pay of his troops. But his cousin SADASHEVAH being present, observed, that the *Marrattas* were a privileged people; that wherever they went, the country and its revenue might be considered as their own; and then asked RAGONAUTH ROW what grounds he had for so extraordinary a demand? To this RAGONAUTH replied by making him an offer of the commission, which SADASHEVAH ROW accepted; and having taken the command of an army of 90,000 horse, he first moved with this force against SALAUBAT JENG, the bro-

* " His brother," it should be.
† Others say " Sixty Lack."

ther

ther of the present NAVAUB NIZAM ALY KHAN. But that Prince having been reduced to great straits since the death of the late NAVAUB NASIR JANG, had but a small body of horse to oppose them; and having been surrounded by the Marrattas on all sides, he was obliged to give up to them the forts of Barhampour and Assir, with a country of fiftyfive Lack of Rupees *per annum*, besides considerable sums of ready money. Thus enriched, SADASHIVAH ROW took his way towards *Hindostan*\*; and on his arrival in the neighbourhood of *Dehly*, laid claim † to the empire and the throne: but his pride was offensive to the Most High, by whose providence it happened that he was, in a short time, hemmed in between two formidable armies, that of the ABDAULEE SHAW attacking him in front, and that of the NAVAUB SHUJAA UD DOWLAH and the *Rohillas* falling at the same time upon his rear. Here ensued that famous battle, of which those who were eye-witnesses report, that it was the greatest ever fought in *Hindostan*: for the *Marrattas* being beset with enemies in front and rear, saw no possibility of flight, and therefore resolved to sell their lives as dear as

\* Meaning from the *Decan* to *Hindostan* Proper.
† He did not pretend to sit on the throne himself, but set up J. . . . . . . . . .

they

they could. Eighty *Marratta* Chiefs that rode on elephants were killed on the spot: but concerning SADASHEVAH Row himself there are different accounts, some asserting that he was killed in the engagement, and others as confidently affirming that he escaped alone from the field of battle; and that having reached *Poonah*, disguised as a private soldier, he waited privately on BAULAUJEE ROW, who, in wrath for what had happened, ordered him secretly to prison in the fort of *Poorendher*; and there, say they, he lives to this day: and yet it is pretended that this is so carefully concealed, that PARABATTY BAUHER, his wife, who is still living at *Poonah*, and even bears a part in the councils of the *Marratta* Chiefs, knows nothing of the matter; which surely gives this story a great air of improbability: for how can it be credited that so considerable a man should thus be shut up in prison, and the circumstances not transpire?

AFTER these events MALHAR ROW marched to the side of *Hindostan*, and fixed his quarters a long time at *Kaulpee*, whence he afterwards moved to *Korajehanabad*, to succour SHUJAA UD DOWLAH; but General CARNAC engaged him there, and gave him a total defeat. MALHAR Row is since dead, and has been succeeded by his son TUKKOJEE HOLKER, and his wife AHALEYAH BAUEE, in the possession of the

*Soobah*

Soobah of *Endour*, which was his jagheer. They have 50,000 horse at their command, and are of the *Dhanker* cast.

The next army the *Marrattas* sent into *Hindostan* was that commanded by Mendejee Sendheean and Bessaujee Pundit, who placed Shah Aulum upon the throne of *Debly*; a great subject of boasting to the *Marrattas*, who say the Emperor of *Hindostan* owes his kingdom entirely to them. But it is well known, that when Colonel Champion marched to *Mehendee Ghaut*, after his success against the *Rohillas*, he engaged this very Sendheeah, and put him and the whole *Marratta* army to flight; so that having crossed the *Ganges* and *Jumna* with great precipitation, they have never from that time ventured over either of those rivers again. At present, indeed, Ragonauth Row's revolution hath produced such dispersion among the *Marratta* Chiefs, and thrown their affairs into such confusion, that Rajah Himmut Behauder, Rajah Dhatanekah the Rajah of Gunud, and others, have united to take advantage of this crisis, and now collect the revenues of all the countries between *Kual'pee* and *Narwer*. The *Marratta* Chiefs, however, meditate an invasion into those parts, whenever matters shall be perfectly settled in relation to Ragonauth Row.

of

## OF THE PRODUCTIONS AND PECULIARITIES OF THE MARRATTA COUNTRY.

THE kinds of grain chiefly produced in this country are *jouár*, *bájerá* \*, &c. Rice grows in the *Kokun* Province †, and is also brought from the *Soobah* of *Khandaiſſe*; it is sold for ten or twelve seer for a rupee, and wheat flour, also, bears the same price. Grain is in general very dear, and there is but little trade in other commodities. Silk is brought hither from *Bengal*. Of linen manufactures there is abundance; but they are not to be compared with those of *Bengal*. Pearls are here a great article of merchandize; they are brought from *Mocho* and *Juddah*. The fruits of the country are grapes, pomegranates, water-melons, mangoes, and pears.

Of manufactures, here are only some of white cloth, chintz, *Burhaunpoor* turbants, &c. but *Europe* goods, such as broad cloths, &c.

---

\* These are different kinds of pulse.

† The *Kokun* rice is like that commonly used in *Bengal*, and is indeed generally sold at 12 or 13 seer for a rupee; but the *Khandaiſſe* rice, called in *Hindoſtan* pattey chauvel, which is the only species brought from that province, is generally used by the higher ranks of people, and is seldom at a lower price than six or seven seer per rupee. It is a long and small-grained rice, like that used for pillaus by *Muſſelmen* of high rank on the *Coromandel* coast.

and

and silk, opium, and *Bengal* cloths, are imported hither from *Bombay*, and dispersed on all sides as far as *Debly*.

EXCELLENT horses* are to be had here in great abundance, but the market-price is high. In every province, and in every place dependent on the *Marrattas*, there are stables and herds † of horses; and in most places there are herds the property of the Paishwah. The principal men also have all herds of horses on their respective jagheers, and inlist horsemen, who serve on them in time of war, of whom the bodies of horse called Bargeer are composed. Accompanied by these the Chiefs offer their services to government; and each of them has from a thousand to two thousand horses of

---

\* The horses most esteemed by the *Marrattas* are those bred on the banks of the river *Bheema*, which runs into the *Krishna*, about thirty cofs west of *Bidder*, in the province of *Bhumky*. They are of a middling size and strong, but are, at the same time, a very handsome breed, generally of a dark bay with black legs, and are called, from the place which produces them, *Bheemertidy* horses. Some of them bear a price as high as 5000 rupees upon the market. Mares are commonly the dearest.

† These herds are called in the *Marratta* language *Flouk*, and are composed of the horses of several individuals, who send them to feed on the open plains as long as they have no immediate occasion for them. But those that are the property of the Paishwah are called, as well as the places where they are kept, *Paugah*.

his

his own. In a word, stout men and good horses are the chief boast of this country: besides these it has but little to show but rocky hills and stony ground. The soil, indeed, in some places, is black, which creates an excessive quantity of mud in the rainy season, and the roads at that time are rendered also in most parts impassable by the torrents that come down from the hills.

The city of *Poonah* hath nothing extraordinary to recommend it: it is about three or four cofs in circuit; but there are no gardens to be seen here like those of *Bengal* or *Benares* \*, and the houses of the principal people are like the houses of the *Mahajins*.—Few of them have any extent of building or ground, and fewer still are adorned

---

\* There are, it seems, a few gardens to the east and to the south of *Poonah*. Among the latter, that of *Moorooperneveses* is the best; but even that has few or none of the ornaments here mentioned. On the north and west of the city runs a small river called the *Moolamootha*, but it is full of rocks, and not navigable. NARRAYEN ROW began to build a bridge over this river, which was intended to be open during the rains, and shut during the hot months, in order to preserve water for the use of the town; but he was killed before it was finished, and it has not since been carried on. This idea was suggested by a dreadful season of drought, which happened under his reign, during which a cudgeree pot of water was at one time sold in *Poonah* for half a rupee. This excessive scarcity, however, did not continue above ten or fifteen days.

Vol. II.      D d      with

with courts, parterres, rivulets, or fountains. The inhabitants are, nevertheless, most of them wealthy, and merchants, and the best part of the offices and employments are held by *Brahmans*.

As to beauty and complexion, the people of this country resemble those of *Panjaub* [*]; few are to be seen of a very dark colour. The women of all ranks, both rich and poor, go unveiled; and those of distinction go in palankeens without curtains. The wives of soldiers ride about on horseback. Curtain-selling [+] is very common in this country.

Many *Brahmans* [‡] sell their own daughters, and girls that they have brought up, for a great price.

Other casts [§], besides *Brahmans*, bring up fowls in their houses, and eat the eggs; but the *Brahmans* eat neither flesh nor fish.

Cows

---

[*] From other accounts it should appear, that the people of *Panjaub* are of a very different feature and make from the *Marrattas*; and that there are more people of a dark colour among the latter than would be understood from this description of them.

[+] By this he means prostitution.

[‡] A *Marratta Brahman* to whom this was read discovered great indignation at this assertion, and denied that they ever sell their own daughters, or bring up girls for sale, though he acknowledged it was not unusual among the inferior casts.

[§] The fact is, that not only the *Brahmans* abstain from fish and flesh, but all the different divisions of the *Vies*, or *Banian*

Cows are not allowed to be killed in any of
the countries dependent on the *Marrattas*.
*Muſſulmans* are here but very few in number,
and the influence of *Iſlam* at a low ebb.—But
idolatry flourishes, and here are idol temples in
abundance.

## OF THE CUSTOMS AND MANNERS OF THE MARRATTAS.

SOME of the *Marratta* customs appeared
excellent to me. One was the good understanding and union that has in general subsisted among their Chiefs, insomuch that no instance of treachery had ever occurred among them till RAGONAUT ROW made himself infamous on that account. Another was, the attention and respect paid by the Paiſhwah, and all the great men, to people of the military profession; so that in the public Durbar the Paiſhwah is used to receive the compliments of every single Jammatdar of horse, himself standing till nine o'clock in the morning, and

*Banian* caſt, are equally abſtemious, while the *Chettri* and *Sudder* indulge in both.

bracing them by turns\*. At taking leave, also, he gives them betel standing: and whoever comes to wait upon him, whether men of rank or otherwise, he receives † their salams, or embraces them standing.

ANOTHER ordinance current among them is, that if an eminent Chieftain, who commands even an hundred thousand horse, be sent into some other country with his forces, and happens there to be guilty of some offence, in consequence of which he receives a summons from the Paishwah, far from thinking of resistance, he instantly obeys, and repairs to the presence

---

\* According to the present custom distinctions are made in this matter, which were not formerly observed; for the Paishwahs used to embrace all that came without discrimination, till advantage was taken of this custom by BAPUJEE NAIK, who having a grudge at SADESHEEVAH BHOW (commonly called BHOW SAHEB), at the time that he held the office of First Minister to the fourth Paishwah BALAUJEE ROW (called also NANAH SAHEB), attempted to stab him with his cuttaar when he went to embrace him. From that time a regulation has taken place, according to which none but people of distinction, and they unarmed, are permitted to embrace the Paishwah, or others of his family.

† This, it should seem, is too generally expressed; but the custom does still subsist on one particular occasion, to wit, on the day on which the army marches on any expedition, the Paishwah then stands at the door of his tent, and, after delivering the golden standard to the General who has been appointed to the command, receives in that posture the compliments of the troops of every rank and denomination.

in perſon with all expedition. The Paiſhwah then pardons him if the offence be ſmall; if otherwiſe, he is impriſoned for ſome months, or kept in a ſtate of diſgrace till it is thought proper to admit him again to favour.

A THIRD is, that if an eminent Chief goes upon an expedition which ſubjects him to great expences, ſuch as his own jagheer is not ſufficient to ſupply, and he is obliged on that account to run in debt to the *Mohajins*, though the ſum ſhould amount to even ten or twelve lack, it is all freely allowed him; and though the government have demands upon him to the amount of lacks of rupees, yet if, in ſuch circumſtances, he pleads the inſufficiency of his means to diſcharge thoſe arrears, he is excuſed without heſitation, nor has he any thing to apprehend from being called to account by the Dewan, the Khanſaman, or other ſtate Officers. The Chiefs are all their own maſters, and expend * what ſums they pleaſe; ſo that a general

* This muſt be underſtood with ſome limitation. They do, indeed, often laviſh great ſums when on ſervice, and that not merely on the ſoldiery, but on feaſts given to Brahmans, preſents to ſingers, dancers, &c. and on their return theſe ſums are generally allowed them under the head of *dherrem*, or charitable diſburſements. But they are ſo far from being without any check in their expences, that the officer named the *Karkun* is ſent with each Chieftain expreſsly for that purpoſe.

satisfaction prevails among them, and they are always ready at a call with their quota of troops, and march with alacrity upon whatever service they are ordered to take. At present SAKHARAM BABOO causes great discontents among the Chiefs, by canvassing their accounts, and making demands on the Jagheerdars, in a manner very different from the usage of former Paishwahs; hence numbers are disaffected, and time must discover what it is that Providence designs to bring about by that means.

ANOTHER custom is, that when one of their Chiefs that held employments, or jagheers, &c. dies, his son, though of inferior abilities, or an infant, succeeds * immediately to the employment, the business of which is conducted by deputy till he becomes of age, and the monthly stipend, or jagheer, &c. is given to his family and relations. Nor are the effects of deceased persons ever seized and appropriated by Government, in the manner that has been practised under the Emperors of *Hindostan*.

---

* This is also liable to some exceptions; for though great attention is paid to the claims of representatives of great families, when those representatives are themselves men of merit and ability, yet when it happens otherwise, the jagheers and employments are at length usually taken from them and given to persons from whom the State has better expectations.

To

To the south-west of *Poonah*, at the distance of fifty cofs, is the fort of *Sattarah*.

*Bombay* is about fifty cofs distant due west.

*Surat* and *Guzerat* are to the north-west about 130 cofs distant.

*Aurungabad* stands east of *Poonah* about 70 cofs.

*Bombay*, *Salfet*, *Baffern*, &c. stand on the shore of the salt sea towards the west.

And the country of *Kokun*, which belongs to the *Marrattas*, lies south-west of *Poonah*.

KOKUN is a fine country, and produces rice and other such things in abundance, with which it supplies *Poonah*. The Paishwah and the other Chiefs are mostly *Kokun* Brahmans. This province is called a *Soobah*. The Brahmans of *Poonah* may be divided into two sorts; the Désy Brahmans, who are those of *Aurungabad* and those parts: the other those of *Kokun*.

To the south and east are also many countries under the government of the *Marrattas*, extending from the parts adjacent to *Poonah* to the boundaries of the *Carnatic* \*, and *Ramefer*

(which

---

\* The *Carnatic* must by no means be understood here in the confined sense in which the *English* receive it. The country governed by MAHOMMED ALY KHAN is only part

of

(which is a place of worship of the *Hindoos*, as famous as that of *Kasy*, at 500 cols distance from *Poonah*) and *Panalah*, a jagheer of the *Bhosalahs*, and to the boundary of *Nellor*, &c. the country of HEIDER NAIK.

To the east and north are situated the Circar of *Asair*, *Burhaunpoor*, and the Soobah of *Khandaiss*, at the distance of eighty cols from *Poonah*.

AND to the north and west are the half of the country of *Guzerat*, the Pergunnah of *Broach*, &c. which are in the possession of the *Marratta* Paishwah.

of the *Carnatic* properly so called, and should always be termed the *Carnatic Payeen Ghaut*, i. e. "that *Carnatic* which is below the Passes." In the name *Carnatic*, standing singly, is to be comprehended all the countries lying south of *Merch* and *Bidder*, which composed the antient kingdom of *Viziapoor*. In fact, the name of *Carnatic Payeen Ghaut* appears to have been given to MAHOMED ALY KHAN's country by the *Moors*; for the *Marrattas* allow that appellation to a very small part of it, and denominate the whole Soobah of *Arcot Dravid-des*, while the *Malabars*, natives of the country, call it *Saramandalam*, from whence our *Coromandel*.

What he says here with respect to the extent of the *Marratta* dominions southward, applies only to the possession they once had of the country of *Tanjore*, and the tribute they collected from the *Tondemans*.

BESIDES

BESIDES all these countries, the Pergunnah of *Bhilsa*, the Soobah of *Endoir* *, the Soobah of *Udgein*, the Pergunnah of *Seronje*, the Soobah of *Kalpy* †, were all made over to the Marrattas in jagheer, by GAUZY UD DEEN KHAUN, in consideration of the support and assistance afforded him by the *Marratta* forces, and they still remain in their possession. The above Mahals are included in the jagheers of TUKKOJEE HOLKER and SENDHEEAH; that is to say, there are about 50,000 or 60,000 horse appointed on the side of *Hindostan*, which those two Chiefs pay out of the produce of those countries, and transmit the balance to the Paishwah.

THE actual revenue derived from all the countries dependent on the *Marrattas* is about twelve Crore, from which when we deduct the jagheers, and the expence of the troops stationed on the side of *Hindostan* Proper, there will remain about five Crore at the disposal of the Paishwah; and out of this he has to pay all those troops who receive their allowances in ready money, and to defray the charges of the

* *Endoir* is a Pergunnah.
† *Kalpy* is not a Soobah, but a Pergunnah. To these must be added the Pergunnah of *Dhor*; the fort of which, bearing the same name, is very famous for its strength, and is said to have been built by the celebrated Rajah Bhoj, who made it his capital. It is situated at the distance of about twenty-four *Bengal* cofs from the city of *Udgein*.

forts,

forts, which are, large and small, in number about seven hundred; so that there is never a balance of so much as one Crore of rupees in ready money remaining in the treasury of the Paishwah *.

THE full number of the troops is about two hundred thousand horse and foot; but, including the garrisons of the forts and other places, we may reckon it four hundred thousand.

THE *Marrattas* are always at war with HEIDER NAIG, or the Navaub NIZAM ALY KHAN, or others. Their country is never in perfect tranquillity, and hence it is exceeding desolate and waste.

THEY are at present at peace with the Navaub NIZAM ALY KHAN BEHAUDER, but their country is in much confusion on account of their discontents with RAGONAUT ROW; advantage of which has been taken by the Zemindars on the hills on every side, and by HEIDER NAIG. On the side of *Hindostan* the *Gosayn* Rajah HIMMUT BEHAUDER, and the Rajah of *Gohud*, &c. have seized the Soobah of

---

* This, it seems, is true at present; but MAUDEVEROW, it is said, had two Crore of Rupees in his treasury at the time of his death, most of which fell afterwards into the hands of RAGONAUT ROW, and was dissipated by him on his accession to the government, and his expedition towards the Carnatic.

*Kalpy,*

*Kalpy* \*, &c. and the Circar of *Gualier* †; and HEIDER NAIG has also possessed himself of some of their countries on his side; but as soon as they can promise themselves security with respect to RAGONAUT ROW, their armies will issue forth on every side.

\* It ought to be written "The Pergunnah of *Kalpy*." Rajah HIMMIT BEHAUDER did indeed take *Kalpy*, in the time and under the the orders of SUJAH UD DOWLA, but was soon driven out of it again by the *Marratta* forces, under the command of VITTHEL SIVADEO, NAUROO SUNKER, GOVIND PUNDET, &c.

† The Rajah of *Gohud* got possession of the open country, and a few mud forts in the Circar of *Gaulior*, but was never able to get possession of the fort of that name till the *English* took it for him.

THE END OF THE SECOND VOLUME.

www.ingramcontent.com/pod-product-compliance
Lightning Source LLC
Chambersburg PA
CBHW030551300426
44111CB00009B/940